Outsourced Children

# Outsourced Children

*Orphanage Care and Adoption in Globalizing China*

Leslie K. Wang

Stanford University Press
Stanford, California

Library of Congress Cataloging-in-Publication Data

Names: Wang, Leslie K., author.
Title: Outsourced children : orphanage care and adoption in globalizing China /
Leslie K. Wang.
Description: Stanford, California : Stanford University Press, 2016. | Includes
bibliographical references and index.
Identifiers: LCCN 2016007827 (print) | LCCN 2016008470 (ebook) | ISBN 9780804799010
(cloth : alk. paper) | ISBN 9781503600119 (pbk. : alk. paper) | ISBN 9781503600126
(ebook) | ISBN 9781503600126 (e-book)
Subjects: LCSH: Orphanages—China. | Orphans—China. | Abandoned children—
China. | Intercountry adoption—China. | Children with disabilities—Institutional
care—China.
Classification: LCC HV1317 .W36 2016 (print) | LCC HV1317 (ebook) |
DDC 362.7340951—dc23
LC record available at http://lccn.loc.gov/2016007827

Typeset by Thompson Type in 10/14 Minion

*To Jin Jin, Huan Cong, Le Qi, and all of the children in China who touched my life. I have been humbled by your extraordinary resilience and courage.*

# Contents

# Acknowledgments

THIS BOOK WOULD NOT EXIST except for the generosity of the organizations, volunteers, families, and children who graciously allowed me into their lives. Over the course of more than a decade their acceptance of me as a researcher, a caregiver, and a friend has been a great source of inspiration.

My interest in the topic of adoption dates back to when I was a study abroad student at Peking University during the late 1990s. There, during a visit to the Forbidden City, I was surprised to see two white American couples with strollers that each held a Chinese baby girl. I pondered for the first time why these children were being abandoned and adopted and how their movement across borders was shaping China–U.S. relations. These questions became my constant companions.

Along the way I have been supported by a group of incredible peers. At the University of California Berkeley, Barrie Thorne and Tom Gold served as shining exemplars of mentorship. Thank you for your unfailing support and investment in my research, career, and overall well-being all of these years. Marion Fourcade-Gourinchas, Jennifer Johnson Hanks, and You-Tien Hsing also helped to guide my path. While at Berkeley I benefited from the camaraderie and scholarly feedback of other colleagues, a group that included Zongshi Chen, Jenny Chio, Julia Chuang, Mark Dallas, Shannon Gleeson, Amy Hanser, Jon Hassid, Jennifer Jones, Charlotte Lee, Elizabeth Logan, Jennifer Randles, Rachel Stern, Chris Sullivan, Chung-Min Tsai, and Suowei Xiao.

In Boston the ideas in this project continued to be shaped by Sofya Aptekar, Kimberly Hoang, Miliann Kang, Jennifer Musto, Jillian Powers, Saher

Selod, Nazanin Shahkrokni, and Cinzia Solari. Thanks to Jessica Cobb for her superb editing help. At Stanford University Press, I am indebted to the reviewers, and especially, to Jenny Gavacs for her guidance throughout this process. Lastly, I regret not being able to share this book with Norman Apter, whose historical research on child welfare in China has made a lasting impact on my work. I count myself lucky to have enjoyed his presence as a friend and colleague, although it was for far too short a time.

Financial support for research and writing was made possible by a Fulbright-Hays Research Award and by UC Berkeley, in particular the Department of Sociology, the Graduate Division, the Institute of East Asian Studies, and the Center for Chinese Studies. I also received support from the University of British Columbia, the Association for Asian Studies, and the University of Massachusetts Boston to update and present this research. Over the years I have benefited from the insights of audiences at Princeton University, Harvard University (the Transnational Studies Working Group and the Harvard China Gender Symposium), the University of British Columbia, and the Chinese University of Hong Kong. I presented portions of this work at the annual meetings of the American Sociological Association and the Association for Asian Studies.

Earlier versions of parts of this book have appeared previously in "Unequal Logics of Care: Gender, Globalization and Volunteer Work of Expatriate Wives in China," *Gender & Society* (2013), 27(2): 538–560; "Importing Western Childhoods into a Chinese State-Run Orphanage," *Qualitative Sociology* (2010), 33 (2): 137–159; and "Missing Girls in an Age of 'High Quality': Government Control Over Population and Daughter Discrimination in Reform-Era China," *Social Transformations in Chinese Societies* (2009), 4: 245–270. Thank you to the publishers for permission to use these materials.

Of course, through it all I could not have ventured along this unpredictable, yet immensely gratifying, journey from California to Vancouver to Michigan to Boston (with many trips to China in between) without the unconditional love and support of my friends and family. This includes Shaana Berman, Marianna Eyzerovich, Diane and Jasson Flick, Karin Iwasaka, Willis Jackson, Iris Ponte, my siblings Elaine and Steve, and my parents Harry and Kim Wang. I'm in gratitude to you always.

Outsourced Children

# 1 Introduction

*Children and the Politics of Outsourced Intimacy in China*

AT THE END OF A FREEZING COLD JANUARY DAY in 2007, I made my first visit to the infant hospice unit at the Haifeng Children's Welfare Institute (CWI).[1] My breath escaped in white puffs as I ventured tentatively down the dark un-heated hallways of the large Chinese state-run orphanage. I had just begun serving as a full-time volunteer for Tomorrow's Children,[2] a Western faith-based organization that provided medical care to abandoned special needs youth. The group had recently opened a large infant hospice, which occupied one full floor of the CWI—a "model" orphanage located in Henan Province, in central China. Tomorrow's Children used first-world medical practices to care for the institution's most disabled and ill babies and toddlers until they passed away. Many infants survived and after rehabilitation were returned to the regular state facility, sent out to local foster care, or occasionally even adopted internationally.

I was there to pick up Emma, one of the unit's young residents. A happy one-year-old girl with a severe bowl haircut, Emma suffered from a rare child-hood cancer that had claimed the sight in her left eye. The aggressive dis-ease was threatening her vision in the other eye and possibly even her life. Although it was impossible to know for certain, this illness was most likely the reason she was cast out of her family. As part of my volunteering duties for Tomorrow's Children, I was given the task of escorting Emma to Beijing on an overnight train. From there, she would fly to Hong Kong for immediate surgery and chemotherapy.

I soon found myself standing nervously on a dark, crowded train platform holding the girl in my arms. Her urgent medical situation filled me with fear, but Emma had the energy of a healthy, rambunctious toddler. She attempted to squirm out of my grasp as several old men rolled past with rattling metal carts, loudly hawking a diverse array of instant noodles, red cellophane-wrapped sausages, and cheap cigarettes. It was late at night when we boarded the train, settling into the bottom bunk of a dimly lit soft-sleeper car filled with businessmen. Emma bounced up and down on the bed and babbled cheerfully as the men snored noisily overhead. Burdened with an overwhelming sense of responsibility, I lay awake anxiously the entire night, terrified to let her out of my sight. When we reached Beijing the following morning, I passed the girl to an American volunteer waiting at the station and heaved an enormous sigh of relief.

Emma spent the next two years in Hong Kong undergoing multiple costly procedures to save her young life. Through the organization's monthly online newsletters, I learned that her cloudy left eye was removed and that she underwent chemotherapy, laser treatment, and radiation to maintain vision on the other side. In 2009, the group asked its foreign funders for US$20,000 in donations to cover Emma's latest course of radiation treatment. Against tremendous odds, the child's cancer went into total remission, and she returned to the Tomorrow's Children main foster home near Beijing. Then, at the age of four, she was adopted by an American family.

Emma's uplifting journey of rescue and redemption through international adoption is the type of feel-good story that is often featured in the Western media. However, the positive outcome she enjoyed is rare among abandoned disabled youth. More common are the situations faced by children like Henry, another memorable resident of the Tomorrow's Children special care unit. Born with severe cerebral palsy, Henry was stick thin, ghostly pale, and nearly catatonic when he first arrived; his dull eyes lacked any sign of awareness, even when you peered directly into them. Without a birth certificate or other identifying information, the doctor estimated that Henry was roughly six years old. Yet after only a few weeks of a specialized nutrition and medical regimen, the boy doubled in weight and grew six inches in height— shocking everyone with his transformation. Facial hair began sprouting from his chin, making clear that he was in fact a teenager. As Henry's physical health continued to rapidly improve, he blossomed into an intelligent and perceptive adolescent. His Chinese caregiver (*ayi*) used physical therapy techniques learned from a Western volunteer to stretch his stiff limbs and teach him to grasp objects.

After several months of being nursed back to health, Henry's hunger for mental stimulation became a source of frustration within his confined surroundings. When volunteers entered the room he howled loudly; using pleading eye contact, he asked to be taken outside in his wheelchair. His *ayi* believed that he was demanding too much of her time (as she also had two other high-needs children in her care) and ceased his physical therapy. Instead, he was placed in front of the television for hours on end with his back facing the rest of the room. With only three volunteers tending to more than forty children, it was impossible to give Henry the individual attention he craved. In desperation, the boy began to bite his own hands, drawing blood on several occasions. Volunteers attempted to provide him with more one-on-one time, but their efforts could provide only temporary relief.

Both of these children were likely cast out of their families due to their costly life-threatening illnesses. They then embarked on an odyssey of care and rehabilitation within state-run orphanages, and their lives were totally transformed by an intricate set of collaborations between the Chinese government (their official guardian) and the international humanitarian aid groups that assumed full responsibility for their well-being. Within four short years, the vast emotional, medical, and financial resources of global child savers "remade" Emma into a desirable Western adoptee, transporting her from the very bottom of Chinese society to the top of global society. By contrast, Henry's severe disabilities and long-term dependency limited his chances of adoption. Nonetheless, even though he remained institutionalized, the first-world care and resources he received also remade him into a very different kind of person than he would have otherwise been.

A complex global migration of children is carving an indelible circuit between China and the industrialized world. Since the 1990s, intensive Western investment into certain highly marginalized youth living in the People's Republic of China (PRC) has been a phenomenon that would have been unimaginable only a few decades earlier when the nation was inaccessible to the outside world. This new predicament raises a number of questions. First, in this time of unprecedented prosperity, why have many Chinese parents abandoned their children to state care? Why have Chinese state authorities allowed foreign humanitarian nongovernmental organizations (NGOs)—whose intentions are often viewed with deep distrust—to become so enmeshed in their nation's child welfare system?[3] And finally, what is the relationship between the international adoption of Chinese children to countries in the global north and the involvement of Western NGOs in domestic state-run orphanages?

The trajectories that Emma and Henry embarked on could not have been more different. Nonetheless, both children participated in the dynamics of what I term *outsourced intimacy*: the process by which the Chinese state has outsourced the care of locally devalued children to Westerners who, using their own resources, remake them into global citizens. This book highlights the two main ways that outsourced intimacy has operated as an ongoing transnational exchange: (1) through the *exportation* of mostly healthy girls into Western homes via adoption and (2) through the subsequent *importation* of first-world actors, resources, and practices into orphanages to care for the mostly special needs youth left behind.

Because of the power inequalities that exist between countries, international adoption typically involves the migration of children from developing areas to advanced industrialized regions. Thus, nations that place their vulnerable children in the care of outsiders are typically perceived as having lower global status. However, I contend that since beginning its international adoption program in the early 1990s, the PRC has been able to further a range of state objectives through outsourced intimacy; these include funding its child welfare system and fostering closer relationships with first-world countries, especially the United States—the destination of most adoptees.[4] Moreover, the outflow of healthy girls through adoption has propped open a window of opportunity for international humanitarian aid organizations to enter China and take over the costly care of thousands of other vulnerable, and locally stigmatized, sick and disabled children.

Drawing on a year and a half of ethnographic fieldwork in Chinese state-run orphanages that collaborated with Western NGOs, this book represents the first systematic analysis of the lives of institutionalized youth in the PRC. *Outsourced Children* considers the cooperation, tensions, and ethical dilemmas that were embedded in these transnational care partnerships to examine China's changing relationship with the industrialized world and to highlight the key role that children are playing in globalization processes.

This analysis is not meant to condemn practices of international adoption and foreign assistance to institutionalized children. Indeed, I worked closely with vulnerable youth in orphanages and foster homes in the PRC for more than a decade and developed trusting relationships with many of the individuals and organizations that appear throughout these pages. Yet, to provide an honest depiction, I give certain descriptions of orphanage conditions or childcare that may be emotionally distressing to some readers. These observations are not meant to shock but instead are intended to raise awareness and foster an informed dialogue about the lives of the children who exist, largely forgotten, at the edges of the world's fastest-growing economy.

## Children as Symbols of Chinese Modernity

The PRC initiated the process of "reform and opening up" (*gaige kaifang*) to the outside world in 1978, embracing a capitalist market economy while maintaining an authoritarian political regime headed by the Chinese Communist Party. Since then, the nation has experienced meteoric rates of growth credited with alleviating poverty for more than 600 million people.[5] A tidal wave of first-world investment, knowledge, and goods has crashed onto Chinese shores, transforming the country into a global center of manufacturing and consumption.

As the second-largest U.S. trading partner, the PRC is often presented dichotomously in the Western media as either a land of freewheeling opportunity or a dangerous threat to the industrialized world. In 2007 *Time Magazine* boldly announced that we had entered "the Chinese century," predicting that the commercial giant would soon surpass the United States as the most powerful national economy.[6] Despite this unprecedented prosperity, the PRC remains a developing country with dramatic and escalating inequalities based on gender, class, and geography. Expectations of cradle-to-grave employment security once guaranteed by the government through the socialist "iron rice bowl" (*tie fanwan*) have completely disappeared, making individual families completely responsible for their own well-being. Rising prosperity has fueled a pervasive sense of anxiety among citizens who engage in a fierce competition over limited resources.

China's unprecedented economic growth has inspired a flood of research and speculation about the long-term implications of the country's rapid development and industrialization. Yet few studies have considered the fundamental ways that global capitalism has also transformed the seemingly "private" realm of families or how these macrolevel changes have reshaped individual lives. Children in particular have received inadequate attention, even though many have been acutely affected by socioeconomic transformations.

Studies of contemporary Chinese life that do focus on the family tend to highlight society's most highly valued youth: urban middle-class only children. Referred to as "little emperors" and "empresses" who are doted on by two parents and four grandparents, these stereotypically spoiled offspring are the outcome of the one-child policy that was first enacted in 1980 and eventually discontinued in early 2016.[7] Mocked for their selfishness and rising obesity rates and even labeled by their own government as "wimps . . . with no fighting spirit,"[8] these coddled city kids nonetheless shoulder the heavy responsibility of boosting their country's international reputation and economic productivity.

Parents and state authorities have expended significant effort to mold this group into industrious future workers. Vanessa Fong points out that today's urban only children, like Chinese emperors of the past, are expected "to bring glory and prosperity to their empire."[9] As the most "modern" of Chinese citizens, little emperors have become the standard against which all other offspring are judged. Indeed, the pervasive sense of insecurity that governs Chinese society has even caused certain children to be "recognized as having more value than others and therefore more deserving of the rights of citizenship."[10]

Studies of pampered singletons can tell us solely about the "winners" in the new market economy. In contrast, this book exposes the dark underbelly of modernization by highlighting the experiences of those who were cast out of their families. Within a context of financial insecurity, limited fertility, and an existing cultural preference for sons, Chinese parents now carefully choose which offspring to invest their resources in.

Particularly in the countryside, parental desire to bear at least one healthy male heir who can care for them in old age has negatively impacted two main groups of kids, healthy rural daughters and special needs children. First, in what has been labeled a "gendercide," parents have turned to sex-selective abortion, abandonment, hiding, or even killing of *tens of millions* of daughters to protect the possibility of having a son. Of these "missing girls"—so-called because their names are missing from official records—a small fraction have been abandoned to state orphanages. Second, meteoric economic growth has been accompanied by a rapid increase in the number of children born with congenital illnesses and disabilities. Between 2001 and 2006 birth defects jumped by nearly 40 percent, an increase that many have attributed to environmental pollutants, particularly in coal-producing regions.[11] The

Chinese government estimates that now every year between 800,000 and 1.2 million babies are born with birth defects of which 30 to 40 percent are life threatening.[12] With few financial, medical, or social supports available for families with special needs offspring, many of these children have also been abandoned to state care.

The stakes surrounding children in the PRC are high because they "not only represent the future, but their bodies are the site upon which the terms of the national future are being worked out."[13] In the contemporary period, parental preferences for perfect offspring align well with the Chinese government's goal of producing a new generation of so-called "high quality" (*suzhi gao*) citizen-workers who can further the country's global economic and political ambitions. It should be noted that, even though the Chinese government halted the one-child policy in early 2016, many urbanites are deeply ambivalent about bearing a second child due to the high cost of child rearing. An online survey on *Sina News* that received over 164,000 responses found that 43 percent of individuals were not interested in having two children, while 28 percent said they would have to wait and see. Only 28 percent said that they would definitely do so.[14]

Hence, in an era defined by stringent restrictions on family size and growing social inequality, the country's youngest members have been separated into opposing groups with radically different life opportunities. Compared to healthy urban singletons who receive immense parental and state resources, disabled, poor, and/or female children in rural areas are considered less able to support their parents in the future, contributing to their relinquishment to state care. Because individual identity in China is defined in relationship to one's ancestral lineage, parentless children are deeply stigmatized. Through residing in orphanages, which tend to have little contact with broader society, they are also shut out of civic participation.

Global child rights organizations such as UNICEF (the United Nations Children's Fund) define orphans as children who have lost either one or both parents (and therefore may still be living with and/or supported by family members).[15] However, this book relies on the narrower official Chinese state definition, which refers only to children under age eighteen who have lost their parents through death or abandonment and do not receive support from others.[16] The first government survey on orphans in China, which was released in 2005, stated that 573,000 orphans were spread across the country, with the vast majority (86.3 percent) residing in rural areas. Those with special needs constituted 37.3 percent of institutionalized youth in cities and 66.6 percent of the total in rural areas.[17]

A follow-up study released by UNICEF China in 2010 found that the number of orphans had risen to 712,000, a 24 percent increase in only five years.[18] This figure, however, may still exclude more than a quarter of a million children whose parents never officially registered their births to avoid government penalties, thus disqualifying these offspring from state benefits.[19] Because most of China's orphans reside in the countryside, there are fewer children housed in urban welfare institutes—only about 78,000 in 2008.[20] Chinese authorities estimate that now up to 98 percent of children in welfare institutes are disabled.[21]

Within institutions that participate in international adoption, healthy girls converge with mentally and physically disabled youth such as Emma and Henry before being adopted. This situation, which was the norm in most of the orphanages I visited, challenged my own personal assumptions about abandonment and institutional care. Because I had closely followed China's highly gendered adoption trends for years, when I first began visiting orphanages in 2005 I knew that the majority of the children were abandoned rather than truly orphaned. Like many other Westerners with a surface-level understanding of these issues, I expected to find myself surrounded by countless healthy female babies. Yet, on my first visit to a well-regarded orphanage in the historic port city of Tianjin, I was surprised to discover that most of the young inhabitants had some kind of mental and/or physical disability. Over the course of a week I watched with fascination as a six-month-old infant with the wizened face of an old man sat patiently in a booster seat while a physical therapist fitted tiny, undoubtedly painful, braces onto his severely clubbed feet. During one of these sessions, I asked one of the caregivers in the room where all of the healthy girls were. She responded matter-of-factly, "*Dou bei waiguoren shouyang le* (They've all been adopted by foreigners)."

Between 2005 and 2014, I visited nine different state-run orphanages across the country and seldom ever met a healthy female child. It quickly became apparent that due to their immense desirability for adoption—both internationally and domestically—healthy girls generally leave institutions quite early. Hence, through an ironic twist of globalization, adoption has turned the local disadvantage of being born female into a benefit within orphanages that participate in this practice. This means that nowadays institutions are mostly filled with special needs children and youth, a group that includes a large percentage of boys.[22] In other words, orphanages serve as temporary stops for healthy girls on their way to new families and as permanent homes for sick and disabled children. Because special needs youth will likely never be adopted, their stories are rarely told. This book seeks to give voice to their experiences and examine their lives in relation to the unfolding of modernity in the PRC.

## Chinese Orphanages in the Global Spotlight

As a volunteer with the faith-based organization Tomorrow's Children, I spent several months at the Haifeng Children's Welfare Institute. Located in the primarily agricultural province of Henan, this urban facility cared for about 600 mostly special needs children from the surrounding region. The impressive six-story main structure was covered from top to bottom with thousands of sparkling white square tiles. Inside, the eerily empty lobby was furnished with expensive black leather couches and shiny mounted plaques that attested to the CWI's reputation as a national exemplar in the field of orphan care.

However, when I ascended the wide cement staircase to the second floor—out of sight of most visitors—the general conditions quickly deteriorated and began to resemble an aging hospital. One day early in my work at the CWI, I learned from another volunteer that the babies in the Tomorrow's Children unit were sent up from the main orphanage's "dying room," the place where infants with the lowest chances of survival were housed. Determined to see this room for myself, I ventured down a long hallway whose walls were gray from years of built-up grime, peeking furtively into rooms lit by naked fluorescent bulbs dangling from wires affixed precariously to the ceiling. As casually as possible, I walked past a worker pushing a dirty mop across the floor and entered a doorway at the end of the hall. Pulling aside a heavy rattling wooden bead curtain, I stepped into the small space and let out a quiet involuntary gasp.

Arrayed in front of me were eighteen extremely dirty, very sick babies and young children who lay in pairs on thin bamboo mats. All were swaddled tightly in thick, festive-looking red cotton quilts that matched the rough, rosy circles the intense cold had painted onto their cheeks. At least half of the babies had their heads shaved on one side—a startling image—indicating their recent arrival from hospitals where they had been given fluids intravenously through their scalps. (I learned later that this was a common treatment in Chinese hospitals.)

The atmosphere in the room was unnervingly quiet as two weary older women in stained white lab coats fed the entire group. All of the babies were drinking powdered formula out of plastic bottles that were propped up on little pillows next to their faces; within seconds several rolled out of their limited reach. After only a few minutes, the *ayi*s quickly circled the room and retrieved all of the bottles, even those that were still half-full. Sparsely furnished, the room noticeably lacked toys, medication, or even toothbrushes for the children. The words of a British volunteer echoed through my head: "This orphanage is a fantastic place to be if you survive to the age of four, but up until that point, it's definitely survival of the fittest."

Filled with conflicting emotions, I quietly backed out of the room and continued up the staircase three floors to the brightly lit Tomorrow's Children unit. Stepping over the threshold into the brand-new facility was like entering a sanitized alternate reality. A host of freshly painted Disney characters smiled down from the walls at chubby, laughing toddlers who raced around the warm, clean space in colorful new plastic baby walkers. Two white Western volunteers sat on the shiny wooden floor helping children play with expensive sensory-enhancing toys that they had brought from home in their luggage. Cradling babies in their arms, Chinese nannies in matching red uniforms rushed by to change diapers, give baths, or retrieve medicine from the British nurse.

In advanced industrialized societies, the term *orphanage* is generally associated with a bygone era, conjuring up sentimentalized images of Little Orphan Annie or the pitiful coal-smeared street urchins of Charles Dickens's novels. This type of group-based institutional care was mostly phased out in the United States in the early twentieth century.[23] In China, however, state-run institutions have served as the preferred method of caring for parentless children since the founding of the People's Republic in 1949.[24] Even so, Chinese orphanages operated largely unknown to the outside world until the 1990s, when several damning Western media exposés captivated international audiences. The images they showed of deplorable conditions in these facilities continue to inform dominant global perceptions of the PRC today.

In 1995, a television station in the United Kingdom aired "The Dying Rooms: China's Deepest Secret," a scathing documentary pieced together from undercover footage shot by British filmmakers in several state-run orphanages. Followed by a sequel in 1996, the films revealed never-before-seen images of severe child neglect in these institutions. Heart-wrenching scenes depicted toddlers strapped down against their will to high chairs or with their legs tightly bound together with rope. The cameras zoomed in on the blank faces of extremely malnourished babies lying ignored on urine-soaked blankets. The films were dedicated to a little girl caregivers referred to as Mei Ming (translated literally as "No Name"), a desperately ill child who was allegedly isolated for ten excruciating days before starving to death in a Guangdong orphanage. These "dying room" documentaries quickly gained global notoriety—reaching their height of pop culture awareness when they were featured on an episode of *Oprah*—and have reportedly been viewed by over 100 million people around the world.[25]

In coordination with these films, in 1996 the advocacy group Human Rights Watch/Asia (HRW) released a scathing indictment entitled *Death by Default: A Policy of Fatal Neglect in China's State Orphanages*. The report was based on Chinese government documents and eyewitness testimonials of workers at the Shanghai Children's Welfare Institute in the late 1980s and early 1990s. Within the hidden confines of orphanages, the report charged, death rates among child "inmates" were astonishingly high: up to 50 percent nationwide and 90 percent at the Shanghai CWI. A former orphanage doctor testified that caregivers were occasionally required to implement a macabre process known as "summary resolution," in which food and water were intentionally withheld from certain children until they succumbed to malnutrition. State-run institutions were described as cruel spaces that operated "as little more than assembly lines for the elimination of unwanted orphans."[26]

This unfavorable media exposure directed a global spotlight onto Chinese orphanages, spurring immense international outrage and straining relationships between the PRC and countries in the global north. In response, the *People's Daily*—the official mouthpiece of the Chinese Communist Party—took a decidedly defensive tone, claiming that the British documentary was "fabricated" and the human rights report was "distorted and exaggerated."[27] Charging moral hypocrisy, Chinese authorities drew attention to children's human rights violations in the United States. Using publicly available statistics on guns in American schools, high rates of child poverty, and the large numbers of adolescents involved in violent crimes, one statement charged that "Americans who seem to care about the conditions of Chinese children are totally indifferent to the plight of children in their own country."[28] The damaging publicity stemming from these horrific portrayals led the Chinese government to close off all foreign access to orphanages for several years and to completely revamp the Shanghai CWI, which is now considered a "model" orphanage.

This heated global exchange over purported abuse and neglect in Chinese state orphanages demonstrates how children are deeply interwoven with notions of national autonomy, identity, and global status. All too often their "bodies and minds [are] appropriated as the unprotected terrain upon which cultural battles are fought" at local, national, and global scales.[29] As the PRC solidifies its position as an economic leader and fierce competitor to Western democratic states, international discussions about the welfare of its most vulnerable youth have taken on even more acute political connotations. Anne Thurston, a China-based correspondent for *The Atlantic* who visited a dying room repeatedly in the mid-1990s, confirmed the existence of such spaces but also argued that these types of media depictions reinforce unfair cultural stereotypes that impact international relations. She writes, "The exposés have demonized China just as U.S.–China relations are settling into a more troubled period. American public opinion toward China has typically swung between extremes of admiration and mistrust, as we project our own hopes and fears on a country we have consistently misunderstood."[30]

After a chilling period that lasted several years, in the late 1990s state authorities quietly began welcoming more involvement in orphan relief from outside groups such as NGOs and foreign adoption agencies.[31] Yet the dearth of empirical data means that the controversial allegations of malign neglect in Chinese welfare institutes have never been resolved. Without other more current representations of these settings, the shocking images remain imprinted on the world's imagination.

My observations in the dying room of Haifeng CWI, which I visited several more times over the following months, proved that spaces where very sick and disabled children are housed together and given few resources or individualized care still existed more than a decade after the films' release. But dying rooms cannot be taken as the basis for all institutionalized care in China. This book provides a more accurate perspective by taking into account how the influx of global actors and first-world resources has improved conditions within many orphanages, while at the same time also creating a new set of dilemmas for parentless children.

## Outsourced Intimacy through International Adoption

*There is an ancient Chinese belief that an invisible, unbreakable red thread connects all those who are destined to be together.*[32]

In the popular children's book *The Red Thread: An Adoptive Fairy Tale*, a white king and queen reign over their beautiful, peaceful kingdom. Even though all appears well, something is painfully missing from their lives. Soon a "brilliant red thread" emerges from both of their hearts and leads the couple on an unpredictable journey overseas. Following the thread, the royal pair is led to a small Asian farming village where the inhabitants are poor but welcoming: "The people stared at them; they were so strange, with their clothes ripped to rags, hair tangled, and faces as pale as the moon. But the villagers smiled a greeting, for they were a friendly people." The couple, still unclear about the purpose of their travels, continues on toward a small bundle left in front of an old house. Inside, they find a smiling Chinese baby girl who has the other end of their red threads looped around her ankles. As the locals look on approvingly, an elderly Asian woman steps forward to tell the king and queen that this adorable infant now "belongs" to them.[33]

The myth of the red thread is woven throughout Western narratives of adoption from the PRC. Stemming from a Chinese folktale about a matchmaker—the Old Man of the Moon—who ties a red thread between prospective marriage partners from the moment they are born, the story originally justified the centuries-long practice of arranged marriages in premodern China. Since the mid-1990s, however, it has become a dominant theme within the discourse of international adoption and proliferates through a range of consumer items geared toward adoptive families, including bracelets, necklaces, wall hangings, and even a novel of the same title. Because abandonment renders the exact details of children's early lives largely unknowable, the red thread serves as an open-ended origin story. Symbolizing predestined connections between Western adoptive parents and Chinese babies, the myth helps to "mitigate the unsettling arbitrariness of adoption procedures that initiate a lifelong link between perfect strangers."[34]

Primarily white adoptive parents have used this folktale to solidify family bonds that span biological ties, race/ethnicity, and nationality. However, the sense of fatedness that underlies the story altogether bypasses the larger structural inequalities that gave rise to international adoptions in the first place. *Outsourced Children* aims to show how adoption is a wide-reaching political and economic institution that operates on individual, institutional, and global levels. Specifically, adoption is a key form of outsourced intimacy that has allowed Chinese state authorities to fulfill certain aims. I argue that, for the PRC, sending children abroad to join Western families has served as a form of "soft power," which refers to a country's ability to persuade others to do what it wants without force, coercion, or payments.[35] Through using globally desirable children as cultural bridges and representatives of soft power, Chinese officials have been able to enhance the nation's image abroad while also funding the local child welfare system.

The PRC first began its international adoption program in 1992 after sweeping family planning campaigns filled state orphanages with relinquished offspring.[36] Since then, over 140,000 children have joined predominantly white middle-class "forever families" throughout the global north.[37] The trend has been remarkably gendered, with young healthy girls comprising roughly 90 percent of adoptees.[38] These children experience a sudden escalation in social class and status through their global movement, comprising "one of the most privileged forms of diaspora and immigration" in the contemporary era.[39]

Facilitated and regulated by Chinese state authorities, international adoptions have arguably been motivated by the same market logic that has underlay the PRC's transition to global capitalism. At approximately US$15,000 to $30,000 per placement (of which nearly US$6,000 is brought over by prospective parents in their luggage, usually in cash, as a mandatory orphanage donation), Chinese adoptions and postadoption services and donations have mushroomed into a lucrative multimillion dollar industry. Although these funds have undoubtedly improved conditions in state orphanages, lax oversight and the vast profitability of international adoption have resulted in many (proven) allegations of baby buying, forced confiscations, and deception of birth families for the sake of sending children abroad.[40]

Since 2000, the PRC has been ranked the top "sending country" of adoptable children in the world. Although the total population of adoptees pales in comparison to the roughly *20 million* babies born in China every year, they have nonetheless garnered a disproportionate amount of attention in Western societies. Readily accepted into mainstream American culture, these girls have been featured in numerous documentaries, *New York Times* feature articles, Walmart commercials, and even HBO's *Sex and the City* when Charlotte, one of the main characters, adopts an adorable, if eerily silent, "Mandarin child" after a series of failed in-vitro treatments.

Researchers have also displayed an intense interest in this relatively homogeneous group, studying topics such as their behavioral adjustment, physiological development, language acquisition, and emotional attachment, as well as racial/ethnic identity formation in white families. Yet even as these mostly healthy girls have been studied extensively within first-world contexts, far less attention has been given to their early experiences in China. Because of this imbalance, international adoption is often viewed too simply as a one-way migration of babies from poor developing countries to rich industrialized regions.

This unidirectional perspective overlooks how this form of migration has established ongoing, crisscrossing transnational flows of people, resources, and knowledge between the PRC and Western countries. Most important for this analysis, adoption has enabled international humanitarians to use their own resources to assist Chinese state orphanages. Hence, adoption simultaneously functions as a means of individual family formation as well as an influential global institution central to the "cultural economy of circulating relationships of power and exchange" between the PRC and Western countries.[41]

## Outsourcing Intimacy to Western Humanitarian NGOs

The involvement of civil society and international actors in caring for China's marginalized youth is not a new phenomenon. During the late nineteenth and early twentieth centuries, the nongovernmental sector was integral in providing shelter and services to parentless children. Many private individuals, churches, and charitable organizations ran their own orphanages, some of which were founded by Western missionaries or wealthy Chinese philanthropists.[42] Early children's homes sought to instill into young people positive traits of self-sufficiency and self-reliance in the hopes of developing their human capital for the sake of the burgeoning nation-state. Historian Norman Apter explains that, contrary to today, when abandoned children are seen as detrimental to Chinese modernization, early-twentieth-century philanthropists viewed these disadvantaged children as "an untapped resource to be mobilized in the grander project of national construction."[43]

After the founding of the PRC in 1949, social welfare services became integral to the state's political legitimacy. In the early 1950s, private orphanages were either closed down or taken over and reorganized as state welfare institutes by the government, which took sole responsibility for finance and operations. Implementing a new approach toward child welfare, the regime prioritized collective well-being over that of the individual, reinforcing beliefs that orphaned and abandoned children would be best cared for in institutional settings.[44]

State-run orphanages—both then and now—tended to be located only in urban centers. In rural areas, on the other hand, families and agricultural collectives were responsible for providing for parentless youth. This unequal distribution of services and resources for children mirrored larger regional divides between cities and countryside that have continued to the present day, giving urbanites better education, health care, and material goods while leaving rural residents to fend for themselves. In combination with a rigid household registration system that has prevented peasants from becoming legitimate city residents, the PRC has been "essentially divided into two separate societies: a privileged urban society and a disenfranchised countryside."[45] Today, the government continues to maintain separate rural and urban child welfare provisions. Orphaned and abandoned children in cities are cared for in state-run institutions (the focus of this book) whereas those in the countryside are expected to receive care from informal kin networks; some rural orphans who lack relatives to care for them are eligible to receive a government subsidy known as the "Five Guarantees" system (*wu bao*) that generally doesn't include housing.[46]

Following the shift to a market economy, the Chinese government decentralized social welfare provisions and decreased service funding.[47] In turn, the brunt of responsibility for the care, health, and education of parentless children was transferred to local authorities. Although state welfare institutes were long prohibited from accepting outside sources of financial support, in the early 1990s they received permission to pursue a variety of income-generating endeavors and partnerships with private organizations. Nowadays, financing for orphanages operates according to the principle of "multiple levels, multiple channels, and multiple means."[48] International adoptions and involvement with foreign NGOs rank high on this list—pursuits that reflect the increasing globalization of Chinese society.

## The Realm of International Orphan Relief Organizations in China

The first-world volunteers I met in China who moved there specifically to work with orphanages had two goals, to improve the lives of unwanted youth and to "set an example" for local people. Many became aware of the plight of institutionalized children through negative media portrayals they had seen in their own countries. According to online commentator Nathalie Rothschild, the Western media presents a one-sided view of childhood in China that inspires both humanitarian interest and moral judgment:

> With numerous news reports and documentaries focusing on stories of Chinese parents dumping their babies in filthy orphanages, aborting female fetuses, putting children to work in factories or disciplining them in strict physical training regimes, we in the West have become used to seeing China portrayed as a brutal and bleak place for children . . . [These media portrayals] encourage a politics of pity, allowing Western viewers to feel both upset and superior in relation to China. Chinese adults are typically portrayed either as cruel child abusers or as hapless victims of an oppressive regime. And the logical conclusion is that they need the West's charity, pity and protection.[49]

Institutionalized youth who receive first-world care and resources are caught at the intersection of local and global understandings of individual rights and best interests. I saw this best through my ethnographic fieldwork as a volunteer for two groups, Tomorrow's Children and the Helping Hands Organization in Beijing. Helping Hands was a grassroots group of Western expatriate wives who assisted the Yongping Orphanage, a small state institution that cared for about forty mostly special needs youth on the outskirts of China's capital. Unlike Tomorrow's Children, the faith-based NGO described earlier that constructed its own intensive care units, took in babies, and hired its own staff, Helping Hands instead brought volunteers into the existing orphanage to care for children during short, two-hour weekday visits.

On one of my first visits to the Yongping Orphanage, my nostrils were overpowered by the distinctive odors of sour milk and dirty diapers the moment I walked through the glass doors. Directly in front of me was the baby room, a dimly lit space that was filled to capacity with metal cribs. An anxious one-year-old boy with a cleft lip repeatedly pounded his head against the cold bars of his metal crib. Disturbed by his behavior, I picked him up, and he clung to me tightly, refusing to be put back down. The only *ayi* in the room—a thin, tall Chinese woman in her early twenties—did not look up or acknowledge my presence. She was a flurry of movement, silently changing each child's sopping diaper, one after the other in a tedious row. "*Lei!*" ("exhausted"), she sighed to herself, blowing wisps of long black hair out of her face.

Out in the hallway I spotted Marjorie Lee, the energetic Chinese American founder of Helping Hands, standing over several *ayi*s who were huddled together tightly on a couch. With an audible tone of desperation, she implored in Mandarin, "I know you're tired, but these children's lives are in your hands. Please just do a little more for them!" The head caregiver, a woman in her late twenties named Xiao Chen, shifted uncomfortably in her seat. Unmistakably irritated, her cheeks were flushed a deep shade of red. Several days later, the *ayi* relayed a stinging message to the Western volunteers: "Our only responsibility is to make sure that children have food to eat and a place to sleep. If you have a problem with that, then you don't have to come here anymore!"

Xiao Chen's words revealed the possible complications that can arise when international groups aid local institutions. Global humanitarians have become an established—and highly integral—part of orphan care in recent years and provide a lens through which to view new forms of international engagement in China. Helping Hands was just one of many foreign NGOs that took advantage of the opportunity created by international adoption and the PRC's open-door policy to become involved in assisting abandoned children. Though often welcomed by local authorities seeking to develop greater economic self-sufficiency, transnational partnerships in Chinese orphanages do not always operate smoothly. Instead, they involve a complex mixture of collaboration, negotiation, and conflict between groups that are influenced by different understandings of what children need and deserve.

China's increased openness to foreign involvement in its child welfare sector has neatly coincided with shifting approaches to Western interventionism in developing countries. First-world humanitarian efforts that were previously guided by colonial conquest and missionary work have moved toward a human rights-infused model of development in the second half of the twentieth century.[50] Therefore, many of the Western volunteers I met through my research came to the PRC with the intention of modeling best practices for local people and inspiring them to care for needy children by emphasizing their individual rights.

In contemporary China there are three main types of Western orphan relief organizations: (1) adoption related; (2) expatriate/overseas Chinese; and (3) faith-based (usually evangelical Christian or Catholic).[51] These groups overlap, commonly sharing resources, knowledge, and even the children they support.[52] To provide a comprehensive overview of the world of orphan care in China, my analysis includes interviews with staff members at several adoption-related NGOs as well as ethnographic research at field sites that correspond with the second two categories.

In general, the first organizational category serves the interests of Western adoptive parents who aim to build cultural bridges between adoptees and Chinese society. These groups provide financial resources to refurbish state orphanages and care for the children who are left behind. Large well-known not-for-profit organizations such as Families with Children from China and the Half the Sky Foundation fit this classification.[53]

The second category involves organizations primarily operated by Western expatriate women and Western-educated overseas Chinese women who relocate to urban centers in the PRC to support their husbands' careers. Helping Hands is a prime example of this type. As the wives of international businessmen, diplomats, and journalists, these women are rarely able to secure a work visa abroad but maintain a desire to feel productive; as a result, many join local grassroots charity efforts to assist needy children in cities such as Beijing, Tianjin, Shanghai, and Guangzhou. The individuals who found and manage these organizations are often fluent in Chinese language and cultural practices, enabling them to build strong social networks and trust with local state authorities. Organizations such as these generally rely on the international business community to raise funds and for a steady stream of female volunteer labor. Despite their best intentions, the transience of expatriate life can make these efforts more superficial in nature.

Finally, faith-based Western orphan relief organizations include such groups as Tomorrow's Children. Unlike adoption-related NGOs, which are nondenominational, these organizations are generally inspired by the teachings of the Christian gospel and seek to provide intensive care to the most neglected and disparaged youth.[54] Typically, these foreign faith-based groups are permitted to operate in China—an officially atheistic state—as long as they avoid openly proselytizing or becoming highly politicized within their local communities.[55] Like Tomorrow's Children, a growing number of NGOs have opened their own foster homes and medical units to fill pervasive gaps in the care provided by urban state welfare institutes. In and around Beijing alone, ten to fifteen different private Western foster homes take in children with specialized medical needs whom state orphanages may not be able to (or may not wish to) serve. These care settings tend to use first-world practices to care for sick and disabled children, arranging for their medical care and postoperative treatment. Certain foster homes are widely known among orphanage directors for specializing in hard-to-treat ailments such as blindness or brittle bone syndrome. Although the children they care for technically remain wards of the Chinese state, most of these homes operate their own independent facilities, employing local staff and interacting with state authorities only sporadically.

Each of these different types of groups performs outsourced intimacy for the Chinese child welfare system by providing resources, training, and volunteer labor. This is true even though state authorities often regard civil society organizations, especially those run by foreigners, with deep suspicion. As Anthony Spires found, individual officials who are under pressure to "save face" for the government exhibit a great deal of ambivalence toward Western aid, often projecting caution or even hostility toward these groups in public although supporting them in private.[56]

This ambivalent approach to foreign NGOs forces them to fly under the radar, where they operate in "an informal, undocumented, and unrecognized manner."[57] In a precarious legal climate where private groups can be shut down at any time by state authorities, the survival of these organizations often relies on maintaining a low profile and drawing little attention to their efforts. However, these NGOs are generally permitted to continue their projects as long as they are willing to credit local officials with their successes.[58] Thus, since the 1990s the assistance of private humanitarians has quietly, though very dramatically, improved conditions in many state orphanages.

Without question, the people who perform the arduous work of caring for some of the world's most marginalized youth deserve immense respect. This is not solely a one-way process, however, because the foreign humanitarian aid groups I worked with accepted the responsibility of performing outsourced intimacy in exchange for the opportunity to import first-world practices and ideas into local institutional settings. In particular, Tomorrow's Children and Helping Hands attempted to import universalistic beliefs about children's "best interests" that frequently clashed with the views of their local state collaborators. At the root of these conflicts, I suggest, were different logics of care or understandings of good care that vary according to the specific circumstances (especially access to material resources) from which they emerge.

In brief, the faith-based volunteers at Tomorrow's Children endorsed an intensive logic of care. Based on ideologies of child-centeredness and redemption of the world's most vulnerable populations, the organization used intensive middle-class childrearing practices to remake special needs babies into priceless individuals who could be internationally adopted. This approach often created tensions with the organization's local Chinese caregivers who generally adhered to a pragmatic logic. These women viewed children more realistically within the highly competitive context of the PRC in which disabled people have limited life opportunities, causing them to push back against the labor-intensive individualized care imposed by the volunteers.

By contrast, the expatriate wife volunteers of the Helping Hands Organization subscribed to an emotional logic of care. Although they participated only when their transnational lifestyles allowed, expat wives' primary identities as mothers and housewives led them to prioritize emotional nurturance and maternal care—expectations that they imposed onto local *ayi*s. This caused disagreements with Yongping's workers, who were situated at the bottom of a rigid socialist institutional structure that espoused a custodial logic of care. Viewing its charges as objects to be minimally maintained rather than intensively nurtured, the institution provided only the most basic forms of physical care for them. As the following chapters will show, despite their good intentions, these conflicting logics of care sometimes backfired in regards to the children they sought to help.

## Methods and Fieldsites

This book draws primarily from participant observation and interviews that I conducted in state-run orphanages that were assisted by the two Western NGOs Helping Hands and Tomorrow's Children. The majority of this research took place between November 2006 and December 2007, followed by subsequent fieldwork trips in December 2008, July 2009, June 2011, May 2013, and June 2014. I originally sought to conduct research in welfare institutes that did not have foreign partnerships but soon realized that the political sensitivity of the topic made it nearly impossible for me—a graduate student from the United States—to gain access to state orphanages unless they already had an existing relationship with an international NGO.

As I have already mentioned, Western evangelical Christians ran Tomorrow's Children. The founders established their first medical foster home in 2002 to provide medical care to infants and toddlers with operable issues and treatable diseases who would likely not be able to survive in an institution. The group then used its global religious and business contacts to obtain pro bono or reduced-fee surgeries for children in regions with more advanced medical technology, such as the United States, Singapore, and Hong Kong. Children were often sent abroad for months at a time for surgery and recuperation. The organization worked hard to develop a close working relationship with the Chinese Ministry of Civil Affairs, the government branch responsible for orphans, the elderly, and the impoverished.

As a result, the organization was asked to build similar facilities in Henan Province in central China to provide hospice care for desperately ill infants and young children. Over four separate research trips totaling three months in length taken during 2007 and 2008, I conducted full-time ethnographic fieldwork in these units. Even though the staff and volunteers were all aware of my researcher status, I was treated like any other full-time volunteer. As the only bilingual staff member, my responsibilities included translation, helping nannies with childcare, dispensing medication, taking children to the hospital, and dealing with Chinese medical practitioners.

By contrast, Helping Hands was comprised primarily of affluent Western expatriate wives and mothers. These women originated from a diverse range of national backgrounds, but they shared high socioeconomic status due to their husbands' work in embassies, banks, international media outlets, and multinational corporations in Beijing. I attended their monthly member meetings and spent time with each of the "day groups": clusters of between four and six women who volunteered regularly one morning per week at the Yongping Orphanage. This small facility was located on the grounds of a larger social welfare institute that also featured a nursing home for several hundred senior citizens and a private-pay facility for developmentally disabled adults. My research was limited to just the children. I accompanied women to the orphanage on approximately thirty different occasions during which I conducted informal interviews, translated conversations, observed interactions between the volunteers and Chinese caregivers, and worked with the children. I also visited the orphanage on my own in about twenty other instances.

Over time I became deeply involved with Helping Hands, collaborating with an American friend to organize a volunteer group of Chinese and Western college students to visit Yongping Orphanage on Saturday afternoons. Together, we developed a bilingual list of guidelines and worked to build strong levels of trust with all of the *ayi*s by, for example, giving them traditional *hongbao* (red money-filled packets given during Chinese New Year) and thoroughly cleaning the facility each time we visited. Although we contributed large donations and held fund-raisers on behalf of the children, the expat wife volunteers largely ignored our group because the Saturday schedule interfered with their weekend family plans.[59]

In addition to studying these two main field sites, I also spent shorter lengths of time as a participant observer in multiple care settings around the country. These included six other official state institutions, five private Western foster homes, and one private rural orphanage run by Chinese Catholic nuns. I supplemented ethnographic fieldwork with over sixty interviews with Western volunteers, NGO staff members, Chinese state childcare workers, American adoptive parents, Chinese adoptees, scholars, and orphanage officials. Finally, I conducted archival research on the topics of state modernization and the changing child welfare regime. Although China is an incredibly complex country in which policies and practices vary significantly by region, these ethnographic case studies bring micro- and macrolevel processes together, connecting daily life in orphanages with the broader implications of outsourced intimacy in the PRC.

## The Chapters to Follow

As literal embodiments of the future, children are equated with China's global potential. Without ties to family, institutionalized youth like Emma and Henry define the outer limits of Chinese citizenship and belonging in a time of extraordinary social change. They are a blank slate on which competing visions of personhood are projected, existing at the juncture of local and global agendas. Chapter 2 provides a broader historical context for the economic reforms, fertility regulations, and policies governing "population quality" that have served as linchpins of the state modernization project since the late 1970s. The converging of these political factors with cultural understandings of gender and disability has largely contributed to the large-scale abandonment of healthy rural daughters and special needs children to state care.

Chapter 3 focuses on the "reversal of fortune" that global processes have created for healthy girls once they reach orphanages. Although strict fertility regulations and rampant son preference have heavily disadvantaged female children in China, the demand created by transnational adoption has transformed them into highly desirable Western daughters who are now also increasingly popular for domestic placements. Because international adoption has served as a form of soft power for the PRC, regulations on foreign adoptive parents have mirrored Chinese economic development since the early 1990s, becoming more stringent as the nation's resources, power, and global status have grown.

Adoption has opened the way for the Chinese state to outsource intimacy to global humanitarians inside its own borders. Given unprecedented access to state-run orphanages, these groups use their own resources to care for the mostly ill and disabled youth left behind in China. Chapter 4 provides a detailed ethnographic examination of life in the Tomorrow's Children special care units. I analyze disagreements that occurred between affluent Western faith-based volunteers who were motivated by ideologies of individual rights and child-centeredness and the units' local Chinese caregivers, who took a more pragmatic approach to children's best interests. Chapter 5 focuses on the collaboration between Helping Hands and the Yongping Orphanage. Using a gendered lens, I contextualize the conflicting logics of care that complicated the partnership and created deep ambivalence for both the Western expatriate wives and local Chinese caregivers.

Chapter 6 explores the recent rise in foreign adoptions of special needs children now that far fewer healthy girls are available to Western parents. Here, I highlight efforts that Tomorrow's Children made in China to transform sick and disabled youth into internationally desirable daughters and sons; this, I argue, connects to the broader American Christian evangelical movement to encourage more international adoptions as a means of promoting U.S. moral authority around the world. The book's conclusion delves into the larger implications of outsourced intimacy, exploring how it is beginning to come full circle as waves of adopted Chinese adolescents and young adults are returning to visit their birth country, one that is far more globally influential than when they left.

Together these chapters consider the interconnections that exist between the lives of institutionalized children and changing relations of power between the PRC and Western industrialized countries, particularly the United States. By redirecting attention toward girls and boys who have been cast out of their families during a time of unprecedented prosperity, we can better understand the human consequences of China's global rise.

# 2 Survival of the Fittest

*Relinquished Children in an Era of*
*"High Quality"*

ONE MUGGY MAY MORNING I was serving as a volunteer for the Western Christian organization Tomorrow's Children when Cathy, the British head nurse, asked me to take a six-month-old girl named Angel to the local hospital. Delivered to the special care unit at three weeks of age, the beautiful, rosy-cheeked baby suffered from stomach issues that had so far evaded clear diagnosis. Angel had recently developed a rough cough. Because she had been unable to eat for the last week, Cathy had taken the drastic step of inserting a feeding tube into her throat. But that morning, the little girl's breathing problems rendered her nearly unconscious. Within a few moments of Cathy's request, three of us—the child's *ayi*; the *ayi* supervisor, a kind woman named Liu Wen; and I—jumped into a cab and sped across town with the baby. I soon began my first (highly surreal) experience with Chinese public hospitals, where the difficulty of obtaining good medical care for special needs children became devastatingly real.

The entrance to the provincial hospital was crowded with throngs of people who were standing around, smoking and chatting loudly. Squeezing past them into the packed lobby, we were directed to a small observation room filled with parents and their sick children. To my surprise, everything was completely open to the public. In the center of the swarm of bodies, a doctor sat at a desk calmly conducting quick diagnoses of young patients. We waited in line for fifteen minutes before finally reaching the table. Despite the severity of the child's condition, the doctor was in no hurry. Pulling out her stethoscope, she listened to Angel's labored breathing for a moment. "The girl might have pneumonia," she stated matter-of-factly.

The other families in the room crowded around us in a tight circle, watching with fascination. Somehow ignoring the chatter, the doctor asked us how much money we were going to pay that day. Like all public hospitals in China, medical care was provided only after receiving a full cash payment up front, with the understanding that anything left over would be refunded later. Slightly flustered, Liu Wen checked her pocket book and answered, "I thought she was just going to have tests, so I only brought 1000 kuai" (around US$160). "That will be fine for now," the doctor responded, directing us to the pediatric ward so that Angel could undergo tests and a twenty-four-hour observation.

Pushing our way onto a full elevator, we headed up to the seventh floor. Accustomed to the sterility of first-world hospitals, I was taken aback by the conditions of the pediatric ward. At the end of a smoky hallway our small group entered a room with three beds, two of which were already occupied by women who were breast-feeding chubby babies with IVs attached to their heads. Fathers stood nearby, looking overwhelmed. Someone had strung a piece of rope from one side of the room to the other and hung up some laundry to dry. Angel's *ayi* placed the baby down on the stained, dirty sheet of the remaining bed. The father of one of the other infants had been sleeping there, and it was covered with a disarray of clothes, newspapers, and wet towels.

Soon, three women—a doctor and two young medical students—arrived to give Angel an oxygen treatment. One of the women placed a filmy, unwashed plastic head cover over the wheezing child's face, into which she inserted a tube that connected to a bubbling vial of liquid oxygen. The doctor then ran her fingernails over the flesh of Angel's tiny feet to check her reflexes; they remained unnervingly still. Clucking her tongue, she murmured disapprovingly, "The children we get from the orphanage are always the sickest ones. I just don't know why."

Five days later, I returned to the hospital with Nurse Cathy to check on Angel, who had indeed been diagnosed with severe pneumonia. In the taxi, Cathy mentioned that she had requested more tests under the suspicion that something was wrong with the baby's heart and stomach. On arrival, we learned that because the girl had been admitted during the May Day holiday—a week during which most Chinese people, including hospital staff, travel away from home—Angel had not yet received any new tests. Instead, the baby had only been given oxygen and medication for pneumonia. Even so, Angel's condition seemed to have greatly improved; her breathing was less labored, and normal reflexes had returned. The doctor assured us that the baby didn't need the additional tests Cathy had requested. We departed feeling much relieved.

Later that evening Cathy called me in a panic. "I just heard from Liu Wen, who said that Angel is dying! Can you go with me to the hospital right now?" My heart sank as we grabbed a taxi to the hospital for the second time that day. As we rushed into Angel's room in the pediatric ward, something was definitely amiss. The oxygen was gone, and the baby was no longer lying under the plastic head cover. Scanning around, I noticed a little bundle on the bed: Angel had died and was wrapped in a sheet. Cathy's hand flew over her mouth. Gasping loudly, she exclaimed, "She's died already?! What happened?" Mustering calm, I translated her conversation with the hospital nurse, who told us that the child had stopped breathing an hour earlier and did not respond to resuscitation efforts. The nurse then began to discuss payment arrangements. Although the child had already passed away, she told us, if we didn't settle the bill right away, the hospital would charge for another night's stay. Cathy glared at me through her tears. "Don't talk to me about money," she whispered through gritted teeth. "I want to know why she died."

Angel's primary doctor was nowhere to be found. Instead, the physician who had tried to revive the girl entered the room. She explained that Angel had very serious pneumonia as well as heart and stomach issues, as Cathy had suspected. "If the child had lived, we would have immediately sent her down for tests," she added. The hospital nurse stood to one side looking shell-shocked. "I've worked a thirty-six-hour shift because so many people are gone for the holiday. When I saw this child earlier today, she looked well. It was very sudden. We're so sorry (*feichang yihan*)," she said plaintively.

Though still teary eyed, Cathy composed herself as we took the child's body back to the welfare institute. During the cab ride back, she stared out the window and spoke softly: "The doctor probably knows a million more things about children than I do, but I just knew that her stomach was not normal." Arriving at the orphanage, we climbed the stairs to the Tomorrow's Children unit where I left Cathy to attend to the body. I found myself mourning for Angel's unknown parents who had no way of finding out about the organization's efforts to save their daughter or the fact that she had just died. The next day, I returned to the hospital with Angel's *ayi* to pick up her death certificate and exit papers. In total, the organization had paid over US$2,000 for inadequate treatment. The final refund came out to less than ten dollars.

## "Economically Useful" and "Emotionally Priceless" Offspring

This chapter grapples with the seeming irony of why, in this time of unprecedented growth and prosperity in the PRC, certain daughters and sons have been cast out of their families in large numbers. Of particular importance are Chinese government policies that have attempted to reshape the population to fulfill national objectives. Since the late 1970s punitive fertility regulations have been implemented alongside economic reforms to create a "lower quantity" of so-called "high quality" citizens—individuals whose bodies, minds, and skills match the needs of the expanding global economy.

This quest for a high quality population has vastly widened divides between children based on physical and mental attributes. Market logic has infiltrated the realm of family as state authorities pressure parents to rear healthy, intelligent, high quality offspring. Consequently, children are increasingly valued according to their perceived future economic productivity. Critics argue that this utilitarian approach to family formation may be gradually reducing human life to stark financial terms.[1]

In *Pricing the Priceless Child*, Viviana Zelizer famously demonstrated how the changing socioeconomic context of America in the late nineteenth and early twentieth centuries transformed the social value of children.[2] When the economy was primarily agricultural, the worth of a son or daughter was assessed in terms of his or her labor power and ability to contribute to the household economy. However, as the U.S. economy developed and expanded, new ideologies of children as sacred, vulnerable individuals needy of adult protection became prevalent. Progressive Era child-saving campaigns that advocated for mandatory schooling and abolishing child labor pushed young people completely out of the public arena and into the private sphere of family, emotions, and domesticity. Over time, children came to be seen exclusively in moral and emotional terms, divorced from the realm of financial considerations. In other words, "While men's lives became more and more entangled with market considerations, children's lives were gradually severed from market ties."[3]

The view that children are "economically worthless" but "emotionally priceless" is now common in first-world societies. Globalization has also carried these ideals into the PRC, where they have taken hold among middle-class parents. As a nation in the midst of capitalist transformation, China provides a relevant contemporary comparison to Zelizer's U.S.-based historical account. However, the shift in discourses about childhood that followed American industrialization is complicated by local cultural norms. In China, although economic conditions have changed quickly, the nationwide improvement in wages and living standards has not overturned the Confucian expectation of filial piety—the idea that offspring are wholly responsible for the financial well-being of their elderly parents. Within the context of an inadequate social welfare safety net, many couples use childbearing as the primary strategy to secure their future livelihoods, meaning that in China one's own children are considered the most reliable form of welfare.[4] Nowadays a hybrid model wherein offspring are seen as both emotionally priceless *and* economically useful predominates family life in the PRC. Hence, the Chinese state's modernization goals and its desire for economic glory in the international sphere, I suggest, has encouraged the unequal treatment of children and deprived some of families altogether.

## The Quest to Create a "High Quality" Population

At the dawn of the 21st century, China is full of images of the poster child of the nation's future. Invariably an urban child, it is the planned progeny, the well-educated, well-dressed, healthy, "quality" child who is playing and laughing as it graces the cities' pleasure spots. Elsewhere—never in the same frame—are cultural images of the unplanned child who is not supposed to exist. Usually the offspring of rural migrants in the cities, it is the uneducated, ragged, unhealthy child who is crying or fighting, disrupting social order, and generally polluting the cities' margins. These two images are never seen together, but they belong side by side, for the creation of the planned child—the marker of modernity, the savior of the nation—has entailed the simultaneous creation of the unplanned child—the sign of backwardness, the obstacle that keeps China from attaining its rightful place on the world stage.[5]

As anthropologist Susan Greenhalgh notes in the preceding quotation, the PRC's stringent population control program has divided children into two opposing categories based on their perceived level of "quality." Although urban little emperors bear the heavy responsibility of building a glorious future for their country, a much larger number of youths from rural areas are viewed at best as a hindrance, and at worst as a dangerous threat, to Chinese modernization. The abandonment of "unplanned children" relates directly to the PRC's quest to become a modern society and achieve "material and moral parity with the West."[6]

For the past century China's vast population has been viewed as both the country's greatest strength and its primary weakness. In 1989, then–Chinese president Jiang Zemin gave a speech that overtly linked the "quality" of the nation's people with its global respectability. In his view, the future of the country "demands raising the quality of the entire nation, to develop the new socialist person with ideals, morality, education, and discipline" who will help the PRC to "stand on its own feet among the world's nations."[7] Jiang's statement echoed a long-standing Chinese belief that a country's level of modernity direct reflects the quality of its citizens. But what exactly is "quality" (*suzhi* in Mandarin)? How does this notion relate to the relinquishment of certain girls and boys?

Child abandonment in China has historically served as a socially acceptable survival strategy for poor rural families. Prior to the establishment of the People's Republic in 1949, the desertion or infanticide of children, particularly daughters, tended to escalate during times of war, famine, and natural disasters.[8] What is different today is the addition of government policies that have defined the social value of offspring. For the past few decades, the unwieldy combination of new economic pressures, fertility regulations, and an enduring cultural preference for (healthy) sons has motivated the abandonment of healthy rural girls and special needs youth.

Although there is no precise definition of *suzhi*, the concept broadly refers to a set of quantifiable categories relating to the physical health, mental ability, and the productive power of individuals, groups, and nations.[9] Like so many other issues affecting contemporary Chinese society, discussions of *suzhi* ignited when the nation began transitioning to a market economy. Intellectuals argued that for the country to be considered on par with the industrialized West and Japan, it was necessary to develop a healthy, well-educated population. Since that time mentions of *suzhi* have abounded in both scholarly and popular culture debates, with the PRC's population quality often discussed in negative terms when compared to advanced industrialized nations.

In my various conversations with Chinese people, they were rarely able to give a clear definition of *suzhi*. They generally associated "high quality" with higher educational level and "having culture" (*you wenhua*). *Suzhi* is also reflected in behavior, as was made clear during a conversation I had with a young Chinese official during a visit to an orphanage in central China. On hearing that I was from the United States the official approached me to talk. His sister, who was studying for a master's degree in California, had told him that cars there stopped to allow pedestrians to cross the street. "This really shows that American society has 'higher quality' (*gao suzhi*) than China, where cars will run you over," he stated earnestly.

By contrast, others raised myriad examples of the PRC's "low quality," including broad national issues like corrupt election practices, low educational levels, and individual behaviors such as cutting in line or spitting in public. In fact, during the time of my fieldwork, Beijing was making bold attempts to combat bad manners in an effort to clean up its image for the 2008 Summer Olympic Games. The city instituted a large-scale "Civility Campaign" that encouraged commuters to line up in an orderly fashion at bus and subway stations. The eleventh of each month was designated as "Polite Queuing Day," and the city enlisted thousands of volunteers sporting satiny red sashes inscribed with the words "It's civilized to line up, it's glorious to be polite" to monitor line jumping at public venues. A related antispitting campaign imposed stiff fines of up to 50 yuan (roughly US$8.00) for those caught doing so in public.[10] Individual behavior was correlated with national image based on the concern that foreigners might think the population as a whole had low quality if some citizens behaved in an uncultured manner.

*Suzhi* is seen as continually improvable through external intervention. Because the country's enormous population is seen "not just as a problem but as a principal causal factor in China's failure to progress in history," regulating childbearing has dominated governmental efforts to raise population quality.[11] Correspondingly, the family has become an apparatus through which children's social value has been shaped and constructed. Although, in general, economic development tends to cause a natural drop in fertility levels, the Chinese state has used heavily restricted childbearing to accelerate modernization.[12] Following the chaotic decade of the Cultural Revolution (1966–1976), the nation began developing the economy to transform itself into a globally competitive socialist society. China's vast populace and traditionally high levels of fertility were seen as a major constraint to economic expansion, and population growth was soon framed as a crisis of epic proportions. Reducing the nation's fertility was understood as "the essential ingredient for a 'modern' Chinese nation-state's survival, without which plans for national development and security were threatened."[13]

The government instituted large-scale birth control campaigns in the early 1970s, dramatically lowering fertility through a combination of voluntary and coercive measures. The *"wan-xi-shao"* ("later-longer-fewer") campaign used financial incentives to promote later marriage, the spacing of offspring at least four years apart, and having fewer children overall. Incredibly, by 1977, the national fertility rate—which peaked at nearly six children per couple in 1965—had dropped by over 50 percent. By the end of the 1970s, Chinese modernization efforts focused on the "twin pillars" of expanding economic production and limiting population growth.[14] In 1980, the government took population restrictions further by instituting the one-child policy, which remains the world's most stringent fertility regulation. Until October 2015, nearly all couples in urban areas were limited to just one birth, although the policy was generally more relaxed in rural areas.

Mandated childbearing limits have been extraordinarily successful in lowering overall fertility rates. According to official estimates, family planning regulations have prevented a staggering 400 million-plus births since 1970.[15] The PRC's national fertility rate has even dropped well below the rates found in many Western industrialized nations. In 2008, for example, total fertility in China averaged 1.77 live births per woman, lower than either Norway or Sweden.[16] Nonetheless, enforcing these laws sometimes involved the use of highly controversial coercive tactics by local family planning officials attempting to stay within state quotas. Numerous reports described stark penalties for "unplanned" births, including steep fines, coerced late-term abortions and sterilizations, destruction of property, detainment of individuals, and, in the most extreme cases, the forcible removal of infants from their homes. Demographer Wang Feng describes the PRC's fertility regulations as "one of the most draconian examples of government social engineering ever seen."[17]

Over time, family planning policies shifted their focus from limiting the overall fertility rate to improving population quality. State campaigns have encouraged and even pressured Chinese parents to bear healthy, intelligent "high quality" (*suzhi gao*) offspring who will advance the new economy. These high quality persons are typically characterized as savvy cosmopolitan urbanites who are educated, entrepreneurial, self-disciplined, physically fit, *and* mentally equipped to compete in the global labor market.[18] Rather than succeeding solely for their own sake, high quality citizens are expected to use their skills to build the Chinese nation. Anthropologist Terry Woronov explains the immense pressure faced by these individuals: "High quality subjects are those who will implement the new economy, bring China into its position of global respect, and fulfill its historical destiny."[19]

At its core, *suzhi* discourse promotes a social Darwinistic ideology espousing the "survival of the fittest" among nations and among individual citizens. This perspective has justified increased levels of governmental control over the intimate realms of family, reproduction, and childrearing. As symbols of the future, children are at the center of efforts to raise population quality as part of a collective project of nation building. By encouraging citizens to invest more energy and resources in fewer children, the government has implemented an effective form of social engineering that appears subtle, noncoercive, and even caring. Its emphasis on *suzhi* "bolsters the government's attempt to cast itself as a modernistic and compassionate regime."[20] (See the photo in Figure 2.1.)

The state-driven goal of producing high quality citizens exacerbates existing parental desires to bear healthy, capable offspring who can provide for them in old age through expectations of filial piety. Although parents today raise far fewer children, offspring are legally responsible for supporting and caring for elderly parents to repay the investment they received growing up. This reciprocal parent–child contract is even codified in law such that parents who are unable to provide for themselves have the right to demand financial support payments from their offspring.[21] This familial obligation maintains Chinese cultural values while also allowing the central government to forgo providing extensive social welfare benefits to its citizens. In light of the lack of retirement benefits, parents willingly make enormous investments in their child's future in an attempt to ensure their child's employability in the increasingly competitive job market. This much more calculated approach to family creation extends to a deepening obsession with cultivating children's mental and physical development. Although the PRC has become a renowned superpower, the nation is still marked by "great uncertainties about family security and political stability that become focused on the child."[22]

The quest to improve demographic quality has profoundly alarming eugenic undertones. According to Gary Sigley, "In its most extreme form, *suzhi* functions as a measure of human value which . . . constructs a hierarchy of worthiness and utility."[23] *Suzhi* discourse plays a key role in ranking social groups, reinforcing social disparities, and placing differential value on the bodies of infants. Within this context of increasingly calculated childbearing and diminishing state support, being born female and/or with special

**Figure 2.1.** State propaganda poster from 1987, artist unknown, "Less Births, Better Births, to Develop China Vigorously," *Shaosheng yousheng zhenxing Zhonghua.*

SOURCE: Chineseposters.net.

needs can push a child into the "low quality" category that renders her or him less worthy of investment. The government's desire to enhance the economic productivity of its population is directly tied to individual parents' decisions. Consequently, countless children have been left out on the street; under bridges; at bus, police, and train stations; and at orphanage gates as parents seek another attempt to produce a "high quality" child. Chinese researchers Shang Xiaoyuan and colleagues describe the utilitarianism that governs parental decision-making under these contemporary constraints:

> In a market economy, people have become "resources" whose value has increased and therefore the economic utility of people has gone up . . . Because there are no relative moral restrictions, those who are considered as having low "economic value" (girls and disabled children), are naturally more likely to be abandoned.[24]

## Gender Inequality and the Plight of the "Missing Girls"

In the fall of 2007 I walked through an old apartment complex in Beijing's university district and spotted a poster of a smiling Asian girl in pigtails playfully holding a large red rubber ball. A series of slogans were printed above her head in large Chinese characters:

> *Care for girls.*
> *All of society needs to pay great attention to girls' healthy development.*
> *Today's daughters are the builders of tomorrow's society.*
> *Caring for girls protects everyone's future interests.*
> *Bearing a boy, bearing a girl, just let it happen naturally.*
> *Girls and boys both enjoy the same rights.*

Beneath the child's photo were three smaller pictures. The first featured a metal scale with a group of baby boys seated on one side and baby girls on the other; more boys tipped the scale precipitously downward. The second showed a laughing father tossing his happy daughter in the air. The third shot depicted a wedding scene between a Chinese bride and groom exchanging vows before an audience made up of entirely anonymous, identical-looking young Chinese men also dressed as grooms. At first sight, the imagery on this poster was shocking. Yet as I traveled around the city, into the surrounding countryside, and further out into distant provinces, I saw many similar examples. All were part of the same governmental "Care for Girls" campaign (*guan'ai nü hai xingdong*) that began in 2003 to combat discrimination against daughters—a campaign that has been largely unsuccessful. This campaign arose in response to the astronomical increase in births of male infants and the corresponding drop in female infants in China since the early 1980s.

To give a bit of background, throughout recorded history, China's population always included fewer women than men, particularly in times of war, famine, or natural disaster.[25] Sons were traditionally valued for their labor power and ability to perform ancestral rites of worship whereas a girl "married out" of her parents' household to join her husband's family. In patrilineal Chinese society, male offspring have historically brought strength and prestige to parents, helping them secure economic and political resources.[26] Even so, it is necessary to differentiate the origins of discrimination against daughters from the more contemporary reasons for its continued survival. The skewed gender ratio among children is an evolving, socially constructed phenomenon rather than an unchangeable legacy.

The infant sex ratio at birth (SRB) for any country under normal circumstances averages between 103 and 107 males per 100 females due to male infants' increased chances of mortality from congenital issues or illness.[27] In the mid-1950s, the SRB was normal—though the mortality rate was still much higher for young girls than for boys due to neglect of daughters.[28] In fact, the highly skewed sex ratio that marks the current era did not develop until after the institution of economic reforms and family planning regulations in the late 1970s. Chinese fertility surveys show that although the sex ratio held close to the average in the two decades preceding the onset of the one-child policy, in the 1980s the country witnessed a startling increase in the ratio of male to female births. According to the last census in 2010, the sex ratio of male to female children rose to 118 boys per 100 girls.[29] Certain regions of China— in particular, central and southern provinces—have experienced shockingly high birth rates of more than 130 boys to every 100 girls.[30]

Facilitated by ultrasound technology that enables fetal sex identification, demographers have found that up to *one million* female fetuses are aborted annually across the country.[31] Economist Amartya Sen calculated that as early as 1992, *48 million* females were missing in China.[32] However, his tabulation accounted for all age ranges. Focusing purely on the abnormal SRB among children born in the reform era, Chinese researchers Zhang Kun and Zhang Songlin estimated that, between 1980 and 2000, over 14 million female fetuses were sex-selectively aborted. Put another way, *for every boy born, at least one female fetus was aborted.* They conservatively calculated that, by 2005, the total number of sex-selective abortions in China would reach an astounding 25 million.[33] Although the government passed laws in 1986 and again in 1993 outlawing the use of ultrasound technology for sex selection, there has been a total lack of enforcement.[34] In addition to sex-selective abortions, countless female children are informally adopted at the local level, kept by their birth families but never registered with the authorities, or abandoned altogether.[35] Because their births are missing from official census polls, these children are known as "missing girls."

In China's rural areas, improvements in the standard of living have done little to erode son preference. A lack of state social welfare support renders the elderly particularly vulnerable if they lack sons to support them in old age. Although the law states that all children must care for their parents, most rural couples continue to believe that sons, rather than daughters, are responsible for bearing this burden.[36] Simultaneously, the economic cost of raising children has skyrocketed. In this insecure environment, Elizabeth Croll argues, parents have become selective and strategic in their childbearing decisions "to ensure and maximize long-term returns."[37] Limitations on fertility have led millions of parents to try to ensure that they bear at least one boy, as "the inter-generational contract is primarily and almost exclusively a parent–son contract."[38]

Despite the rapidly changing social context, a survey of elderly Chinese in six rural provinces revealed that parents of a son experience greater economic security. Among the elderly couples who had only daughters, 50 percent lived alone, whereas for those who had at least one son, the number dropped to 30 percent.[39] Fears about the future spur Chinese parents to bear and rear healthy males, whereas restricted fertility has reinvigorated the long-standing cultural assumption that girls are more expendable. In the logic of the new economy, many parents believe that investing in female children may negatively affect their own future livelihoods.

## The "1.5 Child Policy" and Official Legitimation of Daughter Discrimination

China is not the only country to have an extremely abnormal SRB. Other Asian nations, particularly India, Pakistan, South Korea, and Taiwan, as well as parts of North Africa, have experienced a similar phenomenon of abnormally low numbers of female infants. However, China is the only one of these countries with policies restricting childbearing. As a result, the country has the highest SRB maintained over the longest period of time of any nation in the world.[40] This troubling situation is the outcome of national policies that have sanctioned son preference and encouraged discrimination against daughters.

At the time of its inception in 1980, the one-child policy was intended to severely restrict the growth of China's rural peasants, who accounted for 80 percent of all residents. Villagers resisted birth planning, sometimes violently, because of their intense desire for sons.[41] Consequently, beginning in 1984, the government relaxed the one-child policy in most rural areas to allow for a "one-son-or-two-child-policy," commonly known in China as the "1.5 child policy." This law required couples to stop bearing children if their firstborn offspring was male but allowed them a second birth after a period of several years if their firstborn was female.

This led to a bifurcated system of birth planning enforcement across urban and rural areas. During the thirty-five years of its implementation, the one-child policy was strictly applied in large cities, particularly the Beijing, Shanghai, and Tianjin municipalities, though enforcement was eventually relaxed for couples in which both partners were themselves only children or whose first child was disabled as well as for members of ethnic minority groups. As a result, majority ethnic provinces such as Tibet and Xinjiang have sex ratios that are closer to normal levels. Because of this variability, Chinese people did not use the term "one-child policy" at all, preferring instead to use the all-encompassing term of "birth planning" (jihua shengyü).

Easing the policy to allow rural couples to try for at least one son appeased many rural residents, but it also officially legitimated gender discrimination within families and inadvertently encouraged the mass abortion or abandonment of female children.[42] Studies have found that most Chinese parents would prefer to have both a son and a daughter. Although a girl typically leaves her household at marriage and contributes her labor to her husband's family, they are valued for the emotional support they provide to their parents, particularly as parents grow older.[43] However, sons are seen as necessary to future economic survival—a sentiment that Kay Ann Johnson has labeled as "wanting a daughter, but needing a son."[44]

In their research on abandonment in rural central China in the 1990s, Kay Ann Johnson and her colleagues found that the likelihood of a daughter being relinquished depended on whether there was a son in the family. Of

the abandoned children in their study, 90 percent were female, and the vast
majority of these were second- or third-born daughters in families without a
son.[45] By contrast, only a small fraction of the abandoned children were firstborn daughters, demonstrating that, under the 1.5 child policy, girls were not
wholly abandoned at will but were sometimes sacrificed to make room for a
boy. A combination of social factors and cultural traditions has thus created
an environment in which "a very different calculus of life chances emerges, in
which some bodies have more value than others and in which some must be
sacrificed."[46]

Even though girls experience broad discrimination in China, not all have
been equally affected. Over the course of doing this research, many Americans who hear about my research have exclaimed something along the lines
of, "The Chinese just don't like girls, do they?" As with most social issues,
the problem of gender discrimination is not that simple. The PRC is a diverse
country where female children face immensely different life chances and opportunities depending on their geographic location and residence permit status (*hukou*). For example, although population regulations have perpetuated
extreme gender bias in the countryside, urban girls have actually benefited due
to their mothers' access to employment opportunities.[47] In cities, women are
able to express filial piety by providing financially for elderly parents, which
has eroded certain patriarchal norms. Promisingly, Zhang Lihong's ethnographic study of a village in central China showed that increased earning opportunities for women have raised their value in rural families. Zhang found
that young couples appear to embrace raising only one child, even when that
child is a girl.[48] Despite this optimistic finding, the nation's steadily rising SRB
demonstrates that it is still not the case in most rural areas.

## The Marginalization of Special Needs Children in the Reform Era

In 2011, the Chinese government opened a series of "baby hatches" (*ying'er
anquandao*)—safe houses located in large cities where desperate parents can
legally abandon their infants to state care. Painted in happy pastel colors with
cartoon animals adorning the walls, the small spaces are empty save for an air
conditioner, an incubator, and a baby bed. Parents (or other relatives, in some
cases) set the baby inside and then press a button to alert a nearby orphanage.
If all goes according to plan, someone from the orphanage will retrieve the
child within ten minutes. Over the past few years, more than thirty of these

hatches have opened across the country in an effort to combat the high mortality rates suffered by sick and disabled infants who would otherwise be left on the streets.

Outside one baby hatch in Jinan, the capital of Shandong Province, a film crew documented a young mother's final moments with her daughter, who had cerebral palsy. Dressed casually in a striped orange shirt and gray sweat pants, her hair swept up into a messy ponytail, the woman cradled the child tightly as she strode toward the front door. The baby's grandmother trailed a few steps behind; she clutched a bag of belongings with one hand while her other hand grasped a pink baby blanket that she used to dab tears from her swollen eyes. Through the glass door, the mother could be seen laying the girl down onto a bed, covering her mouth in anguish as she took one last glance and quickly departed. Several moments later, a nurse arrived to take the child away.[49]

Although it is unknown how many girls and boys have entered state care this way, these facilities are the subject of intense debate. Their use reveals a critical social issue in China—the lack of state support or other affordable options for parents who bear special needs offspring. One baby hatch that opened in the bustling industrial metropolis of Guangzhou, Guangdong Province, at the end of January 2014 was forced to suspend services after it received 262 babies in less than two months. The deluge of abandoned infants was far greater than anyone had predicted, overwhelming the nearby orphanage and its staff. Tellingly, *all* of the children left at the hatch were ill or disabled, reflecting a broader societal shift away from the relinquishment of healthy girls. Indeed, the gender disparity of babies left at this hatch ran counter to the expected direction. Perhaps because male infants have higher chances of being born with many congenital illnesses, the total number of boys heavily outweighed that of girls: Among these babies, 148 were male while 114 were female.[50] Of the group, 110 children had cerebral palsy, 39 had Down syndrome, and 32 suffered from congenital heart disease.

The socioeconomic changes in China that disadvantage healthy rural daughters have also deepened divides between children based on physical and mental ability. Even as state authorities roundly condemn the trend of daughter discrimination, bias against ill and disabled people remains widespread.[51] Children who are born with any kind of abnormality—but especially those with mental disabilities—are stigmatized for disrupting the "natural" order of family and expectations of filial piety.[52] This situation speaks to a startling new population trend: While the nation's overall fertility rate has plummeted, the number of babies born with congenital issues has skyrocketed. According to official statistics, a disabled or sick child is born in the PRC *every thirty seconds*.[53] Of the 20 million babies born in China each year, roughly 800,000 to 1.2 million are now born with some form of illness or disability—a 40 percent increase between 2001 and 2006. Rural regions in particular have been disproportionately affected, leading some to speculate that environmental pollutants, particularly the widespread burning of coal, are to blame.[54] According to estimates, only 20 to 30 percent of these infants can be cured or treated. Another 40 percent suffer from lifelong problems, and the remaining 30 to 40 percent die soon after birth.[55] The financial costs of caring for these children number well into the billions of dollars.

The growing rates of relinquished special needs children are yet another unintended consequence of modernization, one that reflects changes in the Chinese health care system. From 1952 to 1982, all hospital and medical facilities in the country were government owned and funded. Rural health care was provided through agricultural communes that owned the land, organized cultivation, distributed the harvest, and provided social services to members.[56] During this era, the Chinese health care system gained worldwide attention for achieving enormous improvements at low cost. Thanks to the work of roughly one million "barefoot doctors"—young people who received basic medical training and provided health care and hygiene lessons in villages—rates of infectious diseases and maternal and child mortality plummeted. Amazingly, life expectancy nearly doubled, increasing from about thirty-five to sixty-eight years in the span of only a few decades.[57]

However, in the early 1980s, the rural communes were dismantled and villagers' access to subsidized health services and prenatal care all but disappeared. In the process, the funding base for health insurance fell through, leaving around 90 percent of China's 900 million peasants totally uninsured.[58] As individuals assumed responsibility for their own livelihoods, shared funds that were once used to care for vulnerable citizens dried up, placing the entire burden of caring for sick and disabled children onto individual families.[59] As the central government's share of health care spending has plunged, China's medical system has been plagued with rising costs that hospitals have attempted to offset with expensive high-tech services and pharmaceutical sales. This has created a major disparity in health care access that privileges the rising urban middle class and disadvantages rural working-class and poor citizens. According to one study, "In less than two decades, China's health care system was transformed from one that provided preventive and afford-able basic health care to all people to one in which people cannot afford basic care and many families are driven into poverty because of large medical expenses."[60] Analysts have drawn parallels between the decline of health care in the PRC and the much-critiqued U.S. health care system.

In 2006, the average bill for a single hospital admission in China was nearly equivalent to the annual per capita income.[61] As Angel's story showed, to receive services at public Chinese hospitals patients must undergo a consultation to estimate their cost, which must be paid up front and in cash. After treatment is completed, the hospital returns any unused money to the patient. These out-of-pocket medical costs can easily bankrupt families with ill or disabled offspring. The story of Chen Dafu and his wife Zhen Yuling, a poor migrant couple living in Guangzhou whose daughter was born with Down syndrome, a cleft palate, and breathing issues, sheds light on the financial difficulty that rural residents face on bearing a disabled child. Averaging a combined income of only US$800 per month, the couple was told that they would have to pay US$1,000 *per day* for their daughter's medical treatment. Unable to afford this cost, they decided to abandon their one-day-old infant outside a baby hatch in Guangzhou late one morning. Tragically, they did not realize that the hatch was closed during the day. The baby, who had been placed in a large shopping bag, went unnoticed and died after twelve hours. Chen Dafu was arrested the next day for child abandonment, even though his actions would have been entirely legal if the hatch had been open.[62]

Seeking to understand this situation more clearly, I engaged in a series of informal conversations with local people to get their perspective. One evening in the Tomorrow's Children facility, I asked two *ayi*s why they thought so many special needs children were abandoned. "These people are poor," one woman stated, "and parents can't afford to treat children's illnesses." Playing devil's advocate, I pointed out a large billboard next to the road that led into the orphanage. In large bold characters it stated that cleft palate surgeries were available for free from the local hospital—a clear attempt to prevent parents from giving up their children. As she rocked a sleeping baby back and forth in her arms, the other *ayi* elaborated, "There are some people who still wouldn't want the kid. Chinese people really care about 'face' [*mianzi*]. If there is going to be a major noticeable scar, a lot of people would abandon them even if the surgery was free." She continued, "Because people are allowed to have only one child, everyone wants one that is 'normal' (*shei dou yao zhengchang de haizi*)." It was clear from the conversation that by "normal," she was referring to offspring without any physical or mental abnormalities.

The *ayi*'s explanation points to the strong cultural stigma against congenital disease or deformity in China, which has historically been interpreted as symbolic punishment for the wrongdoing of ancestors. Ellen Holroyd's study of parental caregivers of intellectually disabled youth in Hong Kong explores this cultural bias, finding that a person with "an imperfect or diseased body or mind is seen as incomplete and without moral standing."[63] This cultural stigma also affects family members, who often find themselves socially isolated and marginalized alongside their children. Even more important, parents can find it especially difficult to care for special needs youth because they disrupt cultural expectations of the parent–child contract. As Holroyd explains, "The 'natural' progression of patterns of reciprocity" between parents and their intellectually disabled offspring "is neither immediate, in the form of gratitude, nor generalized, in the form of delayed care, with debts never able to be reclaimed."[64] Within Mainland China, these cultural attitudes, in combination with the lack of government assistance, high costs of treatment, and parental desire for a "normal" child, have contributed to the flood of ill and disabled boys and girls given up to state care.

## Special Needs Children as a Threat to Chinese Modernity

In a time of cutthroat competition for scarce resources, the disabled population has been framed as a societal burden hindering China's economic progress.[65] State authorities themselves have promoted this sentiment, including Jiang Fan, vice-minister of China's National Population and Family Planning Commission. In October 2007, Jiang delivered a speech at a conference on the prevention of birth defects that linked China's international competitiveness with population quality. The speech called for the eradication of physical and mental abnormalities in children to improve the nation's global profile. According to Jiang, special needs children endangered "China's comprehensive national strength, its international competitiveness, sustainable socioeconomic development, as well as the realization of our strategic vision to construct a full-scale well-off society."[66]

The disparagement of individuals who may not be able to perform productive labor is a key feature of socialist societies. In her research on reproduction in socialist Romania, Gail Kligman found that people were given rights and treatment according to their ability to work. Individuals who were considered "nonproductive" were stigmatized and isolated in their communally based social circles. "Those who did not or could not labor in the interest of achieving socialism," she writes, "were deemed 'parasites' eating away at the healthy, disciplined body of 'the people.'"[67] Likewise, in China the terms used to refer to the disabled reflect the categorizing of people according to their usefulness to the larger collective. Since the 1980s, the government has promoted usage of the term *canji* ("injured and diseased"), but many still use the pejorative term *canfei* ("injured and wasted/useless"). Anthropologist Qian Linliang argues that the continuing widespread usage of *canfei* "indicates the public concern with the lack of 'ability' or 'productivity' of 'the disabled,' who are perceived as unable to survive on their own and having to depend on others; in other words, they are useless."[68]

In the reform era, individual bodies are tightly interwoven with state goals of economic progress, thus excluding ill and disabled people from a "modern," productive national body. Some influential Chinese authorities have suggested that families and society would be better off if special needs children were never born at all.[69] For example, in the early 1990s, former premier Li Peng was officially quoted as saying, "Mentally retarded people give birth to idiots. They can't take care of themselves, they and their parents will suffer, and they'll be detrimental to our aim of raising the quality of the people." One newspaper succinctly summarized his message as "idiots produce idiots."[70]

In a proactive effort to prevent so-called inferior births, in 1995, the government implemented the Maternal and Infant Health Law. Originally named the "Eugenics Law," it required couples to submit to an in-depth health examination that tested for serious genetic, infectious, and mental disorders or diseases before they were allowed to marry. If a detected disorder was deemed serious, the couple was not permitted to marry without agreeing to contraception or sterilization. After years of negative international media attention, premarital health checks were made voluntary in 2003 under the guise of protecting individual rights. As a result, very few couples now choose to undergo these invasive exams. Foreign observers have lauded this shift, but many in China now worry that the lack of governmental oversight has contributed to the large increase in births of disabled children.[71]

Concerns about disabilities are not new to the reform era but are instead a modern incarnation of long-standing angst over the future of the Chinese nation. After the Qing dynasty fell in 1911, intellectuals looked to improvements in science and technology to create healthier citizens and to cultivate Chinese civilization and modernity.[72] During the early twentieth century, eugenic practices of "selective breeding" prevalent in some Western societies were proposed as the key to preventing societal degeneration in China—a struggling nation that native intellectuals often referred to as a "sick person" comprised of peasants with poor physical quality. Historian Frank Dikötter writes that, at this time, "The strengthening of the population and the improvement of the race were the essential prerequisites for national survival, an immense effort in which every single individual was meant to participate actively by closely monitoring his or her reproductive potential."[73]

Although the PRC closed itself off to the outside world after 1949 and rejected Western influence and scientific practices for nearly thirty years, discussions about population quality became prevalent again during the transition to capitalism. Bodily and mental ability now operate as a powerful mechanism for sorting youth into advantaged and disadvantaged groups depending on their perceived future utility. Unlike rural daughters, who are valued for the emotional care they provide to parents and would likely be raised by their birth families in the absence of fertility regulations (something that will be easily measured with the nation's switch to a two-child policy), disabled youth are often seen to lack social value. Because good health and mental capacity are considered indicative of a nation's productive potential, ill and disabled youth are seen as not merely incapable of contributing to national progress but as actually impeding it through their very existence. State media warn against the potential harm these children may wreak on families and broader society. A recent article in the *China Daily* reads:

> It goes without saying that a baby with a birth defect will greatly diminish the happiness that the addition of a new member brings to the family. The medical expenses and worries about the future of such babies will affect adversely the family's economy and psychology. The increasing number of such newborns will, at the same time, become a heavy burden on social security.[74]

Such pronouncements reinforce the idea that individual reproductive desires are secondary to the goals of the nation. Western observers have tended to fixate on the coercive aspects of China's fertility regulations, particularly on the now defunct one-child policy. In doing so, they have overlooked the immense ideological influence of *suzhi* discourse, which works "not so much by op-pressing people as by changing who they are—their sense of self, their bodies, their desires and their hopes for the future."[75] The power of this discourse lies in its ability to govern both thought and behavior.

## Conclusion

Within the space of a single generation, the PRC's embrace of global capital-ism and neoliberal values has radically stratified its citizens. From the 1970s until now the Chinese government has linked its population quality with the nation's ability to fully modernize, resulting in pervasive surveillance of fami-lies and heavy intervention into childbearing practices. *Suzhi* discourse has justified the need for smaller families and transformed perceptions of chil-dren's social value. In an era marked by competition, insecurity, and an in-adequate social safety net, offspring viewed as having less future economic potential have faced a much higher risk of relinquishment.

Discussions of population quality reflect long-standing concerns about China's position as a "modern" and "civilized" nation. As such, boundaries between socially useful or useless bodies have been created, establishing "their eligibility for inclusion in or exclusion from an idealized socialist body poli-tic."[76] Chinese economic development has come at significant cost to certain youth. New models of social acceptability have rendered invisible millions of children who fall outside the state-sanctioned norm: a form of social engi-neering that has articulated new categories of personhood—literally, the right to become a living person in many cases. Now the new policy that all couples are allowed to have two children without penalty provides some hope that the numbers of sex-selective abortions and abandonments of healthy girls will be reduced. However, it is unclear whether this policy change will similarly ben-efit special needs youth without a corresponding attempt to change societal stigmas towards disability.

The Chinese government has used its population-related concerns to con-trol, dominate, and manipulate its citizenry during an unstable period. By attempting to create an ideal population and make individuals responsible for their own quality and that of their offspring, this discourse "diverts atten-tion away from deficiencies and inequities resulting from structures, institu-tions, and practices either created, or endorsed by, the state."[77] Which chil-dren are seen to have acceptable quality and which are considered expendable reflects the government's long-term global ambitions. Some of these socially devalued daughters and sons, however, are being pulled into larger processes of outsourced intimacy through international adoption and being cared for by Western humanitarian NGOs. Although these processes can bring a great deal of hope and opportunities for abandoned youth, they do not signal the end of conflicts and ethical dilemmas over their lives and well-being.

# 3 From "Missing Girls" to America's Sweethearts

*Adoption and the Reversal of Fortune for Healthy Chinese Daughters*

IN THE LATE 1990S CHEN ZHIJING, a grandmother and former orphanage employee in Hunan Province, would occasionally find infants who had been abandoned in public places and bring them in to her workplace. At first, the orphanage reimbursed only her travel costs, but in the year 2000 orphanage officials asked her to supply more children. By 2005 Chen was earning up to US$500 per infant—an exorbitant sum for a low-wage worker. This also happened to be the year that transnational adoptions from China reached their peak, with a total of 14,493 infants sent to sixteen different Western nations.[1]

Seeing the potential for profit, Chen soon enlisted the help of her son Duan Yueneng, who recruited his wife, aunt, and other family members to the baby-selling business. They located a supplier 600 miles away in Guangdong Province who claimed to have a steady source of "unwanted" female infants. These children had allegedly been abandoned at local hospitals, although, according to reports, many of the girls had actually been abducted from migrant worker communities bordering the city of Guangzhou.[2] Babies were transported by train to Hunan—sometimes, disturbingly, packed into cardboard boxes—and then sold to six social welfare institutes.

Duan has spoken openly to the media about his role in this industry, sharing documents such as receipts, bank transfers, and orphanage logs with journalists. These documents all contain falsified information such as made-up abandonment locations and purported "finders" of the infants. The former baby broker also kept children's adoption papers and accurate records of foreign parents, including copies of their passports. Speaking to the *Washington Post*, Duan matter-of-factly described trafficking as a business that sprung up in response to Western demand for Chinese children: "We sold babies to orphanages. Others did, too. They bought them because foreigners wanted them, and then made big profits when the babies were adopted."[3] These "big profits" came from the large cash "donation" (totaling nearly US\$6,000 in 2016) that foreign parents were required to pay directly to their child's orphanage.

One particular orphanage—the Hengyang Social Welfare Institute (SWI)—was at the center of this trade in infant girls. Officials there began purchasing babies from traffickers in 2002, selling them to other orphanages for roughly US\$1,000 apiece. Two years later the Hengyang SWI joined China's international adoption program, at which point it kept the donations for itself after sending children abroad.[4] Through a transnational circuit of money and small bodies, between 2002 and 2005 these six orphanages alone provided roughly 1,000 trafficked babies to foreign families. Chinese authorities uncovered these illicit activities in late 2005. In a highly publicized trial, nine of the suppliers and one child welfare institute director were convicted of child trafficking and given sentences ranging between one and fifteen years. In Hengyang County, twenty-three officials were fired for their participation, and international adoptions from Hunan Province were suspended for several months.[5] More generally, since that pivotal time the number of children that the PRC sends abroad has plummeted.

Duan was set free after five years imprisonment to care for his elderly parents. Staunchly unapologetic, he and his mother asserted that they always kept the children's best interests in mind. Though it remains unclear whether the babies they sold to orphanages were purchased for profit or were legitimately abandoned, they believed they helped give underprivileged girls better life opportunities. "Many of those babies would have died if nobody took them in. I took good care of the babies," Chen Zhijing declared. "You can be the judge—am I a bad person for what I did?"[6]

This story highlights the dark side of outsourced intimacy that has fundamentally altered the lives of institutionalized children in the PRC. Since the Chinese government first began allowing foreign adoptions in 1992, over 140,000 mostly healthy girls have joined families in the global north. This circulation of children among Chinese birth parents, orphanages, and Western families—and the central role that state policy has played in all of this—involves a complicated mixture of care and commodification in an expanding international market. The PRC's usage of outsourced intimacy through international adoption brings to the fore uneasy tensions between consumerism and more romanticized notions of family as a private, sacred realm untouched by market forces.

Critics argue that the spread of global capitalism has created a "free market" in children wherein altruistic motivations have been overshadowed by parental preferences.[7] As the Hunan child trafficking case (and many others like it) makes clear, foreign adoption incentivized procuring healthy female babies by any means possible, in the process transforming "once-unwanted Chinese girls into valuable commodities worth stealing."[8] It is evident that the financial transactions involved in international adoption complicate standard notions of how families should form. Yet, there are also many different sides to this story.

Strict fertility regulations and rampant son preference have heavily disadvantaged female children in China, especially in rural areas. This chapter, however, explores how the PRC's international adoption program elevates the social value of these abandoned daughters once they reach orphanages, transforming locally disparaged "missing girls" into priceless Western sweethearts. The foreign investment made in these children through adoption can be considered a form of outsourced intimacy that transforms them into "high quality" offspring who can further the PRC's population project. I suggest that, by sending children abroad, the Chinese government has been able to exert a form of "soft power," which refers to a country's ability to persuade others to do what it wants without the usage of force or other types of coercion.[9]

Even though adoptees reside abroad, Chinese people still consider them to have a deep cultural connection to their mother country due to an essentialized, blood-based understanding of race and ethnicity, an idea prevalent in the PRC and other East Asian countries. As Lyn Pan writes, belonging does not depend on "language, or religion, or any other markers of ethnicity, but some primordial core or essence of Chineseness which one has by virtue of one's Chinese genes."[10] By allowing Western families to raise children who are considered Chinese regardless of their passports into global citizens, adoption has promoted foreign interest in the PRC that will have long-term economic, cultural, and political benefits for the country. Even so, in recent years the Chinese government has severely restricted Western parents' eligibility to adopt, while encouraging domestic placements.[11] These shifts in adoption policy arguably demonstrate the country's enhanced ability to assert itself on the global stage through the symbolic circulation of its children.

## Adoption and the Revaluation of Chinese Girls

International adoption has long been the subject of intense ethical debates. In the United States, this practice emerged out of American wartime occupation of Asia in the 1950s. These early adoptions had clear religious overtones and were primarily motivated by Christian "narratives of love, altruism, salvation, and redemption."[12] South Korea soon became a primary sending country; since 1955 the nation has sent roughly 200,000 children abroad, half of whom have joined American families.[13] Compared to Korean adoptees, however, Chinese girls have garnered a disproportionate amount of media attention. Popular interest in their lives relates to numerous factors, including the speed and scale of their adoptions in the 1990s and 2000s, the embrace of multiculturalism in the United States, and technological advances that have facilitated discussion and information sharing. Yet perhaps most relevant is the growing awareness and interest in the PRC as an international superpower.

Although Chinese children make up only a tiny fraction of adopted youth in the United States, the transracial and transnational nature of their families makes them stand out.[14] The journey that transforms these girls from "endangered daughters"[15] to priceless objects of Western love and affection is well documented, in part because these adoptees have been remarkably homogeneous until recent years. According to U.S. Immigration Statistics, in 2006 the composite of Chinese children adopted by Americans was 91 percent female, with 44 percent less than one year old and 52 percent between the ages of one and four.[16] These adoptees have tended to originate from a relatively small number of southern Chinese provinces that have the highest sex ratio disparities, such as Guangdong, Jiangxi, Anhui, Hunan, and Guangxi.[17] Table 3.1 lists the numbers of children sent to the top five Western receiving nations between 1992 and 2012.

During the 1990s, China's "overabundance of abandoned female infants correlated almost perfectly with the desire of adoptive parents in the West to adopt female infants."[18] The PRC quickly developed a stellar international reputation for running a smooth, reliable, and honest adoption program that all but guaranteed the arrival of a healthy girl within a brief one-year time frame. Orphanage officials and adoption agencies assured eager parents that Chinese birth mothers did not drink or smoke—evidence that they actually "wanted" their pregnancy. It soon became accepted fact that Chinese women abandoned their daughters as a result of the pressure to produce a son under

**Table 3.1.** Adoptions from China, 1992–2014.

| State | 1992–1997 | 1998–2002 | 2003 | 2004 | 2005 | 2006 | 2007 | 2008 | 2009 | 2010 | 2011 | 2012 | 2013 | 2014 | 1992–2014 |
|---|---|---|---|---|---|---|---|---|---|---|---|---|---|---|---|
| United States | 10,383 | 24,193 | 6,857 | 7,038 | 7,906 | 6,492 | 5,453 | 3,912 | 3,001 | 3,401 | 2,589 | 2,697 | 2,306 | 2,040 | 88,268 |
| Spain | 105 | 3,300 | 1,043 | 2,389 | 2,753 | 1,759 | 1,059 | 619 | 573 | 584 | 677 | 447 | 293 | 229 | 15,830 |
| Canada | 2,947 | 3,610 | 1,115 | 1,007 | 960 | 625 | 662 | 334 | 377 | 424 | 288 | 254 | 216 | 157 | 12,976 |
| Netherlands | 479 | 1,893 | 567 | 800 | 666 | 362 | 365 | 299 | 283 | 306 | 197 | 192 | 136 | 137 | 6,685 |
| Sweden | 339 | 947 | 373 | 497 | 462 | 314 | 280 | 206 | 248 | 190 | 111 | 89 | 59 | 50 | 4,165 |

Data from Peter Selman, *International Adoptions from the People's Republic of China, 1992–2014*. Working paper, Newcastle University, UK, 2015.

the one-child policy. Western parents commonly assumed that all adoptable babies were left anonymously in crowded marketplaces, at hospitals, at police stations, and outside orphanage gates where they were sure to be found, a presumption that unraveled with the Hunan trafficking case in 2005. However, even revelations about illegal baby trafficking have not diminished the interest of Western parents in adopting these children.

### Gendered and Racialized "Flexibility" of Chinese Daughters in American Society

Exactly why Chinese girls are so highly desired by foreign families is somewhat unclear. Their overwhelming popularity goes far beyond issues of supply and demand, as Western applications have vastly outweighed the number of available children for years. Research suggests that American adoptive parents—who are typically white, middle-class, highly educated individuals—tend to favor Asian girls for reasons relating to gender and race. The explanation, at least in part, lies in shifting understandings about children's inherent purpose within families. As Viviana Zelizer has shown, the historic cultural transformation that altered American views of childhood during the late nineteenth and early twentieth centuries also profoundly reshaped adoption practices. In previous eras, parents viewed children as economically useful workers, thus preferring to adopt strong teenage boys who could contribute their labor to the household. As broader industrialization and urbanization transformed children into sentimentalized objects of affection, adoptive parents began expressing preferences for babies and for "pretty little girls" in particular.[19]

These inclinations remain strong today, as shown by a recent large-scale study of prospective adoptive parents in the United States that measured a distinct preference for girls. The authors propose that this preference may reflect societal perceptions of boys as being more difficult to raise. In other words, they suggest, adoptive parents may "fear dysfunctional social behavior in adopted children and perceive girls as 'less risky' than boys in that respect"—a perception that rests on heavily gendered stereotypes of male and female behavior.[20] Furthermore, a recent psychological survey of heterosexual, lesbian, and gay male preadoptive couples found that roughly half expressed a gender preference. Of those with a preference, every group except gay men heavily preferred girls.[21] The gender preference for children may also differ by the gender of adoptive parents. Because women are usually the initiators of adoption and tend to take the lead in the process, they may make a concerted effort to secure a daughter.[22] In comparison, scholars have found that American men often prefer sons as their biological children. Men who have a biological son are slightly more likely to marry or to stay married than those who do not.[23]

The popularity of Chinese adoptees has hinged, at least in part, on the overwhelming likelihood that the child will be female. Many adoptive parents I spoke with mentioned gender as a motivating factor in their decision to adopt. For example, a white adoptive mother I interviewed in California in 2004 stated that she and her female partner chose China because they considered it "a privilege to give a girl a chance." Adoption administrators are overtly aware of this preference for daughters and have tried to counter it to encourage the adoption of boys. On the colorful red website of the child advocacy organization Love Without Boundaries, "Being a Boy" is listed as a special need alongside physiological issues such as infectious diseases, neurologic conditions, and heart/blood conditions.[24] To draw awareness to the plight of boys, the organization created a sentimentalized Youtube video. Interspersed with photos of adorable Chinese male infants and toddlers, stark white words appear on a black background:

> There is one "special need," ironically, that often is the barrier to a child ever finding a permanent home.
> Being orphaned
> And being born a BOY.
> If an adoption agency is given a list of children to place from overseas, the girls will often be chosen quickly while the boys often wait . . .
> and wait . . .
> and wait for a family to step forward.

Accompanied by soothing guitar strums, the video uses a series of masculine stereotypes to encourage prospective parents (presumably fathers) to consider adopting a boy. Some of these reasons include:

> Because it's never too early to buy that first truck.
> Because playing sports is fun.
> Because we need more cowboys.

Because girls are the obvious favorites, the video depicts them as more emotional and demanding. In one photo, a smiling adolescent Chinese boy with a fixed cleft lip stands tightly wedged between his white mother and father. With twinkling eyes, his adoptive parents hold up a handmade sign over their son's torso. Swirly letters drawn on pink construction paper spell out the words, "Less drama, less prima donna." Finally, as the background music rises to a dramatic crescendo, the video asks viewers, "Can you open your heart to a little boy? . . . And open your life to adventure?"[25]

Adoption is also deeply racialized in ways that favor Chinese girls. For example, a survey of mostly white prospective parents found that they were seven times more likely to be interested in adopting a non–African American baby than an African American one. Put into stark economic terms, the study found that parents would be willing to pay roughly *US$38,000 dollars more* to adopt a child who is not black.[26] This points to socially constructed perceptions of race that have created a hierarchy of desirability among adoptable children. Prevalent American societal discourses about poverty and childbearing often depict low-income blacks as being irresponsible bearers of "crack babies." Poor children of color who end up in the foster care system may be regarded as "damaged goods" forever tainted by the immoral choices of their parents.[27]

Whether or not parents are conscious of their racialized preferences, many consider Chinese girls to be more easily assimilable into white families than black children would be.[28] Anthropologist Toby Volkman writes that China–U.S. adoption provides "a less fraught space in which to deal with race than stories about transracial black–white adoptions in the U.S."[29] The perspective of white single mother Patricia Matthews serves as a prime example of how individuals can unconsciously rank children by race. We chatted in her sunny kitchen in West Los Angeles while her five-year-old daughter watched television in the next room. During our conversation, Patricia claimed to be completely "color-blind" in regards to race. Waving her hand dismissively, she said, "The topic of race has always been a silly one to me. People create those kinds of boundaries." Yet when I asked about her attempts at domestic adoption prior to choosing China, she unwittingly revealed a negative view of African Americans. Absent-mindedly twirling a wispy lock of blonde hair around her finger, she recalled: "Both the babies I was considering were mixed black and white." Leaning forward, she spoke in a conspiratorial half-whisper, "Because when you're single and you're domestically adopting, you're kind of the bottom of the barrel."

Other parents I interviewed were highly aware of China–U.S. adoption as a racially "less fraught space." I asked Harry Davis, a white adoptive father who had two white biological children prior to adopting a Chinese daughter, whether the biracial nature of his family had ever drawn negative reactions from strangers. Pursing his lips, he thought for a moment before stating carefully, "If we had African American boys, I bet we'd face a lot more interesting racial-type tension. So I've seen people look at us weird wherever we are, but I've never seen real blatant racism."

Whereas adopted American children might be considered "damaged goods," a different set of discourses more positively frames orphaned children in developing countries as the innocent victims of culturally backward societies. According to Ortiz and Briggs, this discourse asserts that child "victims" can be redeemed through international adoption:

> Unlike the poor of the First World . . . whose families are constructed as perverse rejecters of social norms, the rural Third World poor are romanticized as malleable innocents who can take advantage of the opportunities passed up by the dysfunctional domestic underclass. This makes their children the innocent of the innocent—a bare canvas upon which American-ness can be reproduced, an image not just of (adoptive) parents, but of the supremely modern.[30]

Chinese birth mothers and the female infants they relinquish have generally been framed as powerless victims of a sexist culture and an oppressive communist regime.[31] Many adoptive parents drew on an oversimplified view of the one-child policy as justification for choosing China over pursuing a domestic adoption. "It wasn't like we needed another child," Harry Davis told me candidly. "But we wanted to make a statement against a policy that's causing some problems." Thus, the romantic image of saving a child from a life of political repression and sexism to enjoy the freedom and equality of American society has provided powerful ideological motivation for parents to adopt from the PRC.

Parents' favorable perceptions of Chinese children have been bolstered by the influential societal stereotype of Asians as hardworking, family oriented, and professionally and academically successful "model minorities." This common understanding of Asian Americans has pushed them into the realm of "honorary whites."[32] In her study of white adoptive parents in the Midwest, Kazuyo Kubo found that Asian babies are generally preferred because they are seen as culturally, but not racially, different.[33] Patricia Matthews, the single mother quoted earlier, reflected this sentiment by asserting that she "never really thought about Asians as a different race," instead believing that she and her daughter were from different cultures. Despite this color-blind perspective, she conceded that adopted Asian girls experience less racial prejudice in the U.S. than other children:

> I think that being someone who's black or mixed race is much harder than being Asian. I never worry now that [my daughter] is going to have a hard time being accepted. There'll be discrimination, but it's a different kind of thing, more because we look different than because she happens to be from a race that is *perceived a different way.*

In Western societies, Asian women have historically been stereotypically depicted as highly sexualized "docile dolls" or as "diabolic Dragon Ladies." According to Uchida, in the United States "there is a consensus that the characteristics of a typical Oriental Woman include submissiveness, subservience, obedience, passivity and domesticity."[34] The parents I spoke with did not consciously "Orientalize" their adopted daughters. Yet their imaginings of Asian women were often based more on dominant ideologies than reality. Paula Archer, one of the two Chinese American adoptive mothers I interviewed, noted that even she "bought into" these sorts of stereotypes when she adopted her daughter. She explained:

> I think there's clearly a population of men who believe Chinese women—like the mail-order bride thing—I'm sure there is a macho-type population that like the idea of the petite little Chinese girl who's quiet and submissive. And in some ways we kind of bought into that because with Kyla; here we thought we were going to adopt a sweet little Chinese girl, and she is so rambunctious, and she's also big-boned . . . I thought I was going to end up with this petite, quiet little Asian girl!

Due to their foreign origins, the gendered and racialized construction of children's adoptability situates Chinese girls as unquestionably deserving of rescue. Andrea Louie argues that white adoptive parents tend to consider Chinese girls as "innately intelligent and fairly trouble free to raise . . . and free of problems associated with fetal alcohol syndrome, crack addiction, institutional neglect, and other problems attributed to [those who are] domestically adopted."[35] As culturally redeemable and racially flexible subjects, these girls can "not only be rescued *from* their unfortunate conditions abroad, but also absorbed *into* a new life at home. They are at once strange and familiar, different yet knowable."[36]

## The Gendered Paradox of Bloodline and Domestic Adoption in China

The widespread visibility of transnational adoptions has contributed to the common belief in Western countries that Chinese people do not adopt children unrelated by blood. On the contrary, it has long been common custom in China for parents—especially those in rural regions—to use informal means to attain additional offspring. Throughout history girls have been particularly favored for informal adoption due to issues of bloodline; in essence, because biological sons carry on the family name, females have been seen as less directly related to their birth families. Ironically, this perception has allowed girls to be more easily accepted into Chinese adoptive families than boys.

Prior to the founding of the PRC in 1949, boys and girls were adopted for different reasons. In pre-Communist China, boys were often adopted by families without sons to continue the lineage and ensure care for parents in old age. By contrast, girls were often adopted to usher in the birth of a son, as a child in the household was believed to improve a couple's chances of conception. Poor families also adopted infant girls as *tongyangxi*, or future daughters-in-law, who would become wives to their young sons when they grew up.[37] The 1950 Marriage Law, one of the first major pieces of legislation passed by the Chinese Communist Party, expressly prohibited this practice and gave women the legal right to divorce their husbands. This resulted in a flurry of divorces instigated by women who had been adopted as child brides.

In the contemporary era, informal adoption has been heavily influenced by state limits on childbearing. A large-scale demographic survey of reported births in the PRC showed that adoption has served as an important method for parents to obtain another child. During the 1970s there were roughly 200,000 adoptions per year in China. Yet after stringent fertility regulations were passed in the late 1970s, the number rose to an average of 400,000 between 1984 and 1986 and to over 500,000 in 1987. By 1988 (the final year of the survey) there were an estimated 6 million legally adopted children in the PRC. In total, between 1970 and 1987, adoptions accounted for an estimated 2.5 percent of all live births, up from only 1 percent in the prior decade.[38]

Since the institution of fertility regulations, Chinese couples have often turned to adoption to fulfill their desires for another child while avoiding the steep penalties of an "out-of-plan" birth. Zhang Weiguo's qualitative study of 425 rural adoptions found that rather than involving orphanages, the vast majority of adoptions took place through informal social networks. Nearly 50 percent were arranged through intermediaries and 26 percent between kin, whereas less than 1 percent were processed through state orphanages.[39] The remaining 23 percent of adoptions were of children who were found by strangers soon after abandonment.

Females are increasingly overrepresented among adopted children in China. Between 1950 and 1969 girls comprised 58.9 percent of total internal adoptions, a number that rose to 71.3 percent by the late 1980s.[40] Zhang's study supports this trend, finding that females accounted for three-quarters of the children in his survey, all of whom were adopted during the 1980s and 1990s. Stringent birth control regulations provide the most obvious reason for this gender skew; prior to the loosening of these regulations many Chinese parents defied the one-child policy to adopt, "in part because the same policy create[d] a demand for girls among families who have filled, or overfilled, their quota of births with sons yet still long for a daughter."[41] Kay Ann Johnson found that informal domestic adoption in the 1980s and 1990s reduced overcrowding in Chinese orphanages.[42] Nonetheless, fertility regulations placed many obstacles in the way of domestically adopted children since a reported 80 percent of these arrangements are not registered with authorities.[43] Without official registration, they are considered "black children" (*hei haizi*) who lack basic rights of citizenship such as health care and education. In another major policy shift, in December 2015 the Chinese government announced it would allow this group of roughly 13 million undocumented people, many of whose births were in violation of the one-child policy, to apply for official registration.[44]

In the PRC, adopting a girl through informal means is generally less expensive than adopting a healthy boy; parents in Zhang's study reported paying up to 15,000 yuan for a boy but less than 5,700 yuan for a girl (it was unclear to whom the money was paid). In addition to initial adoption costs, daughters are considerably less costly to raise because parents shoulder the burden of paying for their sons' marriage costs, including bride price and often the purchase of a new home for the couple. Furthermore, within the new economy, sons' filial piety has waned, giving daughters added emotional significance to parents as caregivers.[45] According to Chen Zhanbiao, director of the Marriage and Adoption Registration Division of the Shanghai Civil Affairs Bureau, "Domestic families like to adopt a healthy girl so that when they get old someone can take care of them."[46] Thus, birth control regulations have played a major role in creating "two pools of families: one that gives up its female children, albeit often unwillingly, and the other that readily welcomes the abandoned girls" through adoption.[47]

Perhaps the most important reason for this gendered trend involves patrilineal bloodline. Johnson proposes that, in the past, the "ambiguous position of females, especially children, in the formal kinship structure and bloodlines made girls more readily exchangeable and hence more 'adoptable' as daughters."[48] These issues continue to be salient in the contemporary period, rendering the adoption of daughters of unknown parentage more acceptable even today. Many Chinese parents fear that if a son finds out about his adoption—something that is usually kept secret to ensure a child's loyalties—he might return to his birth parents and abandon all financial and emotional responsibility to the adoptive parents. Parents are less concerned that girls will become disloyal. This perception of devotion may reflect women's lower status in Chinese society. With fewer employment options for daughters, adoptive parents in rural areas may be more assured of their loyalty.[49]

### Preferences for Girls at the Yongping Orphanage

The desirability of girls for domestic adoption became apparent to me firsthand at the Yongping Orphanage, an institution that did not send children abroad. Because orphanages that participate in foreign adoption must meet certain child-to-staff ratios, hygiene standards, and expectations for facilities and equipment (requirements that are difficult to meet in light of the limited state funding they receive) most welfare institutes in China do not qualify for the program.[50] During my first visit to the facility in 2006, I was surprised to see boys everywhere. Like many others who follow international adoption trends, I assumed that all orphanages were overflowing with healthy girls. But out of Yongping's thirty-six children, fewer than half were female. Among the girls, only a few were healthy older babies and toddlers. Others were autistic, and two were wheelchair bound—paralyzed below the waist from spina bifida. The oldest girl in the unit, a muscular teenager with Down syndrome and short spiky hair named Dang Yu, served as an unpaid caregiver, helping with laundry and diaper changing.

One dark winter afternoon, I arrived at Yongping to find only three caregivers instead of the usual five or six. Dang Yu, who was usually friendly, if sometimes aggressive, spotted me and ran over excitedly. Grabbing my hand roughly, she dragged me down the cold hallway and into a side storage room that was crowded with boxes and clothing. Pointing exaggeratedly at a small crib in the middle of the space, she exclaimed loudly, "It's crying!" (*ku le*). Peering inside the crib, I was astonished to find a tiny week-old baby girl. Wailing with hunger, the milky-skinned infant appeared to otherwise be in good shape. I realized that, halfway through my fieldwork, this was the first healthy female newborn I had encountered on any of my numerous visits to different orphanages.

The child was bundled up in two heavy quilts, several layers of clothing, and a large pink baby cap and then left alone in the room without supervision. Instinctively, I scooped her up and hurried back down the hallway toward the *ayi*s. "Put her back down," the woman we referred to as "Big Mother *Ayi*" ordered sternly. "She's too young and might catch a cold if anyone holds her," she said, gesturing at me to return to the storage room. Doubting her logic, I reluctantly trudged back down the hallway with the child. Nonetheless, when the *ayi* returned to supervising the older children I darted back into the room and picked the baby up again. For over an hour I held her close, stroking her downy face to subdue her cries. The following week, I searched for the child again and was relieved to find that she had been moved to the room with the other babies. Then several months later, without any announcement or fanfare, the girl disappeared altogether. On questioning, one of the *ayi*s confirmed with a small, satisfied grin that she had "*bei shouyang le*"—been adopted by a local family.

This healthy baby girl stood out as an exception at Yongping. The majority of children were boys with some type of physical or mental impairment, including minor issues that did not affect brain or motor development such as cleft lips and palates. Others were given up because they were born missing limbs or other body parts. One adorable four-year-old boy who was born without a right arm below the shoulder was known to indiscriminately run up to volunteers, pleading "*bao wo, bao wo!*" ("hold me, hold me!") We referred to another charming, chubby-cheeked toddler as "Pinkies" because he was born with only the outermost fingers and toes on each of his hands and feet. Beyond these more superficial issues, boys at Yongping also suffered from major disabilities: Two toddlers had Down syndrome, three had severe cerebral palsy, and several others had intellectual disabilities.

The two boys with Down syndrome were of similar age and size and were always kept together. Slower to walk than the other children, they were frequently placed in a squeaky metal cart with prisonlike bars on the sides that was rolled from room to room. Extremely sweet tempered, the two toddlers would sigh contentedly with closed eyes when volunteers spread lotion onto their rough, sandpapery faces. I sat with them one afternoon in the corner of the playroom and watched, transfixed, as they used their small hands to make animal shadow puppets on the wall. My heart grew heavy when I thought about the lack of investment these children received.

Over time, I learned that three of the male infants and several of the older boys at Yongping were completely healthy, debunking my earlier assumptions about the gendered nature of child abandonment. Though scholars have yet to address the issue of healthy boys in state care, some speculate that the growing prevalence of prostitution, premarital sex, and out-of-wedlock births in the reform era have increased rates of relinquishment for sons.[51] Healthy boys remained at Yongping long-term, whereas healthy girls disappeared one-by-one into the homes of local couples, much like the child who was kept in the storage closet. Over the span of two years, nearly all of these girls left the facility, including those who were already of preschool age. On one occasion I spotted the orphanage's associate director speaking in a low tone to Dang Nian, a shy but highly intelligent four-year-old girl. As a group of young boys with fixed cleft lips hovered close by, listening in with obvious envy, the official placed her arm around the girl and stated, "You're going to live in a big house. But," she warned seriously, "you had better behave, or else you'll have to come back here!" Dang Nian left soon after and to my knowledge was never sent back to the orphanage.

In December 2007, I arranged to bring an American licensed clinical nurse with me to Yongping to perform physical examinations on all of the children. Over the course of several hours, we compiled details about each child's condition, including age, sex, and medical issues. This confirmed my suspicion that healthy girls really were leaving the institution while boys were being left behind. Out of a total of thirty-six children, twenty-nine were boys. More surprisingly, the nurse found that ten of the institution's children were perfectly healthy—even when excluding those who had entirely recuperated from surgeries to heal their various conditions. Among this healthy group, seven were young boys.

The presence of physically and mentally capable male children at Yongping and their lack of desirability for domestic placements forced me to rethink the role of gender in abandonment and adoption. Even though several of these healthy boys had arrived as newborns—the age when children are most likely to be adopted—when I returned to the facility for a visit nearly three years later in 2009, I discovered that all of them still remained in the institution. Meanwhile, each of their healthy female peers had left to join a family.

## China's Rise as Reflected in Adoption Laws

The popularity of healthy girls for adoption, both internationally and domestically, has reversed the fortunes of countless youth. But adoption has also served another purpose beyond locating loving homes for children. In particular, the laws that regulate the circulation of China's children across international borders reflect the PRC's own economic reversal of fortune and its growing ability to assert influence over Western industrialized countries. China's first national adoption law came into effect in April 1992. Prior to this time, there was no official route to obtain children from institutions.[52] This policy, though best known for opening the country to international adoption, actually applied equally to foreigners and native Chinese citizens. The 1992 law specified three major qualifications for prospective adoptive parents: (1) childlessness; (2) demonstrated ability to rear and educate the child; and (3) aged thirty-five or older.

These seemingly simple, straightforward rules were carefully chosen by the Chinese government to dually encourage international adoptions while simultaneously reinforcing stringent domestic birth control regulations. The eligibility requirements favored Westerners for whom childlessness in one's midthirties is both commonplace and socially acceptable.[53] In China, however, couples customarily marry in their early to midtwenties and have usually borne a child by age thirty-five. Hence, the requirements excluded most Chinese people from eligibility. According to Johnson, the 1992 Adoption Law prioritized local fertility regulations over children's best interests:

> [The] law was not written with an eye to serving the interests of homeless children in need of families. Instead, the main purpose of codifying these restrictions into law was to provide birth-planning officials with additional regulatory weapons to shore up the one-child policy by eliminating adoption as a potential loophole for those who sought to hide the birth of a child, typically a daughter, in order to try again to have a son over quota.[54]

Another important aspect of this law was that it did not require adoptive parents to be married. This had little effect in the PRC where unwed motherhood is very rare, as it is both socially stigmatized and technically against the law (unwed mothers must pay heavy fines to bear their child legally). But in

Western societies, this provision opened up eligibility to single people, giving China one of the world's most liberal international adoption policies. Consequently, thousands of single Western women rushed to adopt Chinese children, as did numerous lesbian couples who had one partner register as a single mother.

By 2000, the PRC's surprising openness toward older parents and atypical family compositions, its seemingly endless supply of healthy girls, the total lack of birthparent involvement, and the efficiency of the adoption process all converged to make China the top sending country of adopted children in the world. The founding of the Chinese Center for Adoption Affairs—since renamed the China Center for Children's Welfare and Adoption (CCCWA)—streamlined the process even further. Created in response to the negative international attention and controversy provoked by the "Dying Rooms" documentaries, this government agency oversees foreign adoptions and care for orphans in welfare institutes. The CCCWA standardized China's international adoption guidelines, bolstering the country's reputation for running a clean program. Despite the millions of foreign dollars entering China through the adoption industry, it was not until the eruption of the 2005 Hunan baby trafficking scandal that any doubts were raised about the legitimacy of the country's international program. In comparison, domestic adoptions still lack clear guidelines and a centralized regulatory agency.

### The Intermingling of Love, Money, and Adoption

Throughout the 1990s and early 2000s, foreign adoptions poured untold resources into China's child welfare system at a time of decreasing central government support for orphanages. Care for each institutionalized child, including room, board, medical care, and educational expenses, costs each facility upwards of 10,000 yuan (over US$1,600) per year.[55] The financial allowances provided by the central government for orphaned and abandoned youth cover only a fraction of these costs and vary substantially according to region. For example, in 2005, children in economically developed cities such as Beijing, Tianjin, and Shanghai each received 3,000 to 4,000 yuan of state support per year, while those in the poorer provinces of Henan, Gansu, and Ningxia received only about 1,000 yuan.[56]

For local-level governments struggling to care for the children abandoned in their districts, it has made logical sense to become approved for international adoption. Although there are no exact statistics, it is estimated that 560 to 575 orphanages scattered across twenty-nine provinces and municipalities send children abroad.[57] Meier and Zhang argue that foreign adoption fees have made adoption central to many orphanages' survival, creating "a funding stream for the social welfare institutions that [has] *depended* on intercountry adoption."[58] Unsurprisingly, the international adoption industry has been extremely lucrative for local officials. The large mandatory parental cash donations required by orphanages are not systematically tracked, heightening the temptation to use the funds for personal profit.

For example, a Chinese news exposé of the Hunan child trafficking case reported that only 5 percent of the standard adoption fee was given to the Provincial Administration while 95 percent went directly to the welfare center, to be used at their discretion.[59] This created considerable incentive to secure healthy female infants by any means possible. Legal scholar David Smolin charges that profit motive has contributed to widespread "child laundering" practices that plague the international adoption system. In his view, the lack of legal accountability within adoption laws in either sending or receiving countries "both legitimizes and incentivizes the stealing, kidnapping, trafficking, and buying of children."[60]

Due to the money at stake, orphanages that participate in the international program may be less likely to make children available for domestic adoption. In 2006, researcher Brian Stuy conducted a telephone survey of thirty-two orphanages that routinely send children abroad. For this research, he asked a female Chinese citizen to pose as a thirty-five-year-old, childless married woman interested in the availability of healthy infants for local adoption. Of all of the orphanages surveyed, only five claimed to have any healthy infants. One of the five welfare institutes asked the woman for a "donation" of 30,000 yuan (roughly US$5,000), a sum that was even higher than the foreign adoption fee at the time.[61]

Because there is no designated agency to regulate local adoptions, it can be difficult for Chinese locals to adopt without first developing *guanxi* (social connections) with an orphanage. According to Zhang Wen, executive director of the Children's Hope Foundation, "If you don't know anyone with the civil affairs department or from the orphanages, basically you can never adopt a healthy child from there." Like Stuy, Zhang found that although there is no official set adoption fee for local parents, Chinese families are sometimes required to pay even more than foreigners.[62] Thus, the potential profit to be made from adopting out healthy girls has placed Chinese citizens in direct competition with Westerners.

There is no real way to verify whether and to what extent adoption fees line the pockets of orphanage directors and other local officials, but it is unlikely that the entire donation goes toward orphan care. In my travels to nine different children's welfare institutes that participated in international adoption in Henan, Hunan, Jiangxi, and Guangdong Provinces, each institute's director rode around in an expensive foreign luxury vehicle entirely unaffordable on his or her civil servant wages. Nonetheless, as evidenced by obvious improvement to facilities and the creation of new programs for special needs children, it was also clear that a good portion of the proceeds were used to upgrade care for those left behind.

Many of the foreign volunteers I met who had been working in orphanages starting in the 1990s remarked on the vast improvement in overall conditions they had witnessed since adoptions first began. Cathy, the British nurse at Tomorrow's Children, first began working in an orphanage in Henan Province in 1998. She described routinely seeing children with rope burns around their wrists and legs from being tied to their beds. The nurse expressed relief that this was no longer common practice and credited the improvements to the oversight brought about by international adoption. An American adoption administrator told sociologist Sara Dorow how the circulation of children to foreign homes caused care and money to become intertwined:

> Care in Chinese orphanages used to be abominable. With the realization that adoption brings in money, now the children are better cared for. The child is "upped in the food chain." Adoption puts a price on children that makes them more valuable . . . valuable to rescue and valuable to take care of.[63]

The informal circulation of children between families—sometimes for profit, sometimes not—has long played a central role in Chinese family formation. In discussions of the Hunan baby trafficking scandal, Western observers unequivocally felt that this form of child circulation constituted a punishable crime. Within the PRC, however, considerable debate erupted over whether children's entrance into foreign families may have served their best interests in the long run, perhaps even justifying the practice. Because of the sustained history of child trafficking in China, some scholars even argue that the practice "is culturally embedded to the point that is not universally viewed as criminal, but simply as a 'tradition.'"[64]

The desire to acquire children using financial means is by no means limited to the realm of international adoption. As class inequalities have deepened, there has been a surge in kidnappings for domestic adoption. Although there are no exact statistics, an estimated 20,000 to 70,000 kidnapped children are sold every year on a thriving black market.[65] The Chinese government has devoted major resources to fighting this illegal flow of bodies, classifying child trafficking as a crime punishable by death. Dramatic news headlines tout the rescue of stolen babies from local trafficking rings such as a case from February 2014 in which a sting operation across twenty-seven different provinces rescued 382 babies and arrested more than 1,000 people suspected of using baby-selling websites and online forums.[66]

In terms of scale, therefore, the role that foreign adoption has played in incentivizing orphanages to procure healthy girls is small relative to the booming domestic market in babies and toddlers. However, because they have emerged from the same market logic that underlies Chinese state-led modernization, both forms of child trafficking signify the utilitarian view that governs many aspects of contemporary family life. Within China's fraught socioeconomic context, the commodification of children is not a clear issue of kidnapping versus relinquishment. For parents who may be living in abject poverty and prohibited from bearing more offspring, trafficking "could be understood as a survival strategy for the family on one hand, and as a possible strategy of social mobility for the children involved on the other."[67]

## Extending Population Quality across Borders by Restricting International Adoption

In April 1999, the Chinese government sought to widen the pool of adoptive parents by dropping the minimum age to thirty, sparking even more international interest in Chinese girls. This new law was, in fact, designed to encourage domestic placements, representing one of the PRC's first major changes to its family planning policies. In addition to lowering the minimum age, the legal change allowed couples who already had one child of their own to adopt abandoned children from orphanages if their parents could not be located, creating an important exception to the existing one-child-per-couple rule.[68]

The number of official domestic adoptions soon climbed significantly and began to vastly outnumber international adoptions at a rate of four to five times. According to the Ministry of Civil Affairs, in 1999, Chinese citizens adopted nearly 32,000 children from orphanages (compared to only around 6,000 international placements). In 2000, the number of domestic adoptions reached more than 49,000, and in subsequent years has tended to fluctuate between roughly 30,000 and 40,000 children per year. These numbers are quite high, especially considering that legal adoption can be a tedious process, requiring parents to provide proof of household registration, marital status, and the ability to raise and educate children.

In 2001, the Chinese government officially limited the number of international adoptions by single women to 5 percent of the total. This was the first in a series of policy changes that demonstrated the CCCWA's employment of increasingly heteronormative and racialized standards for foreign parents. Sara Dorow found that many adoption administrators and officials in China considered white and overseas Chinese heterosexual married couples to be the most appropriate applicants, viewing others as "not normal" (*bu zhengchang*) and therefore less likely to be approved for a child.[69] The amendment appeared to have been provoked by the Chinese government's increasing displeasure with large numbers of children being adopted by single women, many who were in same-sex partnerships. Until that point, single women had constituted about one-third of all placements.[70] After nearly a decade of looking the other way, all adoptions to gay parents were officially disallowed. In a statement that explained these new guidelines, CCCWA's message was unmistakable:

> The People's Republic of China recognizes only families formed by marriage of opposite sex and does not recognize the legality of homosexual families . . . In terms of the Chinese traditional ethics and customs and habits, homosexuality is an act violating public morality and therefore not recognized by the society.[71]

Signaling a major shift in international power relations, this amendment highlighted China's ability to pick and choose among foreign prospective parents for the first time. Unlike most other sending countries, the PRC began to use adoption regulations to assert its own moral standards and extend its project of raising population quality across national borders, ensuring that its children were "placed in homes deemed suitable according to Chinese cultural views."[72]

Adoption policies became even more stringent on May 1, 2007. This time the stipulations pertained only to foreign parents and were exceedingly specific, appearing to some as an attempt to exclude most Western couples from eligibility. The official reason given by the CCCWA for the new regulations was that the supply of adoptable children (for example, healthy and female) had declined and could no longer keep up with rising international demand. The criteria, currently still in effect, designate the following:

- Heterosexual couples must be married for at least two years. If either has been divorced, the current marriage must have lasted at least five years.
- Both partners must be between the ages of thirty and fifty and have at least a high school education.
- Both the husband and wife must be healthy and not have AIDS, mental disabilities, any kind of infectious or long-term disease, blindness, deafness, loss of limb function, severe facial deformation, organ transplantation less than ten years earlier, schizophrenia, untreated mental disorders, or a body mass index of forty or higher.
- Either the husband or wife must have stable employment. The family annual income must reach US$10,000 for each family member and should not be derived from welfare programs, pensions, unemployment insurance, and so on, and the family net assets should be at least US$80,000.
- Neither the husband nor wife has a criminal history and can demonstrate good moral character. Neither has a history of domestic violence, sexual abuse, abandonment or child abuse, drug abuse or addiction, or alcohol abuse within the past ten years.

The announcement of these new guidelines ignited heated debates in Western countries regarding the future of Chinese adoptions. The presidents of the four largest American chapters of Families with Children from China quickly penned a joint letter of concern to urge the CCCWA to rethink its stance. They pointed out that transnational adoptions have served as an effective form of soft power by creating a deeper understanding of the PRC abroad:

> The appreciation American adoptive families express to China leaves a strong and deep impression on other Americans. When others see the way that our families honor our children's Chinese heritage they learn more about China. All of this contributes to increasing the visibility and position of the

People's Republic of China, as well as enhancing awareness of her role in our global future.[73]

Despite this grateful tone, the letter expressed concern over the emotional impact the changes might have on adoptees whose parents would be rendered ineligible under the new guidelines. The letter quotes one worried single mother: "My daughter has such a glowing view of China . . . How can I tell her that the Chinese government no longer thinks that I would be a good parent?"

Other more sensationalistic responses attempted to cast doubt on the legitimacy of the PRC's claim of having fewer adoptable children. In a *New York Times* editorial entitled "The Mystery of China's Baby Shortage," American adoptive mother Beth Nonte Russell drew a direct link between the new regulations and China's concern with its international perceptions prior to the 2008 Beijing Summer Olympics. Based on anecdotal evidence, she wildly speculated that there could be at least *one million* unwanted females still residing in institutions. These girls, in her view, would be "left behind by Beijing's new policies—perhaps spending their lives in institutions because of these arbitrary and artificial limits." Under the new restrictions, Russell pointed out wryly, neither she nor Angelina Jolie would be eligible to adopt from China. She joked that Madonna was still eligible "at least until she turns 50, gets fat, . . . gets divorced or goes broke."[74]

The timing of the new regulations just one year prior to the Beijing Summer Olympic Games was indeed significant, as the government was preparing for an onslaught of international coverage on every aspect of Chinese culture and society. Local officials were well aware that after South Korea hosted the 1988 Olympics in Seoul, it was lambasted by the global media for "exporting its greatest natural resource" to other countries while doing little to promote domestic adoptions.[75] Even so, Russell's widely circulated piece hinged on two false, albeit common, Western misperceptions: (1) that orphanages are hiding untold numbers of healthy girls and (2) that international adoption is the only hope for institutionalized children because Chinese people will not adopt daughters.

The public outcry and skepticism of these changes also reflects longstanding American media representations of the PRC that view the country through the lens of communist oppression. This discourse "has contributed to and underscored the attitude of many Americans that these children would be better off in the United States than almost anywhere else."[76] To be fair,

Chinese people often feel similarly about the superiority of the United States. Within a local context of overwhelming competition for education, jobs, and resources, many view America as a land of untold opportunity. One study of urban Chinese residents showed that they considered international adoptees to be incredibly lucky (*xingfu*). Participants felt that these children would benefit from their adoptive parents' increased ability to provide them with financial resources, emotional support, and a better education—especially English-language education. Moreover, adoptees were envied for having the opportunity to grow up in a country that they considered more socially, culturally, and economically advanced than China.[77]

This perspective was brought to life during a visit I made to an orphanage in rural Jiangxi Province with two American adoptive families in 2007. Over the course of a five-hour drive that wound through lush green countryside, the taxi driver, Mr. Chen, and I conversed about the one-child policy and adoption. Mr. Chen, who in his mid-forties still sported a full head of pitch-black hair, had a twelve-year-old son. Three years earlier his wife bore a long-desired daughter, for whom he had paid a considerable fine and was now spending a large portion of his income to cover preschool fees. The driver glanced in his rearview mirror, quickly surveying the two Chinese American girls seated in the back with their white parents. Giggling at cartoons on a shared iPad, the eight-year-olds were completely oblivious to the outside world. Mr. Chen reflected on the good fortune of these international adoptees while lamenting the challenges of achieving economic success in China. "America is a more civilized (*wenming*) society," he stated earnestly. "As long as I could see my daughter again in the future, I would be happy for her to be raised by foreign parents in the United States."

Based on my firsthand observations and myriad conversations with individuals involved in orphanage care, it does appear that the abandonment of healthy females has diminished substantially in recent years. High rates of sex-selective abortion have reduced the number of female births, but scholars also speculate that rising income levels have allowed parents such as Mr. Chen, the taxi driver I encountered in Jiangxi Province, to afford to pay the fines associated with over-quota children.[78] Furthermore, with the discontinuation of the one-child policy, the abandonment rate of healthy daughters will likely continue to fall.

As the PRC has grown in status as a world superpower, it has also limited foreign access to its children. These new regulations, I suggest, relate to the

**Table 3.2.** Total number of adoptions from China and percentage to the United States.

| | 1992–1997 | 1998–2002 | 2003 | 2004 | 2005 | 2006 | 2007 | 2008 | 2009 | 2010 | 2011 | 2012 | 2013 | 2014 | 1992–2014 |
|---|---|---|---|---|---|---|---|---|---|---|---|---|---|---|---|
| TOTAL | 15,315 | 37,574 | 11,228 | 13,404 | 14,484 | 10,759 | 8,744 | 5,873 | 5,004 | 5,426 | 4,362 | 4,132 | 3,403 | 2,758 | 142,466 |
| Percentage to United States | 68% | 64% | 61% | 53% | 55% | 60% | 62% | 67% | 60% | 63% | 59% | 65% | 68% | 60% | 62% |

Data from Peter Selman, *International Adoptions from the People's Republic of China, 1992–2014*, working paper, Newcastle University, UK, 2015.

state goal of improving population quality: an objective that hinges on the notion that children are extensions of the nation, regardless of their citizenship or where they reside. By placing its abandoned girls with healthy, affluent, well-educated Western parents who have a demonstrated ability to raise "high quality" offspring, the Chinese state greatly extended its modernization project across international borders during the 1990s and 2000s—years that coincide with the country's phenomenal growth and economic transformation.

These regulations demonstrate that the PRC is not embarrassed of its status as a sending country. Rather, it has used adoption as a tool of soft power, furthering its national interests by using foreign money to fund its child welfare system and creating greater awareness and appreciation of Chinese culture in the global north.[79] It is thus no coincidence that the United States, the PRC's largest trading partner, has received the majority of adoptees. (See Table 3.2.)

The wait time for adopting a healthy girl has risen to more than seven years, but this has not deterred Western interest in children from the PRC. Instead, many prospective parents have switched from seeking a healthy girl to join the Waiting Child Program, which matches special needs youth with foreign adoptive families. Almost half of Chinese adoptees to the United States now arrive this way. As I will explore later in this book, this relatively new form of child circulation is another manner in which foreign resources are being used to remake young boys and girls into global citizens—and to potentially improve the PRC's international image in the process.

## Conclusion

This chapter has focused on the reversal of fortune experienced by healthy girls in Chinese state-run institutions who are highly desired for adoption both internationally and domestically. Although gender bias is the primary cause of the "missing girls" phenomenon and their large-scale relinquishment to state care, their gender and good health reverses their fortunes in institutions while special needs youth remain behind. The migration of these girls to Western nations has not only profoundly transformed their social value, but it has also stoked foreign interest in China and involvement with its welfare institutes. More stringent adoption regulations reflect the PRC's own economic reversal of fortune, with Chinese authorities controlling access to its children in a manner that conveys its growing global strength to the industrialized world.

The imposition of increasingly high mental, physical, and economic standards onto Western parents has allowed state authorities to extend the project of improving population quality beyond Chinese borders. Put another way, the PRC has outsourced the intimate care of certain youth to affluent and educated foreign parents who use their own resources to remake marginalized individuals into "high quality" citizens and cultural ambassadors. Due to essentialized notions of race and ethnicity in China, foreign adoptees are seen as maintaining a blood-based tie to their birth country regardless of nationality. They are uniquely positioned to link the PRC with countries in the global north—especially the United States.

Chinese authorities have continued to find new ways to enhance its international image through adoptees, such as through government-subsidized heritage tours for adoptive families. These carefully planned ten-day adventures show off China's vivid culture and history through trips to ancient relics such as the Great Wall, the Forbidden City, and the Terra Cotta Warriors in Xi'an. (They also include the option to hold a baby giant panda.) These trips are specially designed to build stronger relationships between the PRC and Western adoptive families. Thus, in addition to more common tourist attractions, families also visit the CCCWA headquarters to view the room where their adoption match was made, and, for an additional fee, they can tour the child's orphanage.[80]

These trips appear to be at least somewhat financially motivated—costing nearly $2,000 per parent/adult and $1,400 for nonadopted children, excluding international airfare. Nevertheless, adoptees of any age travel for free, sponsored by the Chinese Ministry of Civil Affairs. The price of these summer tours has held steady for several years despite increased food and transportation costs in the country. By promoting sentimental ties to the adopted children's homeland, these tours can be viewed as part of the PRC's larger objective to facilitate interconnections with the global north through soft power.

China is not the first sending country to organize heritage trips. Indeed, they resemble long-established South Korean state-sponsored trips for overseas adoptees. Eleana Kim's study of one such tour found that adult adoptee participants (who are now discussed in government discourse as being part of the "global family" of South Korea) were introduced to a highly scripted, "folklorized" version of culture that "included trips to ancient palaces and courses on Korean 'traditional' food and customs."[81] At the same time, they were heavily discouraged from coming into close contact with regular society. Likewise, some families traveling to China on state-sponsored trips are told ahead of time that their interactions with local people are to be kept to a minimum.

In one travel agency's contract, a very specific clause is interspersed with more generic advice. It states: "I understand that involving myself with Chinese locals, other than for planned activities . . . is to be kept to social situations only, and that at no time, will I bring locals to any part of the homeland tour."[82] By rigidly controlling what adoptive families see, eat, and experience on these journeys, state authorities are able to manufacture positive and lasting impressions of China and Chinese culture. These tours affectively link children with their ancestral homeland and also strengthen ties with adoptive parents, who are generally already strong proponents of the PRC.

Due to its complex mixture of care and commodification, international adoption has been critiqued for incentivizing corruption and child trafficking. At the same time, the migration of healthy girls out of the country has forged a path through which globalization—in the form of Western actors, resources, and practices—has been imported into state-run welfare institutes. Having sketched the broader structural forces that shape the world of contemporary Chinese orphanage care and adoption, I now turn to my ethnographic field sites to explore how outsourced intimacy operates within institutional care settings.

# 4 The West to the Rescue?

*Outsourced Intimacy in the Tomorrow's Children Unit*

I BEGAN WORKING AS A TRANSLATOR and all-around helper for the Tomorrow's Children special care unit in January 2007. Managed by Western evangelical Christians, this medical facility occupied the entire fifth floor of the Haifeng Children's Welfare Institute (CWI). The organization used its own funds to provide first-world palliative and medical care to severely ill and disabled infants. Children like Emma and Henry, whose stories appeared in Chapter 1, were cared for in this unit until they either passed away or were nursed back to health. Some of these youth continued to reside in the unit as long-term care cases whereas others were returned to the regular facility, taken in by local foster families, or sometimes adopted internationally.

One cold morning in February, I entered the grounds of the Haifeng CWI through imposing wrought-iron gates and approached the orphanage with a mixture of excitement and apprehension, not knowing what the day would bring. The six-story structure made for an impressive sight. In the middle of the circular driveway stood a large stone statue of a stern-faced woman holding a baby and standing protectively over two older children. Reminiscent of Chinese socialist propaganda posters of the past, all four figures aimed their steely gazes forward toward the future (even the baby, giving the statue an unintended comedic appearance).

Once inside the building, I moved past the empty, smartly furnished lobby and ascended the wide cement staircase to the second floor. As had become my regular habit, I poked my head into the room designated for the sickest children to see if there were any new arrivals. After nodding a greeting to the two middle-aged *ayi*s inside who were busy mixing formula, my eyes were drawn to a handsome, though shockingly jaundiced, six-month-old boy I hadn't seen before. He had been recently abandoned at a local hospital in the final stages of liver failure. Although the whites of his eyes were tinted a shocking shade of mustard yellow, the small boy's penetrating stare conveyed mental clarity. Wrapped tightly in a thick dirty quilt, he soberly locked his gaze onto mine, quietly sizing me up from his bed. Looking at him, my mind wandered to thoughts of his parents, wondering whether they knew that he had ended up here. Reluctantly, I backed out of the room and climbed three floors to the special care unit to begin my volunteer shift. But, to my immense relief, later that day the orphanage doctor brought the boy up to the Tomorrow's Children unit.

Head nurse Cathy carried the frightened child down the hallway to the gleaming examination room. Cooing in soothing British-accented English, she carefully peeled off multiple layers of dirty clothing. Underneath was a soiled cloth diaper held tightly in place by a thick length of string stiffened by urine. Dropping the string in the trash, the nurse turned to me and asked softly, "What do you think his name should be?" Thinking for a moment, I replied, "He looks like an Aaron. We don't have an Aaron in the unit right now, do we?" She shook her head. "No, we don't. All right, Aaron it is!" Cathy began a file for the newly named baby. Gently she weighed him, took his temperature, and thoroughly examined his tiny body, taking detailed notes throughout. Now settled in comfortably, the boy peered curiously around the brightly lit room.

After the examination, Cathy passed little Aaron over to his new Chinese caregiver, who carried him briskly to one of the brightly colored bathrooms. Placing him in a shallow pool of warm water, the *ayi* used a pricey array of Johnson & Johnson baby products to shampoo and bathe him. The child appeared dumbfounded as sheets of ashy gray skin peeled off his small body. Once he was toweled dry, it took five different Q-tips to clean out weeks of built-up dirt from his ears. Aaron's nanny then spread generous amounts of cream on his bottom to soothe an angry red diaper rash. Pulling on an expensive Huggies diaper, she finished off the look with a soft cotton onesie emblazoned with a festive blue sailboat. "*Hao le!*" ("There you go!"), she exclaimed brightly before whisking him away to the kitchen for a feeding.

In the end, this baby lived for only two more weeks. Yet rather than spend his last days in the cold confines of the dying room, he was cared for with imported Western practices that transformed him from an unwanted burden into an object of unconditional love. Aaron's story speaks to the ways in which the migration of healthy girls out of China through international adoption explained in the last chapter led to an impressive—though far less publicized—influx of foreign actors, resources, and practices into the country's child welfare system. In large part, this type of outsourced intimacy is significant because of the intensive foreign investment of material and emotional resources in terminally ill children, most of whom will never recuperate enough to leave institutional care.

This chapter examines the "rebirth" that I saw kids undergo in the Tomorrow's Children infant palliative care unit at the Haifeng Orphanage, a process that profoundly changed their personalities and markedly altered their life trajectories. These transformations involved negotiation and conflict as affluent Western volunteers attempted to import a highly individualized middle-class approach to care that differed greatly from that of the local working-class Chinese caregivers. Although Tomorrow's Children volunteers were motivated by an *intensive* logic of care that sought to cultivate kids' emotional and intellectual potential, low-paid local *ayi*s followed a *pragmatic* logic that focused more on securing children's immediate physical health. Highlighting the different logics of care at play in this case shows how children's "best interests" are not universal but are instead shaped by the surrounding context and access to resources. More broadly, the everyday tensions regarding care that I observed also reveal some of the concrete implications of the Chinese state's outsourcing of intimacy to private global foreign aid groups that arrive armed with their own moral agendas.

## Tomorrow's Children: Setting an Example for Locals to Follow

In the summer of 2005, an acquaintance told me about the Tomorrow's Children medical foster home, a beautiful facility built on the rural outskirts of Beijing that provided Western medical care to abandoned children. I made my first visit that summer and met the organization's founders, Barbara and Peter Dunlop, a white evangelical Christian couple who originally moved to Beijing in 1994 to pursue career opportunities. After learning about the deplorable conditions in Chinese welfare institutes, they felt a deep religious calling to devote their lives to helping needy orphans. Using their own savings, the couple opened the first Tomorrow's Children foster home in 2002. Barbara Dunlop, a feisty and highly opinionated Western-trained physician, handled all of the children's medical care while her more subdued and serious husband Peter dealt with the administrative and financial aspects of their rapidly expanding organization.

The couple originally sought to provide medical care to children with operable issues and treatable diseases who would have almost no chance of survival if they stayed in an institution. Their foster home near Beijing accommodated nearly sixty children at a time who were sent from various CWIs throughout the country from as far away as Inner Mongolia and Xinjiang. The young patients suffered from an extensive range of illnesses and disabilities seldom seen today in the global north, including minor issues such as cleft lips and clubbed feet and more serious disorders like exposed bladders, spina bifida, and congenital heart diseases. The group used its global religious and business contacts to obtain pro bono or reduced-fee treatment for children in more developed regions, often sending them to the United States, Singapore, and Hong Kong for months at a time for surgery and recuperation. After children were deemed completely healthy, usually by the age of two or three, they were typically placed on the foreign adoption list. The organization could not directly arrange adoptions, which were controlled by the Chinese state, but church-based advocacy groups spread the word about children's availability, leading most to eventually be placed with Western Christian families.

The Dunlops labored to develop a close working relationship with the Chinese Ministry of Civil Affairs, the government branch responsible for attending to the needs of orphans, the elderly, and the impoverished. As a result, the organization was asked to build similar facilities in multiple CWIs in central China that would provide hospice care for infants and young children with little chance of survival. Through these facilities, Tomorrow's Children experienced incredible growth. In 2012, the group operated five separate units that cared for around 350 babies and employed over 550 local staff. In that same year, the units received 293 new admissions and organized hospital surgery or treatment for 193 babies. Furthermore, 261 of its children were adopted internationally between 2006 and 2012.[1] In addition to local staff, foreign financial donations and a steady stream of Western volunteers who provided labor and specialized skills during both short- and long-term stays kept the medical units going.

Tomorrow's Children was founded on Christian principles of self-sacrifice and helping those in need. The Dunlops told me that they were "inspired by God's will" to devote their lives to caring for "the least of these" (a reference to Bible verse Matthew 25:40, "The King will reply, 'I tell you the truth, whatever

you did for one of the least of these brothers of mine, you did for me.'") Because Chinese law prohibits proselytizing, the group funneled its energy into
working with stigmatized youth to model best behavior that they hoped locals
would eventually emulate. This approach mirrors what anthropologist Erica
Bornstein calls "lifestyle evangelism," which she defines as "the process of living a life in the manner of Christ, providing an example, and showing non-
believers Christianity through the life that was led."[2] By using their own funds
to care for sick and disabled babies seen to have little value to local society, the
organization was able to serve a dual purpose: It filled a major gap in the Chinese child welfare system while accomplishing its own goals of using Western
methods to alleviate suffering for some of the world's neediest children.

Other than myself, nearly all of the group's volunteers were evangelical
Christians who learned about the foster homes through global church networks. These volunteers often seemed surprised to find out that people with
secular leanings also performed charity work. While giving a tour of the Beijing foster home, Barbara paused to point out a framed photo of the head sur-
geon of a prestigious American medical school whom she could count on in
emergencies to jump on a plane to China to operate on a dying child. Eyes
opened wide, she praised his generosity and added, somewhat incredulously,
"And he's not even a Christian!" Despite my own lack of religious conviction,
Tomorrow's Children welcomed my involvement due to my Mandarin language skills and ability to volunteer full-time in the Haifeng unit for several
critical months after it first opened.

Using its own finances, the organization replicated the model of the Beijing home inside several different orphanages in Henan Province. At the time,
Tomorrow's Children was one of only a handful of foreign philanthropic
groups granted official state permission to operate within CWIs. This was
especially remarkable as it occurred during the run-up to the 2008 Beijing
Summer Olympics, when the government severely curtailed the operations of
many well-known foreign organizations. During my fieldwork, a range of foreign organizations and NGOs were shut down or had their activities severely
limited by the Chinese government. Several Western foster homes in the
Beijing area were even required to return children to their original orphanages. Most notably, China Development Brief, an independent Western-run
publication founded in 1996 that published articles on NGOs and Chinese
civil society, was forced to cease operation of its Chinese-language website in
July 2007. Many speculated that these new stringent governmental limitations

directly related to the Olympics and official fears over intensified international scrutiny.

That these units administered *only* to children with some form of physical or mental disability was highly significant. As Sara Dorow argues, institutionalized special needs youth bear symbolic importance as "placeholders of true care—a site for modeling the value of all children equally."[3] Although (and perhaps because) a large percentage of its patients were not going to survive very long, volunteers considered them even more deserving of individualized care and intensive nurturance. Nevertheless, there were also times when certain children who were not considered *disabled enough* to receive these resources were unfortunately left even worse off than before.

## Diverse Childhoods in a Chinese Orphanage

Located in a major metropolitan center of a very poor and populous province with high child abandonment rates, Haifeng had earned a national reputation as an award-winning model orphanage. At least half of its 600 children resided in local foster homes or boarding schools while the other half lived onsite; of these, 90 percent suffered from some kind of illness or long-term medical need.[4] The older, able-bodied youth who lived in the orphanage were generally well behaved and good natured; they were instructed to politely greet foreign visitors in English when they passed by on the stairway. During an interview that I conducted with Mr. Fu, Haifeng's progressive and open-minded director, he stated that his primary goal was "to provide excellent educational opportunities to all of the mentally capable children in order to guarantee their future success."

Director Fu made a special effort to increase awareness of the plight of abandoned disabled youth within the broader community. One key aspect of this campaign included dazzling concerts performed by children and nurses outside the orphanage on major holidays. During a memorable Chinese New Year show, I stood on the street alongside hundreds of other audience members in front of a huge elevated stage that glowed dramatically under bright spotlights. Large cameras recorded the event for later airing on several major television outlets. The concert included a series of intricately choreographed dances, such as an unforgettable high-energy solo performance by a one-legged young man; wearing a sparkly sequined silver shirt, he did strenuous push-ups in time to thumping techno music. Nurses clad in white uniforms gave an educational demonstration of physical therapy for children with cerebral palsy. Finally, the audience stood spellbound during a lengthy final act in which a teenage boy born without arms held a brush between his toes to create a remarkably professional-looking Chinese watercolor bamboo painting.

The media attention surrounding Haifeng was due in no small part to the extensive resources, equipment, and personnel that it received from Western groups. In addition to the Tomorrow's Children unit, the orphanage received free infant formula each month from a Western hospital in Beijing, the Half the Sky Foundation ran a childcare center for disabled youth, the Gates Foundation sponsored a physical therapy unit for children with cerebral palsy and provided a large van for their use, a Hong Kong–based group operated a recreation center for children and helped to place healthy babies in local foster homes, and an American teacher was brought in on a daily basis to teach English to the older children. This level of foreign intervention was fairly unheard of, making this orphanage stand out from other state facilities.

In exchange for being allowed to work at the CWI, Tomorrow's Children volunteers were obligated to take part in occasional media pieces that sought to highlight Western involvement as evidence of Haifeng's high level of quality. On a smoggy spring morning, the special care unit received word that several Chinese reporters had arrived and wanted to film the volunteers. At the time, Cathy and Brian Marks, a devout evangelical white British couple in their mid-fifties, ran the special care unit. After having spent several summers volunteering with Tomorrow's Children in the early 2000s, they felt called to serve the needs of institutionalized children and retired early from their careers to relocate to China. Cathy was a nurse practitioner with three decades of professional experience who managed all of the children's care at the Haifeng unit, except for major decisions regarding surgeries and palliative care, which organization founder Barbara Dunlop made in Beijing. Her husband Brian oversaw all of the business aspects of the unit, including finances, building renovations, and deliveries.

Several months into the opening of the Haifeng unit, the volunteers had grown used to these types of spontaneous public relations requests. Serving as translator, I accompanied Brian and Ashley, a twenty-four-year-old blonde American woman who was halfway through a one-year volunteering stint, down to the front of the building. Venturing outside, we were directed to the orphanage playground—a space that was typically deserted. To our surprise, ten children who lived in the main part of the orphanage were playing giddily on the slide and tire swings and in the sandbox. Two journalists from Beijing Chinese Central Television captured their antics on film as a large group of CWI nurses stood off to one side, supervising closely. A jovial Director Fu emerged from the doorway to greet the journalists. As the director breezed past, Brian called him over to ask how the volunteers should answer the reporters' questions. Under his breath, the director answered, "Don't worry; they just want to shoot some footage and won't be asking any questions."

After the playground filming finished, our large group walked down the street toward a building that was usually dark and boarded up. On this particular day, the doors had been thrown open, revealing a fully stocked ceramics center inside. A Chinese man in a lab coat was moving around inside, studiously readying a variety of implements for the pottery session to come. Brian murmured dryly, "I've never seen this place open before. The guy in the lab coat is actually the orphanage plumber." The film crew then instructed Brian and Ashley to sit with several children—whom they had never met before—and help them to decorate cups. I asked the reporters if they would like me to participate as well. Glancing over at me, one responded gruffly, "No, you look Chinese. We want *real* foreigners (*laowai*)!" As the scripted encounter wore on, I realized that these children were the same ones who performed in the CWI's community talent shows. In front of the cameras, the group of strangers feigned laughter and familiarity.

When the reporters took a cigarette break, I asked about the purpose of their shoot. They were producing a segment that would compare and contrast a model orphanage like Haifeng to an underfunded CWI in Inner Mongolia. One of the men stated, "The social welfare system is really good now, and there is food, clothing, and so on for all the kids. But we wanted to show a place like Haifeng, which has funding from the Gates Foundation and other Western groups, to show the kinds of things you can do with these handicapped kids so that they can become workers in the future." He released a stream of smoke into the air before continuing, "Other places like Inner Mongolia don't have anything like this yet, so we would like to encourage it."

This encounter highlighted the ways in which Chinese authorities use foreigners to generate a positive image of itself through media. The conscious decision to not film the Tomorrow's Children unit obscured the largely independent manner in which the Western volunteer organization operated at the orphanage. These types of scripted media performances conveyed to Chinese audiences that state authorities were in charge of Western aid, which was portrayed as a marker of modernity helping the nation to develop necessary and beneficial skills.

## Unequal Childhoods within the Same Institution

Within the state-run portion of the CWI, children were housed together according to disability and severity of prognosis. Over 100 residents had cerebral palsy, and they all lived together on several floors of the orphanage. By contrast, developmentally typical youths lived in dormlike settings and left the grounds each morning to attend local schools. Each day, Haifeng received one or two extremely ill and/or developmentally disabled infants who were abandoned at local hospitals or in the surrounding area. These children were sent directly to the dying room—a cramped, grimy, and depressing space that was poorly resourced and understaffed.

Despite its substantial foreign aid, the institution clearly put most of its funds toward able-bodied children or individuals who could be rehabilitated while investing little in the sickest ones. This calculated, unequal distribution of limited state resources shaped children's life opportunities (including, in some cases, their very survival) in a manner that mirrored broader Chinese society, in which material investments are often linked to one's perceived future economic potential. Nonetheless, babies like Aaron who transferred from the dying room to the Tomorrow's Children unit several floors above were instantly reborn into a fundamentally different reality founded on global middle-class ideologies of childhood. As a private, well-funded foreign organization that placed terminally ill youth at the top of its hierarchy of care, Tomorrow's Children quietly relieved the orphanage of a large financial burden without challenging the power of state authorities or drawing attention to larger social inequities. In this way, the organization served as a primary example of outsourced intimacy in China.

Nonetheless, despite operating under the general guise of international cooperation, in the special care unit I observed repeated conflicts between Western volunteers who were motivated by an intensive child-centered set of practices and local Chinese *ayis* who took a more pragmatic approach to care. It was, however, always clear who was in charge. As Tomorrow's Children founder Barbara Dunlop told me, "There are many different ways to do things. My way might not necessarily be the best, but here it is the *only* way." She added sharply, "Otherwise, they don't have to work here!"

The Haifeng unit attended to the needs of roughly forty-five children who remained under the legal jurisdiction of the CWI. As was true of many orphanages I visited, the vast majority of children were male, with girls comprising only one-third of the unit's residents at the time of my observations. Roughly 75 percent suffered from mild to severe cerebral palsy, which sometimes occurred in conjunction with other illnesses and disabilities. Children's issues were wide ranging, including (but not limited to) autism, spinal cord issues, heart disease, liver failure, imperforate anuses, hydrocephalus, cleft lips/palates, Down syndrome, skull malformations, skin disorders, and severe prematurity. The facility was primarily set up to care for infants and toddlers, although children were often older than they first appeared. Because they were abandoned and their true birthdates unknown, orphanage doctors guessed children's ages based on physical size. Thus, as in the case of Henry, whose story appeared at the beginning of this book, proper nutrition and medical care often caused children to grow rapidly and mature, seemingly by several years, within a short period of time.

For the sake of organization, patients were separated into five spacious and cheerful color-themed rooms according to age, size, and medical condition. Two smaller rooms accommodated toddlers with cerebral palsy while an adjoining room housed twelve infants, many needing only minor corrective surgeries. Once these infants had fully recuperated, they were returned to the regular facility or sent out to local foster care to create space for others. The largest room contained twelve older children ages five and up who had cerebral palsy; these girls and boys stayed on as long-term care cases after their health was stabilized.

Lastly, babies suffering from the final stages of terminal illness or preemies needing intensive care were kept together in a separate room with an adjoining sterile nursery that could be closed off if a child needed to be isolated to prevent the spread of infection. The facility also included a large kitchen run by a full-time cook who prepared fresh food on a daily basis. There was a separate children's playroom, two large bathrooms, a storage room, a laundry room with several new washers and dryers, and a one-bedroom private apartment that could house up to three or four volunteers at once.

Aside from Cathy and Brian, the other Westerners in the facility served on a volunteer basis for anywhere between two weeks and one year, although the typical stay was around three to four weeks long. Every month, the unit

received three or four mostly faith-based volunteers from first-world countries such as the United States, the United Kingdom, Australia, Canada, and
Singapore. Nearly all were trained in some kind of specialized skill that they
hoped to employ in the unit, including nursing/medicine, physical and occupational therapy, speech pathology, and teaching. For the majority, this trip
was their first visit to the PRC. Thus, most lacked Mandarin language skills or
in-depth knowledge of Chinese culture and had to be guided through many
of their interactions with locals.

The unit also employed roughly seventy-five working-class Chinese people who were privately hired, trained, and compensated by the organization.
Most worked as *ayis*, but there were also housekeepers, cooks, a full-time *ayi*
supervisor and a driver/maintenance man—the only adult Chinese male who
appeared regularly in the unit. To enforce uniformity, *ayis* were required to
wear identical uniforms of specially tailored red flowered shirts, red sweaters,
black pants, and black cloth slippers. All were women, and most were mothers, many hired after being laid off from jobs in state-run work units. Their
overall level of attained education was quite low, ranging from junior high
school to high school. Though few spoke even the simplest of English phrases,
the staff assigned each woman a Western name such as "Courtney," "Alice,"
and even "Cherry" to facilitate easy memorization by volunteers. However,
many *ayis* were unaware that they had even been given an English name.

There was a fairly clear division of labor in the unit. The low-paid Chinese caregivers performed most of the physical reproductive tasks—including
feeding, giving medication, bathing, clothing, changing diapers, and putting
kids to sleep—whereas Western volunteers attended to children's medical and
emotional needs. Each nanny was assigned to care for the same two to three
babies every day to promote bonding and, according to Barbara, to prevent
everyone "from just gravitating toward the little cuties." Caregivers were
trained to follow a uniform set of Western standards that sought to provide
unconditional love and keep babies on consistent routines. For their efforts,
*ayis* were paid only between US$60 and $75 dollars per month for working six
days of twelve-hour shifts in a row, followed by a three-day rest period. Although these wages were consistent with the pay for *ayis* in the state-managed
part of the facility, they were exceedingly low not only in comparison with
more developed world regions but even compared to the average salaries of
the local area.

## Using Care to Create Priceless Individuals

*All babies are individuals and although we try to fit them into our routine to make our work easier, please allow for their individual personalities so that they will grow as normal children in a loving home environment and not as "institutionalized" children . . . Get to know your babies well and give them the care that they need.*

**Excerpt from Tomorrow's Children, "Baby Care Policy for Nannies"**

Western volunteers in the Haifeng special care unit were outnumbered nearly ten-to-one by Chinese workers, but the child-centered, individualizing ideologies of care that dominated the unit were imported directly from the global north. Unlike many state facilities where entire groups of children are fed with the same bottle or spoon to save time (inadvertently spreading diseases and infections), in the special care unit, everything was personalized for individual use. *Ayis* were responsible for hand-stitching children's initials onto their towels, washcloths, and clothing using thread matching the color of their assigned rooms. Babies who were becoming mobile were given their own brand-new walkers, while each child with cerebral palsy had an expensive specialized wheelchair and imported feeding chair. On birthdays and with each change of season, children were given a new set of clothing, and on Christmas they each received a large, battery-operated toy.

Another important set of Western individualizing practices involved the surveillance, measurement, and intensive tracking of children's bodies. When they arrived at the unit, very little was usually known about kids' personal backgrounds or medical histories. The intensive intake procedures and medical examination served as a kind of birthing process for each child, providing a new identity while also diagnosing illnesses. The file that Cathy created for every child included his or her Chinese name (usually given by the orphanage), the Western name (given by volunteers), photo on arrival, date of birth, description of illness, and suggestions for treatment. Every day she went through the unit and checked on each individual's condition, noting any changes.

Babies were weighed once a week whereas older children were weighed on a monthly basis. Chinese caregivers were required to fill out a set of four color-coded forms that tracked each child's physical progress during each work shift. An "input/output" sheet monitored the frequency and time of urination and bowel movements (including color, amount, and consistency), as well as the intake and timing of formula or solid food. The second sheet tracked body temperature, which *ayi*s took every four hours or more often depending on the child's condition. The third sheet listed medications, with the dosage times written out next to boxes that caregivers checked off throughout their shifts. The final sheet was used to pass messages between daytime and evening *ayi*s to keep one another informed of changes in a child's medication or general condition. Volunteers also added their own detailed observations in English to individuals' files. This process of rigorous tracking resembled what Olga Nieuwenhuys observed in a study of foreign NGOs that help street children in Addis Ababa, Ethiopia. Constant surveillance and regulation of children's bodies and schedules, she argued, is a primary component of Western aid work that helps to transform stigmatized youths into "normal" (that is, first-world) individuals. Intensive schedules can purify children "from the filth and vice that breeds unchecked in the disorderly [outside] world . . . turning the child in time into a new person."[5]

Though the ultimate objective of this detailed and precise system of tracking in the special care unit was to improve children's health—or at least to make them as comfortable as possible if they were dying—implementing these rules caused continual friction between volunteers and caregivers. Numerous times after a child had fallen ill or major changes were made to his or her medications, I checked the charts and saw that the *ayi* had listed the child's condition as *zhengchang* ("normal"). When asked why they did not record the problem, many *ayi*s answered that they were pressed for time at the end of the day, rushing to give baths and feedings before their shift was over. Several women said they preferred to relay the situation orally to the next caregiver rather than to summarize it on paper.

After spending more time with the *ayi*s and learning about their limited educational backgrounds, I realized that their resistance to recording notes often derived from a sense of insecurity over their writing skills. Considering that children suffered from a wide range of complicated illnesses and conditions that the *ayi*s had never heard of before, they did not want to be held responsible if they wrote things down incorrectly. Nonetheless, Cathy began asking volunteers to "stand watch" over *ayi*s on days when their children became sick by marching the form over to them and pointing at it to make sure they filled it out in a more detailed fashion. (This was purely a symbolic demonstration of authority, though, as I was the only volunteer who could actually read Chinese.) This situation highlighted some of the daily life realities of outsourced intimacy, particularly the complex dynamics that arise when foreigners attempt to import a first-world vision of care that relies on access to education, training, and economic resources outside the reach of most local people.

## Cultivating Children's Potential

Although *ayis* focused primarily on children's physical well-being, Western volunteers sought to encourage their mental and emotional development. Foreign visitors went to great lengths to encourage sick and disabled youth to live up to their fullest potential—regardless of how limited that potential might actually be. For children in stable physical condition, volunteers tried to expose them to a wide range of play and educational activities to discover innate talents and interests that they would support and develop over time to enrich their quality of life. In one case, a group of European volunteers arrived with suitcases full of foreign toys that they used to discern the likes and predispositions of each child. They created a specialized chart that listed children's names alongside their level of engagement with the following activities: painting; drawing; playing with balloons, toy cars, puzzles, and balls; and water play. At the end of the assessment, the large poster served as a guide for future volunteers to organize specialized play regimens around children's preferences. Through small gestures like these, the lives of marginalized Chinese youth were altered by the global spread of rigorous middle-class child-rearing standards into developing country contexts.

Volunteers' rigorous approach aligned with the idea of "intensive mothering," a popular type of contemporary first-world parenting that Sharon Hays describes as "child-centered, expert-guided, emotionally absorbing, labor-intensive, and financially expensive."[6] Such activities also recalled aspects of Annette Lareau's concept of "concerted cultivation," an American middle-class practice in which parents expose offspring to educational and extracurricular activities to foster skills that will enable them to reproduce their own class status as adults.[7] In China's affluent urban areas, well-educated parents are taking a similar individualized approach to raising their only offspring to become part of a skilled class of globally competitive workers. However, children in the special care unit were relinquished precisely *because* they had physical and mental impairments that would likely prevent most from ever living independently, let alone achieving gainful employment. Thus, the presence of foreign charitable aid to orphanages resulted in socially liminal youth receiving similar treatment to that of their fortunate "little emperor" counterparts. Sara Dorow concurs, "Ironically, pockets of abandoned, marginalized children are the objects of some of the same kind of Western child development expertise now being marketed to middle and upper-class urban Chinese one-child families."[8]

This paradox was not lost on the children's *ayi*s, who often watched with blatant puzzlement and curiosity as volunteers helped children splash their hands in water, blew bubbles in their faces, bounced them up and down on rubber therapy balls, and serenaded them with plastic musical instruments. The volunteers' commitment to discovering children's innate capabilities and the unwavering belief that each individual could "improve" often served as a source of confusion, if not frustration, for local caregivers. One afternoon, Cathy assigned me to play with Jenny, a four-year-old girl with severe cerebral palsy and mental retardation. Concerned that both volunteers and *ayi*s were overlooking the child, she told me that given enough individualized attention, Jenny "really had a lot of potential for improvement." I grabbed a bag of toys designed to stimulate infants and sat down on the floor pillows next to the porcelain-skinned girl. Unable to sit up on her own, grasp objects, be potty trained, or make eye contact, Jenny was lying on her side, completely quiet and still.

Looking on with great interest, the two *ayi*s in the room immediately sat down next to me and grabbed baby rattlers, shaking them loudly in front of the child's blank, unblinking eyes. All the while they repeatedly said, "She's not aware of anything. She just doesn't know anything. (*Ta shenme dou bu zhidao*)." I mentioned that Cathy thought the girl could make some progress. Jenny's *ayi* shook her head in disbelief and said, "Yes, but progress to what level? What kind of progress can she really make? (*Jinbu dao shenme chengdu?*)"

Anne, a white thirty-eight-year-old British volunteer nurse practitioner who spent more than three months in the unit, offered her opinion about kids like Jenny:

> With a lot of these children you may not see much of what we would normally think of as improvement. But we need to be okay with the fact that we might work with a cerebral palsy child intensively their whole lives, and the only noticeable difference is that they can make eye contact. All of these children have their own personalities; with some you just have to look a little harder.

Providing for children's medical and daily life needs in a Western middle-class manner was not only labor intensive; it was also incredibly costly in financial terms. Sara Dorow notes that in her visits to orphanages that participated in international adoption, *ayis* were deeply aware of the fact that the abandoned children in their care often experienced better living conditions than they themselves did.[9] This gap in material conditions was especially apparent in facilities run by affluent foreigners. Indeed, the gleaming supply rooms in the unit were filled from floor to ceiling with donated new clothing packed and labeled according to size, item, and season. Large metal shelves were lined with seemingly endless supplies of disposable diapers, toiletries, formula, and snacks. The cabinets in the medical examination rooms were also filled with various over-the-counter and prescription medications as well as specialized tools, such as catheters and pediatric-sized colostomy bags. Many of these items were either unavailable in China or prohibitively expensive. To get around this obstacle, the organization relied on travelers to transport supplies, and even medicine, in their luggage.

## Conflicting Views of Children's Best Interests

*Most of the babies whom we have with us have been rejected and would have had difficult and painful experiences. They are helpless and are totally dependent on us to love them and protect them from harm. At ALL times, be gentle with them and treat them as precious creations of God and let them know that they are loved.*

**Excerpt from Tomorrow's Children, "Baby Care Policy for Nannies"**

In the unit, volunteers and *ayis* engaged in a constant tug-of-war over children's best interests. At issue were different ideas about what children need. Martin Woodhead argues that the very concept of "need" should be viewed as a cultural construction that derives from the heavily value-laden context of Western developmental psychology. In his view, unquestioned notions about needs conceal "a complex of latent assumptions and judgments about children. Once revealed, these tell us as much about the cultural location and personal values of the user as about the nature of childhood."[10] Because the unit's middle-class volunteers greatly prioritized child-directed practices and active engagement with individual kids, they imposed these expectations onto Chinese caregivers. When I asked founder Barbara Dunlop to name the biggest cultural challenges she faced in running her facility, she stated, "Mostly it's been difficult in terms of training the nannies to raise children in a Western way. Chinese people are often very hard on their kids, very strict." As part of their training, the *ayis* were taught to employ Western practices in their work with children. For example, rather than scolding or spanking children when they misbehaved, they were instructed to firmly state "No!" in English.

Bilingual illustrations on the wall instructed workers how to deal with a variety of issues that Chinese people and Westerners tended to handle differently, such as what to do when a child gets a fever or throws a tantrum. One particular poster related to discipline; displaying a large red drawn heart with the word *"ai"* ("love") written in the center, it reminded workers that "discipline is done out of the genuine love for children." Nannies were warned they could be fired for hitting, yelling at, or nagging a child in their care. These were not mere threats, either: One *ayi* in the Haifeng unit who was already under watch after one of her babies mysteriously developed an angry foot-long scratch on his arm was terminated on the spot for smacking the same child on the head when she thought no one was watching.

Volunteers often complained that the *ayis* were too restrictive or too passive or that they appeared uninterested in promoting children's emotional growth and independence. As proof, they pointed to large chests brimming with new toys that were hardly ever taken out. They often lamented that the infants' gross motor and cognitive skills were being delayed by a lack of stimulation and play. Nurse Anne remarked bitterly, "I would love to play with the babies all day long, but I've got real work to do!" In reality, *ayis* typically did not hold infants much or allow them to roll around openly on the floor mats, presumably because their movements were less easily controlled. Instead, babies often sat for hours on end in seats on the ground that *ayis* rocked with their feet as they chatted with one another on the couch.

New volunteers invariably expressed shock at what they considered to be the harsh, rough way that many of the local women treated the children. As a researcher, I attempted to maintain as much objectivity as possible, but I also occasionally found myself conflicted by these same issues. One evening after dinner, I heard a loud commotion coming from one of the rooms. Peeking through the glass window in the door, I spotted Robbie, a severely autistic eight-year-old boy, wailing inconsolably in the corner. Known for throwing inexplicable, terrifyingly violent tantrums that could last for hours, Robbie's unpredictable behavior was a constant source of exasperation for the *ayis*. Most had never heard of autism before (the ailment has only gained attention in China in recent years). The women thus viewed his tantrums as misbehavior. By contrast, the volunteers understood a great deal about autism, but they still could not figure out what triggered the boy or how to calm him down.

Back in the room, Robbie's deafening wails aggravated his two *ayi*s and upset the room's other young occupants. Especially affected was Kevin, a shy six-month-old boy who had just returned from the city of Hangzhou to recuperate from open-heart surgery. His lips were tinted dark blue from the prolonged lack of oxygen in his body. Alarmed by the surrounding commotion, Kevin began to cry in his seat on the floor. Flustered and overwhelmed, one of the nannies stomped over and rocked his chair forcefully with her foot, bouncing his wounded torso up and down repeatedly. The baby shrieked with a mixture of pain and surprise, peering up fearfully at his caregiver. Out of the corner of her eye the woman spotted me in the window, her foot immediately lifting off Kevin's chair. Her panicked voice wafted out from beneath the door as she asked the other *ayi* anxiously, "Do you think she saw that? (*Ta kan dao le mei you?*)" By then, I was already sprinting down the hallway to report the incident to Cathy.

Despite these types of sporadic situations, most of the caregivers were highly responsible workers who cared deeply about the children but were also exhausted by the labor of providing intensive care for long hours and low pay. In private informal conversations, many revealed that their primary consideration was to keep the sick and disabled babies under their care fed, clean, and warm. They explained that bathing, feeding, administering multiple medications, and changing diapers for three children up to six times a day during twelve-hour shifts—as well as keeping fastidious track of these activities—left little time to add "play" to their list of responsibilities. Therefore, if volunteers wanted the children to be entertained, some of the women told me, they should do it themselves.

Furthermore, several *ayi*s stated that the extensive proactive involvement the Western staff encouraged made children less compliant. This, they felt, could negatively affect the others who shared the same limited space. Their comments draw attention to cultural differences in childcare that are exacerbated by the limitations of institutional settings. Scholars such as David Wu argue that the basic tenets of Confucianism are still quite apparent in contemporary Chinese parenting practices despite major societal transformations in the PRC. These include expectations that children obey elders, exhibit impulse control, and accept social obligations; little emphasis is placed on independence, assertiveness, and creativity.[11] In a study comparing Chinese and white American mothers, psychologist Ruth Chao also found evidence of the lasting influence of Confucianism on Chinese childcare practices.[12] She argued that the emphasis Chinese families place on familial harmony through obedience to hierarchical relationships and set roles runs counter to Western ideals of individuality, independence, and self-expression.

Like Tomorrow's Children volunteers, the Western mothers in Chao's study tended to view Chinese parenting as authoritarian and restrictive, although the Chinese mothers—and, by extension, the *ayi*s in the unit—tended to associate stricter control over children with care, concern, and involvement. This perspective was illustrated by an exchange that I had with a nanny at the Beijing foster home. While observing a smiling volunteer patiently encourage a child who was learning how to draw, the woman shook her head and stated in a bemused tone, "Westerners always do what the child wants to do. It's really different from Chinese people. In China, children do what the parents say."

In the special care unit, both staff and volunteers tended to view these issues as the result of insurmountable cultural differences. After spending two months performing medical care at Haifeng, nurse Anne candidly expressed her doubts about the feasibility of the organization's overall mission:

> I know that we're doing good by doing this, but there are such huge cultural differences; how much can you do just by helping this little group? . . . I'm not putting down Tomorrow's Children, but now that I've seen so much more of the cultural differences, I wonder if it can really work. A Western-led voluntary organization in China—can it really work?

Although cultural factors likely played a role in these disagreements, over time I came to see that their conflicts were often rooted in *class-based* understandings of good care. In her study of American parenting styles, Sharon Hays found that different social contexts and access to material resources cause working-class mothers to give children set rules and demand obedience whereas wealthier mothers tend to emphasize negotiation, choice, and self-esteem in their offspring. Akin to the *ayi*s, the working-class mothers in Hays's study emphasized obedience and respect for adult authority in their children because it required less time, money, and labor. She explains,

An obedient and compliant child . . . is less demanding than an assertive and independent one. Establishing a system of standardized and strictly enforced rules requires less time and individualized attention than carefully providing the child with a set of bounded choices and negotiating with the child to establish the rules for proper behavior.[13]

*Ayi*s and Western volunteers thus subscribed to very different logics of care that reveal some of the inadvertent outcomes of outsourced intimacy. Because they were responsible for performing all of the intense physical labor of attending to three high-needs youth over twelve-hour shifts, caregivers preferred children to be docile and less demanding. Ironically, although they worked much more intimately with their charges for longer periods of time, the *ayi*s tended to take a shorter-term view of children's progress by focusing primarily on immediate physical health. In the context of modernizing China where societal membership is contingent on "high quality" offspring who will become productive laborers as adults, physically and mentally challenged youth are seen to lack a viable future. This led *ayi*s to take a pragmatic approach and define children's needs solely in the present tense.

By contrast, temporary Western faith-based volunteers took a long-term and individualized approach to care, emphasizing emotional as well as physical well-being. Despite the very different social and political environment, they treated children in Chinese orphanages as they would those in their own countries, preparing them for life opportunities that would likely never materialize. In the process of trying to serve as "examples" for *ayi*s to learn appropriate childcare practices, they often overlooked the disparities in life options and material resources between themselves and local workers.

## The Backfiring of Best Intentions: Grace's Story

While finishing breakfast in the special care unit kitchen one morning, I heard a cacophonous crash followed by peals of raucous laughter. Poking my head around the corner, I spied Grace in her sturdy black wheelchair, which had just come to rest after colliding with the wall. The young girl was gasping for breath, making a rather poor attempt to contain her giggles. On her lap sat Robert, a cherub-faced toddler who suffered from frightening epileptic seizures. Chuckling irrepressibly after their careening joyride, the boy craned his head around to peer at Grace's gleeful expression, triggering yet another explosion of laughter. An *ayi* emerged from one of the rooms and surveyed the scene. *"Hao le, hao le"* ("okay, okay"), she softly scolded them, her stern tone undermined by the slight twinkle in her eye. "No more playing in the hallway!" she warned as she pushed the pair back to the room they shared.

Grace was unlike any of the other children in the special care unit. Although she was wheelchair bound (the result of spina bifida that deprived her of the ability to walk) she was mentally sharp, perceptive, and incredibly verbal. A social butterfly, the girl displayed a wide-ranging vocabulary she used to incessantly pepper the staff with questions, entertain the young children, and sing songs to herself—all of which occurred between intense sessions of Tetris she played on a small hand-held device. Curious about this unusual child's background, I looked in her file and discovered that she had arrived at the orphanage the year before at the peculiar age of "six and eleven twelfths." Although Grace's advanced language skills and physical appearance suggested that she was at least nine or ten, it appeared that her parents (or at least parental figures) had reported a younger age to persuade the orphanage to accept her. The child herself had no idea how old she was. The nurse's notes also mentioned evidence of severe physical abuse; both of her legs were still dotted with faint gray scars from numerous cigarette burns.

Grace's life was an unending series of upheavals. From the time she was a baby, she had been transferred to at least three different households and continued to move between various care settings even after arriving at the orphanage. Prior to being taken in by Tomorrow's Children, Grace was living in the dying room on the second floor, sharing a cot with a rotating group of extremely ill babies. After meeting the bubbly girl in the room on several different occasions, Cathy decided to bring her upstairs to live. She did this knowingly in defiance of the organization's mission to care for only at-risk babies and toddlers. By the time I arrived at Haifeng, the child had been thriving in the unit for two months.

After we became more familiar with one another, Grace shared her story directly with me. Tightly grasping one of my hands between her pudgy fingers, she whispered into my ear that she had grown up in a nearby city and missed her home dearly. After her older brother had gotten married the year before, his new wife demanded that she be sent away, worried that she brought shame onto the family. When I asked whether her most recent set of parents explained why they took her to the orphanage, she shook her head and remarked glumly, "No, they just brought me here and said they would come back to see me in three or four days. Now it's been over a year, and they've never come back." Her eyes watered as she traced one finger over the screen of her beloved Tetris game, a parting gift from her "*yeye*" (grandfather).

Despite the unmistakable improvement in her quality of life after transferring to the unit, Grace had very little to occupy herself with on a day-to-day basis. Spina bifida had left her permanently incontinent, a condition that disqualified her from attending local schools and eliminated her chances of obtaining a formal education with the other nondisabled orphanage youths. At the same time, daily intensive physical therapy and other types of rehabilitation services provided by foreign organizations at the CWI focused specifically on helping those with cerebral palsy. Therefore, the girl occupied a highly liminal position within the orphanage whereby she was simultaneously quite disabled but also considered *not disabled enough* to warrant specialized services.

Several weeks later, I took a break from volunteering and returned to Beijing. While there, I received an urgent update from nurse Anne that the organization's founder, Barbara Dunlop, had decided to send Grace back down to the second floor. Despite the fact that Barbara had spent very little time in the units and had never even met the girl, she made the executive decision to return Grace to the regular facility to avoid sending the "bad impression" to Chinese government officials that the infant care unit was a place for older children. Deeply troubled, I protested that cerebral palsy–afflicted youths such as Henry were even older. However, as Anne explained, because he would die without specialized care, Henry was considered more deserving of the organization's resources than a child like Grace, whose condition was stable and unlikely to worsen. I immediately spoke with nurse Cathy about the situation, who regretted ever bringing the girl up from the dying room. "I knew that I was going against the rules," she stated emotionally, "but I felt heartsick leaving her there to languish."

The organization had been told by orphanage officials that Grace would be allowed to attend classes with other special needs children in the CWI, so a volunteer reluctantly returned her to the dying room with a supply of diapers and several sets of clothing. Three months later, I went back to Haifeng for a visit and immediately went to check in on Grace. Seated in her wheelchair in the middle of fifteen extremely sick infants, I found her chatting animatedly with an *ayi*. Despite her sunny disposition, the difference in her appearance was obvious. She had lost weight and her short, spiky hair had been completely shaved off, which, according to her caregiver, "made it easier to give her a bath." Yet it was obvious that the child had not been bathed and her teeth had not been brushed for some time.

The front of Grace's shirt was stained with several layers of food. Sitting with a blanket pulled over her lap, she wasn't wearing any pants because she had wet them and run out of diapers. When I asked where her other clothes were, she shrugged and explained that they had disappeared long ago. Despite the grim physical surroundings, Grace remained her same talkative self. As we caught up she mentioned that she had never been placed into any classes and that her video game had run out of batteries. When I asked where she slept, the girl pointed sheepishly to a bed where a sick baby who had just arrived from the hospital earlier that day lay crying. Not knowing what else to do since she was no longer under the care of Tomorrow's Children, I brought her a new toothbrush and more diapers and replaced the batteries in her video game. I also gave her a framed photo of herself smiling with Nurse Anne, which she glanced at quickly before tucking it under the corner of her mattress.

Several days later I went back down to the second floor to take Grace out for a walk. She was sitting at the end of the hallway all alone. Spotting me, she self-consciously drew her blanket up onto her bare lap to cover herself. After receiving permission from her *ayi*, I took her outside with another volunteer who brought along Robert, the girl's epileptic toddler friend. Grace reached over and tickled his stomach, provoking squeals of delight. It was clear how much she had missed him. After several minutes, however, her mood darkened. I offered her a small piece of cake saved from a birthday celebration that had been thrown that day for children in the unit, recalling how much she had enjoyed her own party earlier that year. In a barely audible voice she whispered, "I don't want it." With eyes downcast, she pushed the plate away with her hand.

## Conclusion

Due to globalization, the PRC's increased openness to outside actors has allowed humanitarian organizations seeking to change Chinese society from the ground up by assisting its least-valued members to get deeply involved in its child welfare system. International collaborations of this kind make obvious the financial benefits that foreign aid can bring to local authorities as well as the socially privileged nature of Western volunteerism in developing countries. In particular, the Tomorrow's Children special care unit illustrates the conflicts and ethical dilemmas that can occur for children when Westerners cross unequal national spaces to provide outsourced intimacy for the Chinese state.

Self-financed global groups can be highly valued by state authorities for the expertise and knowledge they bring to the PRC to help modernize the local child welfare system. Despite their good intentions, the introduction of private Western assistance to orphanages like Haifeng can also inadvertently stratify ill and disabled youth according to their perceived level of need. As children are circulated, sometimes back and forth, between areas of the CWI that have access to vastly disproportionate financial and medical resources, foreign humanitarian aid contributes to the development of very different kinds of childhoods within the same care setting.

Tomorrow's Children used first-world, middle-class ideologies and practices to remake each patient into a unique individual who could reach his or her fullest human potential. Indeed, babies who were sent upstairs from the dying room were reborn as personalized medical care and attention immensely improved their quality of life. Many experienced comfort and love during the difficult final stages of terminal illness, and an even larger number of youth had their lives extended or saved altogether. Some even recuperated enough to eventually be placed for international adoption. The many successes of Tomorrow's Children notwithstanding, Grace's story reveals a tragic unintended consequence of outsourced intimacy within certain orphanages. Because neither the CWI nor the special care unit categorized her as disabled enough to receive specialized services or education, Grace was ultimately left to languish, uncared for, in a room filled with dying babies. Being "rescued" by the unit, thriving in a first-world setting for several months, and then returned to a life of institutional neglect served as yet another kind of abandonment—the most recent in a long series that the young girl had experienced over the course of her short life.

Grace's situation, one that remained unresolved when I completed my fieldwork, illustrates that, in their rush to get involved, enact change, and save lives, foreign aid groups can reach a point where their approach does not adequately serve the long-term interests of everyone they seek to help. In other words, the seemingly simple desire to help those in need—when combined with the demands of performing outsourced intimacy for the Chinese state— can be fraught with irreconcilable tensions and moral dilemmas that greatly benefit some while unintentionally allowing deserving others to fall through the cracks.

# 5 The Limits of Outsourced Intimacy

*Contested Logics of Care at the
Yongping Orphanage*

CRISP AIR FILLED MY LUNGS as I stepped off the bus in a nondescript suburb on the eastern side of Beijing and jumped over piles of decaying brown leaves blown onto the sidewalk. After a brisk ten-minute walk down several pleasant tree-lined streets, I arrived at the Yongping Social Welfare Institute (SWI), a local Chinese state-run institution that also contained an elder care home, a facility for disabled adults, and a small orphanage that housed around forty mostly special needs children. The orphanage had been built three years earlier with funds donated by the Helping Hands Organization, a local grassroots group of affluent Western expatriate wives in Beijing.

At the front gate, a baby-faced security guard stood at attention, his slight body engulfed by an oversized navy blue uniform cinched improbably tightly at the waist. As I approached, the teenager stepped forward and raised a slender hand to block my passage. In a surprisingly gruff voice, he barked, "Where are you going?" "To the orphanage," I stammered nervously, before quickly adding, "I'm a foreign volunteer." I was unsure whether this would help me get inside or raise suspicions. In light of Beijing's preparations to host the 2008 Summer Olympics, rumors were circulating around the international NGO community about new restrictions on foreigners attempting to gain access to state orphanages. To my great relief, the boyish guard stepped aside and waved me through.

From where I stood the orphanage looked small and insignificant, sitting off to one side of a modern four-story nursing home that cared for several hundred senior citizens. On my way in, I nodded a greeting to two elderly male residents in their seventies who had donned matching dark rectangular sunglasses, striped winter caps, and the black cloth slipper shoes common among Asian grandparents. They sat together silently on a wooden bench in the courtyard, soaking in the sun and tapping their feet along to the jolting rhythms of Chinese opera that blared from an old-fashioned handheld radio. On my right sat a colorful, but forlorn, children's playground built with donations from a Western multinational corporation where the husband of one of the Helping Hands volunteers worked. Rarely ever used for children's play, the blacktop was littered with broken plastic toys. Sturdy white laundry lines crisscrossed the space, drying an array of bedsheets and children's clothing that flapped in the breeze. Several foreign luxury cars were parked alongside the playground, and their Chinese male drivers were dozing off or playing on their cell phones in the front seats. The Western volunteers had clearly arrived.

The orphanage was a plain, one-story L-shaped structure with large plate glass windows that had oversized decals of animals dancing across the front. Pushing open the heavy doors, I ducked first into the baby room, which was located directly across from me. Measuring only ten by fifteen feet, the space was filled to capacity with metal cribs. Four beds formed an island in the center of the room, and eight more cribs, each holding a toddler or baby, lined the faded periwinkle walls. Some of the children were napping fitfully while others stood upright, grabbing the metal bars for support. No toys were in sight. From one bed, a pasty one-year-old boy with Down syndrome smiled up at me, revealing four emerging teeth. Shy but curious, he reached forward and grabbed hold of my pinkie. Several layers of dried formula formed a white crust on the boy's chin and continued down the front of the ill-fitting set of donated overalls he wore. I picked the child up and carried him around the room. The boy settled in contentedly, wrapping his legs tightly around my waist.

In one corner lay a neglected toddler who had severe cerebral palsy and painful-looking infected sores on his cheeks. He was unresponsive to touch, and his small chest felt bony and rigid under my hand. Across the room another boy began wailing loudly from his bed, large angry tears streaming down his beet-red face. He strained forcefully against the cloth strap that had been used to bind both of his hands behind his back. Peering closer, I saw that his hands were lashed to the side of his crib. Later, another volunteer explained that the child was autistic and gnawed on his hands. The *ayi*s had responded by binding them during feedings and naptimes. The only caregiver in the room, a young Chinese woman in a stained white lab coat that gave her an oddly dignified appearance, ignored my presence. She was engaged in a flurry of movement, carrying infants from their cribs to a changing table in an adjoining room. Mechanically, the *ayi* repeatedly unfastened each child's sopping diaper, dropped it in the wastebasket, wiped the baby's bottom with stiff paper towels, and put on a fresh disposable one. Few babies protested when the shock of cool air hit their skin, mirroring the *ayi*'s own noticeable silence.

Outside in the hallway, two middle-aged white American women volunteers spread a blanket out on the floor and began carrying dirty, dazed-looking infants out from the baby room for one-on-one attention. Cheerfully, the women bounced kids on their laps, clipped their tiny fingernails, and spread lotion on ruddy cheeks as they chatted animatedly about their own children's activities at the local international school. The babies, who were all between three and six months of age, responded well to the stimulation; perching on their hands and knees, they rocked their small bodies vigorously forward and back with obvious excitement. The volunteers soon discovered that they had forgotten to bring baby wipes. "*Ayi!*" one of the women addressed a Chinese worker who was hurrying by with an armful of dirty laundry. "Tissue? Tissue?" she called out loudly in English, gesturing exaggeratedly at a child's runny nose. A flash of annoyance crossed the *ayi*'s face as she continued down the hallway, ignoring the woman's request.

Several days later, the management committee of Helping Hands gathered in one member's spacious luxury high-rise apartment in downtown Beijing to discuss the situation at Yongping. Several volunteers criticized the apathy of the Chinese staff and the absence of individualized attention provided to the children. Ellen, a British mother of two and the group's treasurer, recounted her last visit to the orphanage. With an air of disdain, she scoffed, "The *ayi*s asked me to wash the floor, and I just laughed!" She rolled her eyes. "I mean, come on. I'm there to play with the babies, not do the work for the *ayi*s!"

This book contends that the Chinese government has outsourced the care of some of the country's least valued members to private humanitarian NGOs. The previous chapter detailed a relatively cooperative transnational partnership in which the Western group was viewed as a marker of modernity for the orphanage and allowed to use its own resources to remake unwanted children into global citizens. By contrast, this chapter examines the limits of outsourced intimacy by examining the collaboration between the Yongping Orphanage and the Helping Hands Organization. Unlike what occurred for

Tomorrow's Children, this conflict-ridden relationship was characterized by suspicion—particularly that of local state authorities toward the motivations of foreign volunteers. The different logics of care that the Helping Hands volunteers and Chinese state workers subscribed to are key to understanding the tension that characterized this transnational partnership.

Specifically, I suggest that expat wives' highly privileged global social status caused them to develop an *emotional* logic that equated care solely with maternal nurturance. Compared to the evangelical Christians with Tomorrow's Children, who had purposely relocated to China to assist disparaged youth, Helping Hands volunteers were primarily Western women who moved abroad to support their husbands' careers. As the "trailing wives" of elite men who worked for foreign embassies, international media outlets, and in the financial and legal sectors, many turned to volunteer work to bring meaning to their lives in Beijing. Yet despite their insistence on providing emotional care, in practice, women's transnational lifestyles required them to maintain flexible schedules that made them less committed to their volunteer work and to the children they sought to support.

In comparison, the low-paid local Chinese caregivers at Yongping generally subscribed to what I call a *custodial* logic of care, prioritizing tasks such as feeding, cleaning, and laundry that met children's most basic physical requirements. Unlike other welfare institutes I visited, Yongping's care standards reflected the orphanage's ambivalence toward Western aid rather than a true lack of material resources. Within an institutional environment that did not encourage or reward the expenditure of emotional labor, nurturance was not considered a necessary aspect of care. Instead, children's interests were defined solely in relationship to the state. Viewed as social outcasts rather than redeemable citizens, Yongping's residents were treated as objects to maintain rather than global citizens to invest in. These different logics created continual conflicts over care standards that worsened relationships between adults while also not improving children's lives.

In both of the main field sites highlighted in this book, Western volunteers and Chinese caregivers subscribed to divergent views of what children need and deserve. However, Tomorrow's Children flourished (albeit within constraints) at Haifeng while the Yongping Orphanage's partnership with Helping Hands was afflicted by misunderstanding, instability, and ambivalence on both sides. Two key structural factors accounted for this difference. First, unlike Haifeng, Yongping was not signed up for international adoption, creating no financial incentive to invest in or improve the circumstances of its young residents. Second, while Tomorrow's Children provided "face" to local officials through donations of resources and knowledge, Helping Hands was generally treated as a nuisance—and sometimes even as a threat—to the institution. Yongping's director was highly suspicious of outsiders and heavily restricted volunteer involvement to material donations and short two-hour visits, even though the organization sought to do much more. Consequently, whereas Tomorrow's Children was granted great independence in its operations, Helping Hands was *prevented* from making a lasting difference in the lives of institutionalized youth.

## Foreign Involvement with the Yongping SWI

In recent decades, tremendous economic growth that has attracted substantial foreign investment to China's cities has also inadvertently led many elite expatriate women to form grassroots charity groups that assist local society. The organization Helping Hands was founded in 1997 by Marjorie Lee, a Chinese-born, American-educated grandmother who relocated to Beijing after her husband joined an international law firm. Giving up paid work in health care back home, Marjorie devoted herself to helping needy children in China. Talkative and energetic, the petite woman looked at least ten years younger than her actual age. She possessed a rare combination of medical training, English and Mandarin language fluency, bicultural understanding, and the ability to navigate the Chinese state bureaucracy. Marjorie expertly utilized her husband's vast network of social connections to garner support for her causes within Beijing's Western business community.

Soon after Marjorie developed a partnership between Helping Hands and the Yongping Orphanage in 2003, it became a popular volunteering site for foreigners. The Social Welfare Institute that housed the orphanage was located on the eastern outskirts of Beijing, close to the many elite Western housing compounds that have sprung up en masse as the city has quickly expanded outward. Managed by the local district's Ministry of Civil Affairs, the SWI was originally intended only as an elder care facility but was eventually required to take in locally abandoned children as well.

In addition to the elder care facility and orphanage, the premises also contained a private facility serving roughly 100 severely mentally and/or physically disabled adults who required full-time supervision. Visitors were not permitted to enter this building. The windows were placed too high on the brick walls to see inside, though loud moans and other disturbing noises often penetrated the glass. Helping Hands volunteers whispered about the horrific treatment of those living "in the back." The existence of this profit-driven facility at the SWI reflected the broader decline in central government support for social welfare in the reform era.

When Helping Hands first began assisting Yongping (prior to the construction of the orphanage) about twenty mostly special needs babies resided in three isolated rooms of the nursing home. The children were divided according to age, with infants in one room and toddlers in another. The third room was designated as a "playroom," although there were no toys or activities. Long-term volunteers I spoke with described unimaginable conditions, recalling that the children were attended to only during the day. At 6:00 pm, the children were strapped down to their beds or cribs, the doors were closed, and the *ayi*s did not return until 6:00 am the next morning. Fortunately, one elderly man living in the facility took it upon himself to monitor the kids at night. Heather, a white American mother of four whose husband worked for a large international oil company, described the immense deprivation of that time:

> The smell was awful and the sanitation nonexistent. They had nonflushing little kids' toilets on the ground that used to get filled up, and sometimes they'd get knocked over. They used to put two or three babies in a crib and line them all up next to each other. And if the kids were big enough to stand they'd put them in these metal cage things all day long. There were no toys whatsoever. At first we weren't allowed to hold the babies. We had to prop them up on pillows and look down on them from above because if we held them they'd want to be held again after we left and would cry.

Sensing an opportunity, Marjorie Lee quickly got to work, using her unrivaled communication skills to obtain permission to construct a separate orphanage facility and adjoining playground on one side of the nursing home. Completed in 2004 with the financial sponsorship of several major multinational corporations, the bright one-story structure housed thirty-five to forty mostly male children at any one time.[1] There were separate boys' and girls' bathrooms, a cafeteria, two storage rooms, a laundry room, and a large children's playroom. Helping Hands oversaw building renovations, paid children's school fees and the salaries of three of the orphanage's six full-time *ayi*s, donated washing machines and other large items, and delivered a continual supply of disposable diapers and infant formula.

Volunteers came from a diverse range of national backgrounds, including the United States, the United Kingdom, Australia, South Africa, Hong Kong, Taiwan, Canada, Germany, France, Denmark, and Spain. Despite their differences, they all shared high socioeconomic status, and nearly everyone resided in expat enclaves close to the embassies or financial centers in Chaoyang District or by the expensive international schools that most of their children attended. Volunteer shifts were organized to accommodate women's mobile lifestyles, taking place during school hours between 9:30 and 11:30 am on weekday mornings. Due to the transience of expatriate life, many volunteers simply left each summer as families returned home for extended visits or moved on to their next international assignment. Families typically resided in Beijing for a period of three to five years, with wives and children living abroad during the academic school year and returning to their home countries for a month in the winter and three months each summer. In the fall, members would recruit fresh volunteers from the ranks of newly arrived expatriate women in their social circles and housing compounds.

Helping Hands capitalized on the gendered division of labor that defines many expatriate communities, where men typically work for transnational corporations while their wives travel with them and manage the children and household. Correspondingly, men made financial contributions to the organization while women volunteered their time and caring labor. Although group membership was not limited by gender, during my fieldwork there was a rotating contingent of approximately forty female volunteers and only two male volunteers, a white Catholic priest and a retired Australian evangelical Christian who moved to China specifically to work with at-risk children. Women sometimes brought their children to Yongping on special occasions, but it was rare to see their husbands at the orphanage. Instead, men usually attended events such as formal black-tie events that women organized to raise funds for their projects.

## The Custodial Logic of Care at Yongping

Most weekday mornings, expat women entered through Yongping's gates in a caravan of chauffeured luxury vehicles. Regular volunteers often brought friends along on these visits; many were visibly shaken by their experience and never returned again. At the end of one morning shift I saw a first-time volunteer standing outside with her hands covering her face, quietly sobbing. The young Chinese American mother had spent the last half hour in the cafeteria helping the *ayi*s hastily feed a row of hungry toddlers. With the children still clamoring for more, the caregivers had packed up the extra food and taken it away. The woman appeared shell shocked. Her friends gathered around in a conciliatory circle, gently patting her shoulders and assuring her that volunteering would get easier over time. Her anguished voice punctured the air, "It's like the *ayi*s don't even care!"

Western visitors often reacted similarly with shock and dismay on confronting the conditions at the orphanage. Yongping shared much in common with Erving Goffman's concept of the "total institution."[2] In his classic study of life in a mental hospital, Goffman described the daily lives of inhabitants as routinized, tightly scheduled, and structured in ways that subordinate individual needs to the goals of the larger system. Individualized attention is scarce in places where staff members are responsible for managing the daily activity of a group of people in a limited space with few resources. Total institutions also exhibit a breakdown of barriers between the normally separate spheres of work, play, and sleep. This concept pertains to care in orphanages, particularly those in socialist and postsocialist contexts. One study of Russian institutions found that activities such as feeding, diapering, and bathing were performed in a businesslike, detached manner with very little talking or social interaction.[3] Similarly, conditions within underfunded, understaffed Romanian institutions have been characterized by limited interpersonal contact, poor nutrition, and a lack of sensory stimulation.[4]

At Yongping, caregivers were focused on performing reproductive (physical) labor rather than providing emotional nurturance. With each adult responsible for looking after at least ten children simultaneously, *ayi*s prioritized schedules and adult-directed group activities that saved time through decreasing individualized attention. Caregivers were also burdened with the responsibility of cleaning the entire facility in addition to performing childcare tasks. In comparison, the Tomorrow's Children special care unit employed entirely separate cleaning staff to allow caregivers to give children as much individualized attention as possible. Consequently, at Yongping, *ayi*s spent most of their time performing domestic chores that did not directly involve children, such as laundry and mopping floors.

The task of feeding the kids, an activity that consumed much of each day, clearly illustrated the custodial-type care that predominated in the orphanage. Akin to what I had witnessed in Haifeng's dying room, babies were all bottle-fed simultaneously at intervals throughout the day rather than according to each child's level of hunger. *Ayis* often poured the unfinished formula from used bottles into new bottles for other infants to save resources (while also quickly spreading germs). During mealtimes, any child able to eat solid foods was ushered into the cafeteria, which had high chairs lined across one wall for toddlers and several round tables for the older kids. Even though lunch was not served until 11:00 am, children were often herded into the room thirty minutes to an hour beforehand and told to sit and wait quietly.

Because the *ayis* did not provide any activities or entertainment, during this time volunteers often tried to entertain the fidgety children by singing songs and feeding them fruit or other snacks that they had brought. Eventually two or three *ayis* would enter carrying giant steaming bowls of rice porridge and pork-filled buns that were retrieved from the kitchen of the nursing home. This lunchtime meal, which hardly ever varied, contained few vegetables and consisted mostly of starch and fatty meat. After doling servings into individual bowls for the older children, the caregivers would rapidly mix the porridge and buns together on large plates for the toddlers. By this time, the hungry little ones were usually banging their hands against their high chairs, sometimes even standing on their seats. I often joined in to help as the *ayis* quickly moved up and down the row of wriggling children, using the same spoon to feed the entire group one bite at a time. Like a nest of baby birds, the toddlers chomped away, opening and closing their mouths repeatedly.

Sarah, an American volunteer who had moved to Beijing with her financier husband several months earlier, explained that she found working at the orphanage deeply gratifying but couldn't handle mealtimes:

> I feel comfortable playing with and holding the kids, but I can't watch them be fed. I was surprised to find out that I had the strongest emotional reaction to watching them eat. I mean, they get great meals, but it's the way that the *ayis* shove food down their throats and how quickly they do it that makes me uncomfortable. So I decided that I can't go into the room when they're eating.

In every possible way, kids at Yongping were treated as a unified group rather than as individuals. Babies' diapers were changed just once in the morning and once in the afternoon (and likely once at night, though I was never there to observe), meaning that nearly all of the infants were forced to sit in wet and dirty diapers for hours on end. This both cut down on caregiving duties and led to extreme cases of diaper rash. The older children were all bathed together in the shower in co-ed groups of four or five, shrieking with delight as an *ayi* used a hose to spray them down with water. No soap, shampoo, or lotion was ever used, so all of the children constantly experienced dry and chapped skin. Children also spent much of their time sleeping. Even the older youths who didn't need lengthy naps were required to lie down every day from 11:30 am to 2:00 pm. Heather half-jokingly described the philosophy of care at the orphanage as "Keep them quiet, asleep, and out of the way!" She continued more somberly, "It's like there's no long-term plans and ambitions for the kids."

Natalia, a Spanish volunteer, explained her view of the differences between the volunteers' approach to care and that of the paid Chinese *ayis*:

> Westerners feel that kids need more than just material things, whereas the Chinese just feel happy if they are providing enough beds, clothes, and food. When you talk to them about giving one-on-one attention, they look at you like you're from Mars! I think the Chinese do not think it's that important to build emotional bonds with the children. I think it's important for them to develop more of an idea about covering more than children's basic needs.

Natalia did, however, recognize that these differences were not solely an issue of culture but also of economic development. "The thing I think we forget is that all of our countries were like this maybe fifty years ago," she explained. "So we can't always judge China and say that it's so backwards because we used to be like this, too."

### Subsuming Children's Needs to Institutional Priorities

The custodial logic of care at Yongping also informed the organization and control of children. The thirty-six mostly special needs youth were generally divided along the lines of age and physical ability. Infants and older children slept and ate separately, making the transition to the next group when they were able to walk on their own. The cramped baby room usually contained about ten infants. Although some volunteers were intent on learning all of the babies' names, they were randomly switched between cribs nearly every day, making it extremely difficult to keep track. Christopher, one of the two regular male volunteers, was disturbed by the lack of agency in children's lives. He told me gloomily,

> Ownership is a major problem there. The kids don't own anything, not even their bed. I've seen them get switched around from bed to bed. They don't

have even a spoon that they can say, "This is mine." This leads to them not being connected to anything, not even to people. They have no decision-making capability whatsoever. They aren't allowed to choose what they eat or where they sleep or what they wear. It's like a holding facility, but for what?

The only child never to change cribs was the boy with severe cerebral palsy and mental retardation who appeared at the beginning of this chapter. Of all the infants, he was by far the most neglected and suffered from a serious skin infection that festered on his face for the better part of a year. By contrast, I recalled that when an unidentifiable skin rash appeared on one of the babies in the Tomorrow's Children unit, the British nurse immediately snapped a picture and emailed it to a skin specialist in the United States who diagnosed it from afar and suggested appropriate treatment. Within a few days, the rash had totally healed. Although Tomorrow's Children worked to provide individualized care to ill and disabled youth at all costs (an approach that created its own issues, as I've discussed), the opposite appeared to be true at Yongping. This was particularly apparent to me as I regularly went back and forth between the two field sites.

At Yongping I was surprised to discover how little attention was given to small infants, which seemed to contradict modern Western child development models that view babies as the most time and energy intensive. Children who could not yet speak or walk seemed to be considered the least deserving of *ayis*' time and were placed at the bottom of the orphanage hierarchy. Similarly, a study of Russian baby homes found that institutionalized infants spent the least amount of time with caregivers as compared to their older peers.[5] Back at Yongping, infants were often left in their cribs all day long and were rarely held, stimulated, or talked to; as a result nearly all of them exhibited significant developmental delays. The babies were eerily quiet and complacent, as they learned early on that crying did not necessarily garner attention.

Although the lack of individualized care created major developmental setbacks, I also noticed that over time the healthy babies were able to teach themselves important motor skills. When I first began volunteering, there was a cluster of three- to six-month-old healthy babies with extremely floppy bodies who were unable to hold their heads up, roll over, or tolerate being on their stomachs. Yet despite a lack of adult stimulation aside from their short interactions with volunteers, by the time they had reached eighteen months of age, the children were incredibly mobile, intelligent, and inventive. One afternoon, I arrived to find that the *ayi*s had blocked the door of the baby room with wooden shelves to keep the infants from escaping. Without toys to occupy them, the toddlers entertained themselves by performing impressive gymnastic feats—pulling themselves up, into, and out of one another's cribs. Their increased mobility had an unfortunate downside, however, as the *ayi*s began to tie kids' arms to their cribs during nap times to prevent escape.

Furthermore, though they lacked consistent nurturance in their lives, the young children were able to express deep levels of care and empathy toward one another. On one occasion, I was supervising five rambunctious toddlers while the *ayi*s fed the older kids. A bedridden baby began crying loudly in obvious discomfort. In a flash, three youngsters scampered over to his crib; with genuine concern, their eyes implored me to help. I quickly repositioned the baby and dried his eyes, at which time he stopped wailing and the group moved onto playing with something else. Once toddlers could walk without assistance they joined roughly twenty older children, a group that was usually watched by only one *ayi*. Kids ranged in age from two to sixteen years old and mostly included those whose age, gender, and physical and/or mental limitations gave them little chance of adoption by local families. Due to the group's high level of energy, caregivers contained their movements by locking them into a large playroom. For the sake of order, children were divided according to disability. Two small boys with Down syndrome were usually kept together in a cagelike metal cart, and three adolescent boys with cerebral palsy were always placed side-by-side in their wheelchairs in one neglected corner of the playroom.

There were rarely any toys for children to play with in the sizeable space despite the presence of a locked cabinet in the room that was crammed full of donated books and materials. This reflected a culture of scarcity that existed at the facility, whereby nicer items were not used even though volunteers brought more each week. The children, who were understandingly bored, invented their own games or fought over scraps of discarded paper that they used to make paper airplanes. The only entertainment was a television mounted high on one wall, which had been donated for the purpose of playing educational DVDs and kids' shows. Instead, it was nearly always tuned to a dramatic Chinese soap opera that the *ayi* watched with one eye while supervising the group.

Although Yongping was certainly not the most resource deprived of institutions, the absence of individualized care fostered major behavioral issues that were readily apparent in the older children. Research has found that children and youth without a consistent and responsive caregiver tend to exhibit a similar range of behaviors, including indiscriminate friendliness, a shift from early passivity to later aggression, overactivity, distractibility, inability to form deep or genuine attachments, and difficulty with establishing peer relationships.[6] A significant number of Yongping's older children displayed many of these behavioral traits, especially indiscriminate friendliness. During my first few visits to the orphanage, I was charmed when the children would launch themselves into my arms despite not knowing who I was. Jostling against each other, arms outspread, they would call out plaintively in an attempt to be heard above the rest, "*Ayi, bao wo!*" (Auntie, hold me!) After learning more about child attachment issues, my initial pleasure turned to concern when I realized that most of the older children were completely unable to distinguish between trustworthy and dangerous adults.

Compared with the relative calm of the baby room, the general dynamic of the playroom was far more chaotic, competitive, and aggressive. A group of five boys with fixed cleft lips and palates—first and second-graders who attended a local elementary school during the week—set the tone during our Saturday visits. Although they were mostly well behaved and could even be quite caring and considerate, the boys were filled with nervous energy from being confined to such a tight space, leading them to career around the room wildly, steal items from smaller children, hoard snacks, and practice martial arts moves on one another. This unruly environment changed the temperament of some of the group's youngest members as they transitioned into their new setting.

In one case, within weeks of being placed with the older children, Dang Wu, a two-year-old deaf boy who had been a very mild-mannered baby, began to act out aggressively. As I sat on the floor of the playroom one day, Bing Bing, a typically sweet-natured five-year-old boy with a fixed cleft palate, plopped down into my lap and began to chat animatedly. For no apparent reason, Dang Wu ran over and with unabashed enthusiasm fiercely kicked Bing Bing's leg. In a flash of anger, the much larger five-year-old jumped to his feet and reared his leg back to kick the boy in return. With children running amok and no *ayi*s in sight, I physically restrained them until their tempers subsided.

An American volunteer named Laura believed that children's issues stemmed from the institutional environment. Having volunteered at Yongping for four years, she ultimately did not hold out much hope that the situation would improve:

> I've noticed that kids who are raised there create their own problems. Whereas [Westerners] think, "If kids have a problem, let's not create a new problem while we're trying to avoid the old problem." You need someone with a professional background, but what you have is uneducated *ayi*s and a director who really doesn't care.

### Separating the Public Care of the State from the Private Realm of Kinship

Although the care provided to children at Yongping baffled and frustrated Western volunteers, it resembled that provided in other postsocialist contexts. Rosie Read's study of caregiving in a Czech nursing home offers important insight into the custodial logic of care.[7] Like Yongping's *ayi*s, the Czech nurses Read studied did not personalize the care they provided to their patients because they "simply did not see emotional work, i.e., communicating and empathizing with patients and creating a warm and supportive environment of care, as part of their job."[8] The Czech nurses did not identify with patients and their needs but instead identified with their employer and the broader socialist model of care that focused solely on maintaining physical health. Read argues that this approach resulted in "an entrenched and pervasive culture of indifference towards patients' emotional well-being."[9]

This was also the case at Yongping, where *ayi*s were at the bottom of a socialist institutional hierarchy that devalued abandoned children and equated official work responsibilities with reproductive labor. Like Czech nursing homes, Yongping Orphanage was governed by an enforced separation between what Read calls the "public care of the state and the private care of kinship." In other words, state-employed caregivers were not expected to provide personalized care to their patients because love and commitment were considered part of the private, emotional realm of the family.

This separation between public and private forms of care at Yongping was a major source of frustration for twenty-eight-year-old Angela, a Filipina occupational therapist hired by Helping Hands. She lived at the orphanage for several months to provide intensive daily therapy to the children and train the *ayi*s in therapy techniques. During her time there, Angela experienced a serious asthma attack that required hospitalization. I visited her over the course of several afternoons as she recuperated. Normally positive and enthusiastic, the woman was now clearly homesick, exhausted, and dissatisfied with her experience. Angela bitterly noted that her job duties had expanded beyond therapy to including physical labor. "Here, they expect you to do caregiving," she complained. "I can't just do therapy but am also supposed to clean and give the children a bath!" Thoroughly dejected, Angela questioned whether she could make a difference at Yongping:

> It's totally disorganized here. There's no real schedule for the kids to follow. The *ayi*s should teach the children, but they don't. I get frustrated because we are giving them an example, but they're not following it. It's like they [the *ayi*s] think, "You do your thing, and we'll do ours." I wonder, why are we here?

Angela was constrained in her work by Yongping's rigid institutional culture. "There are real limitations to what you are allowed to do here," she explained. "I have a lot of ideas, but they are always turned down by the director or reversed by the *ayi*s." Her most pronounced disappointment stemmed from an incident where she was blocked from having special shoes made for Dang Yan, an extremely intelligent seven-year-old girl who was wheelchair-bound from spina bifida. Disabled children who required bathroom assistance were not allowed to attend regular Chinese schools, but the shoes would have allowed Dang Yan to use a walker and obtain an education. But, as Angela recounted angrily, "I found a doctor out here who was willing to work with her and set everything up, and then we asked the director and she said no! So nothing happened." Soon after, the frustrated therapist was transferred to another location.

It's important to note that Yongping's paid caregivers did sometimes provide emotional care to the children. However, they seemed to consider personalized care exchanges to be separate from work duties. On numerous occasions, I spotted *ayi*s giving individualized attention to their favorite kids—usually the cutest, most sociable, and able-bodied of the group. Yet these brief moments were special indulgences that took place only when the physical work was complete. Caregivers appeared to treat their work responsibilities as unconnected to their personal identities as women and mothers.

### The Political Sensitivity of Foreign NGOs in China

This scarcity of personalized care at Yongping could not be explained by a lack of resources, as Helping Hands was happy to provide generous financial support and connections to services to improve children's lives. Rather, I argue that the routinized way the institution managed its young wards reflected the state's ideology of "high quality" and "low quality" people that marginalizes individuals with special needs. Socially stigmatized and considered incapable of contributing to China's global future, the children at Yongping were treated as if they were unworthy of financial and emotional investment—regardless of who provided the money. This attitude was amplified by the director's resistance to Westerners setting the terms of conduct or bringing in unfamiliar practices that would give them more control over the children.

Helping Hands founder Marjorie Lee met regularly with Director Huang and repeatedly offered to pay for cleaners, teachers, and therapists to lighten the *ayis'* workloads and give children a chance for education and rehabilitation. Over several years she attempted a variety of different strategies to improve care, such as offering to pay for more *ayis*, but the director told her that having more caregivers would encourage laziness. Marjorie also tried to implement a foster care program—going so far as to locate local families willing to participate—but the director backed out on learning that the families were Muslim (a group that is highly discriminated against in the PRC). Still undeterred, after a number of Helping Hands volunteers expressed interest in adopting children from Yongping, Marjorie tried to help the orphanage sign up for international adoption but found that the children did not have the appropriate documents. Some of the children lacked *hukou* (official birth registration) altogether, meaning that they did not officially exist as citizens. Director Huang eventually accepted one more full-time cleaner, but she refused nearly every other offer of assistance. This incensed volunteers, who could not comprehend why the director—herself a mother, they often noted—would turn down free opportunities to improve children's lives.

Volunteer Christopher gave an insightful critique of the lack of investment made by the institution, and by extension, the Chinese government, in special needs children and its suspicion of foreign volunteers:

> The government is too shortsighted in their approach. If the government was interested now and invested in these kids now, they could actually contribute something to society later . . . The Chinese government is really ashamed of having Westerners doing volunteer work here, but what they don't understand is that our own countries would not be able to function without volunteers!

As was apparent at different orphanages I visited throughout my fieldwork, the situation at Yongping had become increasingly politically sensitive in the run-up to the Beijing Summer Olympics. Because foreign journalists were allowed to freely tour the country, the government was careful to block access to orphanages. The air buzzed with rumors of crackdowns on foreign NGOs after an established and widely respected Western faith-based foster home near Beijing had been required—without warning—to return sixty of its special needs children to their original orphanages, many of which were unequipped to tend to their severe disabilities.

Director Huang's refusals reflected the broader political climate of suspicion in which foreign NGOs operate in China, a sentiment exacerbated by the Olympics. Though local officials have turned to independent civic groups to meet financial needs, China's authoritarian context has nonetheless ensured that relationships between the state and grassroots groups are "always tenuous, contingent on a continuing perception of mutual benefit."[10] Located in the nation's capital, organizations like Helping Hands faced the constant threat of repression by government authorities seeking to maintain power by limiting outside involvement. Furthermore, in general, NGO donations are never truly free of obligations and can instead "become a form of patronage and a means of control" over recipients.[11] This suggests that, from the perspective of Yongping's director, allowing volunteers to fully implement their plans would have granted them major influence over the state-run facility. These uneasy power dynamics were evident in the struggles over childcare that I observed.

## Orphanage "Voluntourism" and the Emotional Logic of Care

Although Yongping was a workplace for low-paid caregivers, it served as an extension of the domestic realm for foreign volunteers who equated care with maternal nurturance. Yet, within the larger context of transnational migration and the gendered limitations of expatriate life, the care they provided at Yongping ultimately appeared less like the long-term commitment of motherhood and more like the temporary, sometimes self-indulgent, work of volunteer tourists. Volunteer tourism, or "voluntourism" in short, has emerged in recent years from the spread of neoliberalism and the privatization of social services in many developing countries across the globe, including the PRC. This booming market in international travel has brought throngs of Westerners to developing countries in search of unique, intimate experiences of helping local communities. An estimated 1.6 million people spend around $2 billion annually to perform short-term volunteer work.[12]

Scholars have questioned whether local people are truly helped by volun-tourists who provide only short-term, noncommittal forms of assistance. This trend, some critics charge, privileges the interests of affluent aid givers over the needs of receiving communities, thus exacerbating existing global in-equalities.[13] According to a recent CNN news article, the voluntourism indus-try is growing "because more and more people are seeking meaning, fulfill-ment and a sense of purpose in life. If this is not met in their careers and daily lives, volunteering whilst traveling is a powerful way to meet this desire."[14] Though Helping Hands members may not have traveled to China specifically to work in orphanages, their more self-serving motivations for involvement with deprived children and the lack of consistency in their efforts resembled that of voluntourists.

Most Helping Hands members were part of a quiet but growing privileged migration of first-world citizens into urban Chinese society that has accom-panied the country's economic boom. Paradoxically, despite the fact that ex-patriate women in Beijing were among the world's most mobile populations, their daily lives were restricted by social, economic, and geographic bound-aries. Residing in Western-oriented sections of the city produced a sheltered existence for many foreign families. Laura, an American mother of three who had accompanied her journalist husband to Beijing half a decade earlier, self-consciously depicted her family's lifestyle in an exclusive foreign gated com-munity as "grossly out of sync" with local society. As she elaborated in an interview, "We live in a compound—we have to out of necessity. But our kids go to the international school, so the choices that we've made have in some ways separated us from the [local Chinese] community." Another volunteer enthusiastically described the large numbers of establishments catering to Westerners. "You can live here without ever feeling like you're in China!" she remarked brightly.

Just as the work of Yongping's ayis was structured by a pronounced sepa-ration between public and private spheres, so too was life in Beijing's expa-triate community. This divide led to greater social isolation for women than for men because husbands interacted with Chinese society on a daily basis through their jobs. In conversations with Helping Hands volunteers, many fondly recalled their professions back home, which included accountant, journalist, nurse, teacher, physician's assistant, massage therapist, and physi-cal therapist. Yet few pursued paid work in Beijing because, in addition to the difficulty of attaining a work visa, most lacked Chinese language skills or could not find local temporary career options aside from low-paid English teaching gigs. Their husbands' generous relocation packages also eliminated any financial need for women to pursue paid positions.

In many expat communities, international movement can upset more egalitarian gender arrangements that heterosexual married couples with dual careers share in their home countries. Moving abroad, therefore, forces many career-oriented women to choose between work and family, rather than accommodating both. Consequently, only two of the women volunteers I met worked for pay (one was unmarried, and neither had children). Anthropologist Anne-Meike Fechter reflects on this particular gendered characteristic of expatriate life:

> Through the process of becoming expatriates, the relations between men and women are thrown back to those of a bygone era, insofar as even couples who had previously both worked often revert to a more traditional model where the husband is the breadwinner, while the wife has responsibility for home management, childcare and well-being of the expatriate family.[15]

I met Susanna, a thirty-three-year-old Italian mother of two, while volunteering at Yongping. She had earned a doctorate in political science before moving to China three years earlier with her husband, a French diplomat. Her face lit up as we chatted about academia on the drive back to the city after a volunteer shift. Behind the wheel of a dusty green Jeep Cherokee, Susanna expertly wove her way through notorious Beijing traffic while lamenting her inability to find related work: "I'm writing articles, but it's an unpaid job and not so stimulating." She sighed, "I think it's a shame for me, but it's the destiny of the following wife." New patterns of global movement have caused many women like Susanna to become "incorporated wives" whose social identities are conflated with their husbands' professional roles.[16] Rather than giving expatriate wives freedom from social constraints, new transnational spaces can revive earlier forms of women's disempowerment.

These gendered limitations inspire many foreign women to volunteer. Historically, charity work and philanthropy have been a vital part of elite women's lives. Such activities "have traditionally provided—and continue to provide—the means through which women have grasped, wielded, and maintained public power—not only in America, but overseas as well."[17] Charity work is also a primary means of involvement with the local host society. Patricia, a newly arrived American volunteer in the midst of intense culture shock, explained: "It's nice to be able to get involved with Chinese society in this way, which is otherwise so closed to us." Many women that I met used charity work as a key way to participate in the public sphere. Nonetheless, a study of British expat trailing wives in Dubai revealed that volunteer work served as one of only a very limited number of socially valid pursuits for women that allowed them to preserve their primary roles as full-time homemakers.[18] Around the world, then, expat wives use unpaid community work as an "adaptive strategy" to fulfill self-serving purposes such as alleviating boredom, filling free schedules, and providing a sense of purpose while husbands are at work and children at school.[19]

Helping Hands founder Marjorie Lee immersed herself in volunteering to lessen her dissatisfaction about moving to China at a later age. Prior to starting the organization, Marjorie ran a foster home full time for three years in another city, visiting Beijing only on weekends. When I asked if spending that kind of time apart from her husband created marital issues, she laughed, "No, he was happy to get rid of me! I was giving him more trouble because I was not happy to come here. [I thought] why am I coming here for? You're working all day long, and I'm just sitting here, doing nothing!" Another volunteer named Shirley, a middle-aged mother originally from Hong Kong who had earned two master's degrees in the United States and Canada, expressed similar feelings. With her son grown and out of the house, she accompanied her husband to Beijing in 1997 and had nothing to do. Mutual friends introduced her to Marjorie, who asked her to join Helping Hands as one of its first volunteers. Shirley described her reasons for getting involved:

> I just had too much time on my hands. I would just sit at home and watch TV by myself. I'm not the kind of person who goes out to buy jewelry and goes shopping all the time and has tea with my friends. So I got involved with Helping Hands to save myself from depression.

In her study of expatriate wives in Beijing, Daniella Arieli argues that women experience "intensified ambivalence" as they attempt to reconcile the feminist-infused values of their home societies with the highly gendered and restrictive structure of life in China.[20] Rather than resist new norms, she found that many women willingly relinquished their careers and provided emotional support for their families in exchange for higher social status and affluent lifestyles. Many expat women thus engaged in a patriarchal bargain that swapped emotional labor for "wealth, leisure, the ability to dominate women of lower status who do most of the housework for them, and the ability to . . . construct for themselves a prestigious identity as privileged women."[21]

In contrast to Arieli, I found that many foreign women were uncomfortable with their lavish lifestyles. Helping Hands volunteers spoke about the instantaneous—and for some, quite unsettling—increase in social status and standard of living on arriving in Beijing compared to their more typical middle-class existences in their home countries. Such women used volunteer work to challenge negative stereotypes of expat wives as pampered debutantes known for their "lack of language skills, arrogance, ignorance and possibly racist attitudes."[22] For example, Natalia, a Spanish occupational therapist married to a Swiss official, devoted nearly all of her time to volunteering to counter this perception. She asserted, "I don't feel like a normal expat wife who just follows my husband around, like one of those women who just does her nails every day." The couple's move to Beijing, she explained, was a mutual decision based on their shared interest in experiencing other cultures. Natalia emphasized that even though she was currently supporting her husband's career, they agreed that in the future the situation would reverse and her professional goals would take priority.

Volunteering helped many women deal with the peculiar combination of elevated social status and gendered limitations of expatriate life. Paradoxically, their involvement in charitable activities that brought them closer to local society relied on the labor of low-paid female domestic servants in their own homes. Almost all foreign families employed at least one full-time helper to perform time-consuming household duties such as cleaning, laundry, cooking, grocery shopping, and childcare. This was such an institutionalized feature of expat life that servants were often included in housing contracts. Only one volunteer chose to not have an *ayi*; she half-joked that other embassy wives gossiped she was "crazy" for doing her own housework.

Many Helping Hands members self-consciously acknowledged that they benefited from household help and their privileged social positions, which motivated them to do something useful with their time. During one management meeting, treasurer Ellen candidly remarked, "We are mostly trailing wives, and we volunteer as a way to close the gap of privilege between ourselves and Chinese society." Similarly, Laura began volunteering at Yongping due to uneasy feelings about the expatriate lifestyle. Although she had stopped working years earlier to raise three children, she was unprepared to have *ayis* perform most of her housework and childcare. Laura stated,

> When you come to China, you walk into this environment where you have [household] help, where I've got somebody full-time watching my kids, doing the cleaning, and I felt a tremendous sense of guilt. I wasn't working, and I had help to take care of the kids, so I felt a need to be productive in some way.

Freed from domestic labor, some women even considered volunteering obligatory. Heather, whose family previously lived in Dubai and was later reassigned to Indonesia, met me in her palatial house located in an exclusive Western-style compound. As a Chinese housekeeper served us tea and cookies at her large dining room table, she openly critiqued other expat wives for not performing charity work:

> I don't understand why there aren't more expats helping out. There are people out here who are just interested in shopping, eating, doing their nails. I mean, I like to shop and eat, but I just think they're missing the whole boat of why they're here. Plus, the fact is that we all have *ayis* who do our housework, cook our meals, and take care of our kids. My *ayi* sends my kids off to school and picks them up in the afternoon, so once they're gone I really have the whole day to do things. So when I ask them to volunteer, and they say they're busy, I think—busy doing what? You don't even clean your own house!

Expatriate life thus thrust Western women into the role of managers of household staff. Freed from reproductive labor, their principle responsibility became providing their families with emotional care and support. This situation harkens back to the nineteenth-century "cult of domesticity," an ideology that viewed women's appropriate place as within the home and their appropriate social roles as virtuous, submissive, loving mothers and wives. Even now, at home and abroad, affluent women uphold this vision of ideal womanhood by hiring less privileged women to do their dirty work.

## Unequal Logics of Care at Yongping

I've suggested that because *ayis* subscribed to a custodial logic that emanated from Yongping's institutional setting, they did not conflate their work duties with maternal care. This sentiment was confirmed in an interview a student volunteer conducted with Wang Weiwei, a twenty-five-year-old local woman who had worked at Yongping for three years. The *ayi* described the gratification she received from her job but was careful to distinguish between the care she provided and a mother's love. She elaborated:

> I can do my utmost in taking care of these children in a loving and caring way, but the kids will know that my love for them is not maternal love. Receiving love from your parents is so important. Having to miss that in your life is one of the worst things imaginable.[23]

By contrast, expat wives viewed themselves as maternal substitutes who used their brief two-hour shifts to shower children with love. Heather noted that charity work bolstered her sense of maternal responsibility and described feeling a deep imagined emotional bond with the mothers of Yongping's children. "I feel like I have to be the arms for the mothers who had to give their kids away," she exclaimed emotionally. "It's important just to hug a child and let them know that someone loves them when their mothers couldn't." The parent of four drew great fulfillment from her volunteer work and included it in her list of life priorities: "I put my family and my children first, but I put orphanages right under them."

During their shifts, Helping Hands volunteers held babies and brought educational activities for the older youth, using exaggerated body language to bridge the language divide as they worked together on puzzles or decorated Easter baskets. They often organized parties at Yongping, bringing McDonald's Happy Meals, cake, and once even a clown to entertain the children. Similar to what I observed in the Tomorrow's Children special care unit, there existed an unspoken division of labor between the volunteers and *ayi*s whereby volunteers provided bursts of emotional care, play, and stimulation to children while *ayi*s performed domestic tasks. On several occasions I observed a French volunteer named Anna conduct a weekly ritual of tucking the older youths into bed for their midday naps. She hugged each child tightly, kissed their cheeks, and lightly tickled their tummies, provoking squeals of delight, as an *ayi* silently folded piles of laundry nearby.

Disagreements often erupted between state caregivers who prioritized order and volunteers who wanted children to learn and explore—two objectives that were highly incompatible within institutional constraints. For example, *ayi*s kept toys and activities locked away so they could easily sweep and mop the floor throughout the day or keep them in good condition. One afternoon, I was playing with a baby on a pastel-colored foam mat made from large thick pieces that fit together like a jigsaw puzzle. The infant pulled up a piece and began chewing on the corner. Seeing this, "Big Mother" *Ayi* rushed over and removed it from her mouth. From a typical Western perspective, this mat could be viewed as a choking hazard, but Big Mother interpreted the situation differently. "Don't let the kids eat the mat!" she commanded me gruffly. "We don't want to have to replace it!"

Helping Hands volunteers, who regularly donated such items to the facility, questioned the reasoning behind denying children access to things specifically intended for their use. Therefore, during their morning shifts the expat wives always retrieved a number of toys for the children, leaving them scattered on the ground when they departed. They seemed oblivious to the great irritation this caused the *ayi*s, who had to put the toys away before they could clean again. Volunteers continually attempted to pressure the *ayi*s to pay more individualized attention to the children, which irritated the local workers as they hurried around performing chores.

The Saturday student volunteer group I organized sought to avoid friction with caregivers by purposely spending the first thirty minutes of each visit scrubbing the facility. One afternoon, an *ayi* told me that she preferred our student group to the expat wives because "you always clean up after yourselves, and they always leave a mess." At the next Helping Hands meeting, I relayed this exchange to treasurer Ellen, along with a suggestion that it might ease tensions if all of the volunteers cleaned the facility during their visits. My words seemed to shock the woman, who employed a full-time Chinese housekeeper. Disdainfully, Ellen replied, "I would be willing to clean as long as I could use my own supplies to avoid catching hepatitis!" The topic was soon dropped altogether.

The bleak orphanage setting stirred a dramatic maternal response from many expat women. Laura, one of the day leaders, recounted a situation in which a new volunteer spontaneously breast-fed infants without permission:

> I had one volunteer that came twice [who] physically nursed two babies. There were two brand-new babies, and I just thought, "Oh, my god!" . . . She just said, "I just couldn't not nurse the child." . . . She was in severe survival mode, and she was emotional because she had a young child herself, and it was almost like something not to be reckoned with.

As this case showed, volunteers sometimes engaged in incredibly intimate forms of maternal care at the orphanage that would not be permitted, or even considered socially acceptable, in their home countries. Nevertheless, the priority that expat women placed on keeping their own families primary prevented them from providing children truly consistent emotional nurturance. Even the volunteer who breastfed the babies visited on only two occasions, never to return. Unlike other organizations with strict volunteer guidelines, Helping Hands did not require women to commit to a regular schedule. Consequently, many showed up inconsistently or sometimes not at all. Natalia, the Spanish physical therapist, expressed concern about volunteers' low level of commitment:

> I think that in some developing countries many expats think they're here to enjoy themselves, and so they do things superficially. I think there are too many people involved in these projects . . . Sometimes I get worried because China can be so open and allow us to do things that would be impossible to do in our own countries! There are no regulations of volunteers . . . [but I think] people need to plan and take their work seriously.

The lack of consistency in most women's work at Yongping was heightened by their transnational lifestyles, which brought volunteering largely to a halt in the winter and summer when families returned home. Because expat wives' charity work is so often contingent on other factors, some researchers question whether they undertake this work with "genuine conviction, or whether it mainly keeps women occupied, such that they would abandon these activities as soon as their circumstances changed."[24] The superficiality of volunteers' efforts was also compounded by their feelings of discouragement about the custodial logic of care at Yongping, conditions that they perceived as unchangeable. Teresa, a Mexican American volunteer, expressed her frustration:

> I understand that there are certain ways of doing things here, and we must respect that. But some of the things that [the ayis] do to the kids you shouldn't do anywhere—China, North America, Africa. Like tying the kids to the beds or tying their hands behind their back—it's like they're animals!

Shrugging her shoulders, she acknowledged that volunteers had limited power at Yongping: "But we're not going to be able to change them. If there's going to be change, then it needs to come from the top . . . it's not going to come from us." After nearly a decade of effort, even founder Marjorie Lee described feeling depressed by the constant tension and lack of change at Yongping. She decided to pass the organizational responsibilities for the orphanage over to another Chinese American volunteer and devote her time instead to different child welfare projects where she "could actually make a difference." Many women continued to volunteer halfheartedly, resigned to their inability to improve the situation.

## Conclusion

This chapter has shown the limits of China's outsourced intimacy by highlighting how Western assistance to orphanages is sometimes viewed as a threat by local state authorities. At Yongping, these conflicts were crystallized in symbolic struggles over children's care. Although in the arena of global humanitarian aid vast inequalities in resources can heighten power disparities between givers and receivers, in this case the recipients wielded tight control over the situation. As an extension of the Chinese government, Director Huang ultimately had the greatest influence over children's care. The distrust with which the director regarded outside help and the institution's prioritization of custodial labor suggest that she did not consider abandoned youth redeemable citizens or symbols of the future. Instead, children's interests were subsumed to state goals even when external resources that could improve their lives were easily accessible.

Compounding matters further, Helping Hands members tended to approach their volunteer work in largely personalized and emotional terms that did not challenge existing patterns of discrimination in Chinese society that marginalized special needs youth. Unlike the evangelical Christians at Tomorrow's Children who described volunteering as a religious "calling," expat wives generally used charity work to create a sense of purpose in their own lives and to escape gendered constraints while keeping their primary identities as wives and mothers intact. Kay Bratt, the pen name of an expat wife who authored an autobiographical account of her experiences working at a local state-run orphanage near Shanghai, epitomized this sentiment. She writes that after her first day of volunteering, "I was hooked—I absolutely loved it. Perhaps I couldn't change their circumstances, but I felt I had an abundance of love to give these deprived children."[25] Overseas charity work made her realize that she was a good wife and mother, prompting her to speculate, "Why did it take being uprooted from my home and moving to a third-world country to achieve and recognize that?"[26]

In their quest for self-fulfillment through finite acts of helping, expatriate women were like voluntourists. Within the growing realm of voluntourism, regardless of whether individuals work with orphans or animals, teach English, or provide needed medical care, these short-term experiences typically seek to produce intimacy between hosts and paying participants. Anthropologist Mary Conran argues that the search for emotional intimacy inherent in voluntourism "perpetuates an apolitical cultural politics" by individualizing larger social problems and overlooking the structural inequalities that allow these encounters to take place.[27]

Around the world, voluntourists seek personal fulfillment through helping neglected, abandoned, and socially disadvantaged youth. However, as one study of AIDS orphan tourism in sub-Saharan Africa points out, the positive effects are questionable: When tourists inevitably depart, kids experience yet another abandonment that negatively impacts their emotional development.[28] Likewise, according to Cheney and Rotabi, "While many orphan tourists coming from afar think they are offering children the love and attention they deserve, in reality they may be causing serious damage to individual children's development as well as broader children protection systems."[29]

Such was the case at Yongping, where the constantly shifting group of Western women who sought to provide maternal nurturance to children at their own convenience conflicted with an existing care structure that already created a host of challenges for its young inhabitants. This situation highlights some of the possible drawbacks of outsourced intimacy in transnational care collaborations and the power struggles enacted through the giving and receiving of humanitarian aid. In the end this infighting between adults adversely affected Yongping's children by heightening uncertainty within their already unstable lives.

# 6  Waiting Children Finally Belong

*The Rise of Special Needs Adoption*

IN THE SUMMER OF 2011 I RETURNED TO CHINA for a long overdue visit. I reconnected with Cathy Marks and her husband Brian, the British couple who ran the Tomorrow's Children special care units during my fieldwork several years earlier. After multiple disagreements with the organization's founders, in 2010 they decided to establish their own Western infant palliative care unit. Located in the chaotic capital city of Hunan Province, known for its red chili–infused cuisine, their facility was similarly located inside a large child welfare institute that received assistance from multiple foreign humanitarian groups. Though they were both nearing the age of sixty, Cathy and Brian signed a five-year contract with the local government to run their unit. Once the contract ended, they planned to pass the unit over to local Chinese medical staff so that they could retire back in the United Kingdom.

I flew down from Beijing on a hazardously smoggy day. After a harrowing half-hour taxi ride to the city, I arrived at the large welfare institute. Located off a busy thoroughfare in the center of town, the nondescript white building looked like many of the other state facilities I had visited over the years. Cathy greeted me warmly at the door and escorted me up to the special care unit. As we chatted amiably, I surveyed the children. There were thirteen infants and toddlers ranging up to three years old who suffered from a variety of conditions that I had grown used to seeing in abandoned children such as eye tumors, spina bifida, and cerebral palsy. A combination of individualized care, specialized diets, and medications produced high rates of recuperation in the unit. Even the sickest child—a nine-month-old boy with liver failure named

Wen Wen—delighted everyone with his playfulness; sitting in his *ayi*'s lap on the soft mat of the playroom floor, he used his tiny fingers to plunk out dull notes on a toy keyboard.

Wanting to get to know the children better, I plopped down next to Li Li. The gorgeous one-year-old had a tousled bowl haircut that sat atop an enormous head, twinkling eyes, and broad rosy cheeks. Having successfully recovered from serious bowel surgery, she had been diagnosed with a host of other ominous-sounding neurological conditions. Doctors were uncertain whether she would ever be able to walk. Despite her mental and physical needs, the girl had been matched with a well-to-do American evangelical Christian family from North Carolina who would be coming to adopt her in just a few months. Li Li was clearly a staff favorite, grinning mischievously while scooting across the floor on her bottom in hot pink wool tights. As I settled in next to the plump child, her face slowly crumpled, and she began to cry. Two large, dramatic tears rolled down her cheeks as she twisted her chubby torso away from me and held out her arms to one of the women sitting on the couch. The *ayis* began laughing in unison, gently teasing the girl for her shyness. One of the women scooped Li Li up, and she quieted down immediately.

Several days later I was in the playroom when I heard a roaring stampede of feet and the distinctive sound of southern-accented American English. Curious, I darted out into the hallway with a baby cradled in my arms. In front of me stood thirteen excited white American volunteers clad in matching neon green t-shirts. The buzzing group of adults and teenagers was touring different regions of the PRC on a church trip to advocate for Chinese adoptions in the United States. Concerned about the large, boisterous crowd, I exchanged glances with Cathy. She murmured, "Just be patient with them. They've been a huge source of support for us." A blonde young woman with a bright pink face reached for the child in my arms and cooed, "Ooh, can I hold her?" Cathy gave me a quick nod. "Of course," I said. "Wow, your English is amazing!" she complimented me as I passed her the baby. "I'm Chinese American," I responded. "Well, it's still really impressive. You should be proud of yourself!" she replied with a wide, toothy smile. The volunteers fanned out through the unit, systematically taking each child's photo. Before photographing several of the infants, they placed bright red headbands around their scalps; I later discovered that this symbolized the group's intention to locate adoptive "forever families" for these children among their church members back home.

The group's leader, a thin, fashionable brunette in her early forties named Sarah, asked where she could find Li Li. In a faint southern twang, the woman told me she had brought gifts from the child's new American family with whom she had made contact through online church networks. Speaking in a low conspiratorial voice, she admitted, "I really wanted to adopt Li Li myself, but I've adopted two children already, and we couldn't afford a third." Spotting the child across the room, Sarah's heavily made-up eyes glistened with happy tears. She pulled the stunned girl into her lap and began flipping through a picture book filled with photos of the child's new family. Every shot looked professionally done, vividly capturing the adventures of two young, tanned, and athletic white parents and their biological son and daughter as they skied, frolicked on the beach, and barbequed with friends in their spacious back-yard. Several of the *ayi*s huddled together as they peered over Sarah's shoulders, their eyes wide and unblinking. Incredulous, they whispered to one another, "This child is so lucky! (*Zhe ge haizi zhen xingfu!*)" Sarah opened her bag again and pulled out a miniscule frilly purple tutu. Puzzled, one of the *ayi*s held it up at arms-length and examined it, tugging hard on the elastic band. "It's like a little skirt," I explained, showing her how to put it on Li Li. The now highly overstimulated child sprawled out on the mat, comically en-gulfed in a sea of lavender tulle.

As a final treat, Sarah pulled out a plush brown and white stuffed bear with an oversized sky-blue satin heart stitched across its chest. "Listen to this!" she exclaimed breathlessly, giving me a sly wink as she pressed on the heart and held it to the child's ear. The bear began to play a tinny recording of a woman's voice layered thick with emotion. Li Li glanced up in wonder as she listened to words that she could not yet comprehend: "Honey, this is your new mom. Your dad, your brother, your sister, and I all love you and can't wait to meet you! We'll be coming to China to get you soon!"

Healthy female adoptees have been the subject of intense concern and scrutiny in academic scholarship and popular media, but surprisingly little has been written about special needs kids like Li Li who have been international-ly adopted with increasing frequency through an alternative plan known as the Waiting Child Program. She and the thousands of other ill, disabled, and older youths who fall under the official Chinese state-defined designation of "special needs" disrupt commonplace understandings about children's ready adoptability and their intrinsic value to foreign families. Kids who face long-term physical and/or mental limitations that may require expensive medical and professional services challenge the notion that young adoptees present a "tabula rasa" that future parents can mold according to their own wishes. Much more invisible labor goes into remaking some of these children into globally desirable daughters and sons, challenging the sense of fatedness symbolized by the red thread story.

The last two chapters examined how outsourced intimacy operates in China through the involvement of Western humanitarian aid groups. This chapter connects these collaborations to larger patterns of international adoption and soft power. The rise in special needs adoptions through the Waiting Child Program relates to two primary factors occurring on opposite sides of the Pacific, China's changing supply of available youth and the American evangelical church-based "adoption movement"—a newly influential faith-based initiative that casts international adoption as central to American foreign policy. Rather than attempting to alleviate systemic issues of poverty and inequality that deprive children of homes in their birth countries, this movement frames adoption by Western families as the main solution to severe global economic disparities. Special needs adoptions, I suggest, allow both Chinese state authorities and the American government to spread their moral influence around the world, serving as a form of soft power for each of the two major global leaders.

## Declining International Adoptions and the Changing Market of Chinese Children

Adoption has long been the subject of intense ethical debates concerning the commodification of children as they are legally exchanged across families, institutions, and nations. Early waves of international adoption to the United States were bolstered by Christian child-saving impulses that emerged from American wartime occupation in Asia.[1] Over time, critics charge, the spread of global capitalism has created a "free market" in children wherein altruistic motivations have become overshadowed by consumer/parental preferences.[2] According to David Eng, "The logics of global capitalism are ones that commodify and colonize not just an ever-expanding field of objects . . . but also and increasingly subjects themselves, including young children."[3]

Throughout the twentieth century, international adoption was relatively unregulated in either sending or receiving countries, creating legal and ethical ambiguity sometimes resulting in a profit-driven free-for-all. Guatemala serves as a worst-case scenario of fraud and corruption, with many proven accusations that children were kidnapped or bought and sold for the sake of foreign adoption over the course of several decades.[4] As a developing country of only 15.5 million people, at its peak in 2006 Guatemala provided 20 percent of *all* internationally adopted children in the world.[5] Investigations revealed that local officials incentivized by this multimillion dollar industry forged visas and separated children from their birth parents so they could be declared orphans and sent abroad. Even more disturbingly, as early as the 1980s U.S. Embassy officials in Guatemala were aware of these illegal practices and communicated their concerns to the U.S. State Department, to no avail.[6]

To create greater transparency, the Hague Convention on Protection of Children and Co-Operation in Respect of Intercountry Adoption (HCIA) was drafted in 1993. Implemented by China in 2005 and by the United States in 2008, the convention was developed to establish safeguards to ensure children's rights and prevent illicit financial gain in sending or receiving countries. Most notably, the Hague Convention includes the subsidiarity principle, which is based on the perspective that it is in children's best interests to be raised by their birth families or at least by extended family members. If this is not possible, local authorities are encouraged to find other permanent family placements within the child's home country. Thus, the HCIA takes a strong stand on foreign adoption by treating it as a last resort. According to an official Hague publication, "Only after due consideration has been given to national solutions should intercountry adoption be considered, and then only if it is in the child's best interests."[7] Consequently, after more than half a century of steady increase, international adoptions to the United States—the top receiving country in the world—dramatically plummeted. At its pinnacle in 2004, Americans adopted 22,991 children from other countries. By 2013 this number dropped to 7,092.[8] This decline, which is not predicted to reverse course anytime soon, in no way reflects decreased demand from prospective parents. Rather, it is the outcome of the HCIA combined with a proactive effort by the top sending countries—namely Russia and China—to lower the number of kids they place abroad.

The recent drop in intercountry adoptions reflects larger debates about children's best interests as well as the United States' tenuous political relationships with Russia and China. In early 2013, Russia passed a bill that officially banned *all* adoptions to the United States—a law that many observers interpreted as retaliation for American sanctions placed on Russian citizens suspected of violating human rights.[9] This ban, which jeopardized several hundred ongoing international placements, was undoubtedly influenced by several highly publicized negative incidents involving Russian adoptees in the United States. In one infamous case from 2010, a mother from Tennessee named Torry Ann Hansen sent her seven-year-old adopted son on a one-way flight back to Moscow by himself. Along with snacks and activities, she placed a note in his backpack that read, "I no longer wish to parent this child. He is violent and has severe psychopathic issues." Russian Prime Minister Dmitry Medvedev labeled her actions "a monstrous deed" and threatened to suspend all adoptions at that time.[10] In 2013, another international controversy erupted after a three-year-old adopted boy in Texas died suspiciously. Although local authorities ruled his death accidental, the Russian Children's Rights Commissioner called the investigation insufficient and publicly accused the boy's adoptive mother of murder.[11]

In the case of China, the reduced availability of healthy infant girls has contributed to a substantial decrease in adoptions since the mid-2000s. Even so, the PRC remains the top sending country due to the popularity of the Waiting Child Program. Thousands of parents whose paperwork was already submitted for the traditional program, but who were unwilling to wait the seven or more years it may now take to attain a healthy baby daughter, switched over to this alternate system. Many others have been inspired to adopt special needs children in response to encouragement from the American evangelical adoption movement.

## Overview of the Waiting Child Program

The adoption of special needs and older children from the PRC through the Waiting Child Program officially began in September 2000.[12] "Special needs" in this case refers to children and youths who have medical or physical conditions and/or who are older (roughly eight to thirteen). Common issues include cleft lips and palates, heart defects, missing or webbed fingers or toes, Down syndrome, cerebral palsy, hepatitis B, and vision or hearing impairments. Even though special needs youth have been available for some time, they were not considered particularly desirable until after 2006 when the PRC severely limited the supply of healthy girls following the Hunan child trafficking scandal. This change was accompanied by stringent new rules placed on adoptive parents in 2007, which I discussed in Chapter 3. These rules included restrictions against individuals with physical or mental illnesses and those with a body mass index above 40.

Priority is now given to affluent, married heterosexual couples between the ages of thirty and fifty, although those who seek to adopt an infant may not be older than forty-five.[13] The China Center for Children's Welfare and Adoption (CCCWA)—the main state body that governs international adoption—has publicly stated that the new rules were not intended to curb foreign placements. Instead, drawing on the language of the Hague Convention, the CCCWA has argued that the regulations were designed to serve children's best interests. Quoted in Chinese state media, one government official rationalized the need for some of the controversial new laws by explaining that "obese people, for example, are more likely to suffer from disease and might have a shorter life expectancy, which is not without consequence for the life of the adopted child."[14]

The Waiting Child Program provides two avenues for prospective parents to adopt special needs kids. The first is the "Shared List"—a catalogue of anywhere from 1,500 to 2,000 available children, which is updated by the CCCWA monthly. Access to this list is shared by multiple Western adoption agencies that compete against one another each month to "lock in" a child's file for review by a particular family, causing the file to disappear from the view of other agencies. An initial lock lasts for seventy-two hours, at which time the agency must submit the adoptive family's information and intention to adopt; otherwise the file will be "unlocked" and returned to the Shared List.

During this window, prospective parents typically consult with a physician to assess the child's needs, possibly deciding to reject the referral or even turn down several different referrals in a row. This process of assessing and rejecting potential daughters and sons can provoke extreme anxiety and guilt. One adoptive mother spoke candidly to me of being pressured by her agency to take in a child with a serious neurological syndrome that would delay his mental and physical growth and strain her young family's resources. Ultimately, she and her husband decided to adopt a boy with a fixable heart defect, one that fortunately healed on its own without surgery. For quite some time, however, the couple was plagued by a sense of remorse for rejecting other needy babies.

The second avenue to adopt a Waiting Child is through the "Special Focus" Program, an initiative the CCCWA began in September 2010 to place older kids and those with more significant and complicated medical conditions. Children whose files remain on the Shared List for more than thirty days without being locked in are automatically put into this program. To facilitate speedy placements from this particularly high-needs group, prospective parents are allowed to adopt two unrelated children at the same time. Additionally, parents who have adopted from the PRC within the past twelve months are permitted to reuse the same dossier to obtain a Special Focus child.[15]

As a final incentive, after more than a decade of severe restrictions on single women, in 2011 the Chinese government enthusiastically welcomed them back to adopt through the Special Focus Program (though they were limited to adopting children with the most severe needs). In 2014, the rules were relaxed again for single women, who became eligible to adopt children with more minor special needs.[16] At the same time, not all single applicants are welcome. They are required to have minimum net assets of US$100,000, have childcare experience, not have more than two children under the age of eighteen in the home, and not be living with a male partner.[17] Thus the PRC's foreign adoption program has experimented with narrowing and expanding prospective parent eligibility while incentivizing special needs adoptions. I suggest that these decisions reflect the Chinese state's desire to find "high quality" families for children who, unlike healthy girls, are usually locally unadoptable while also needing to expand the pool of Western parents willing to adopt individuals with complex needs.

The switch to the Waiting Child Program ended a fifteen-year period in which an estimated 90 percent of adoptees were healthy girls. In 2009—the last year for which figures were published—special needs youth comprised nearly *half* of all foreign adoptees. This was a huge jump from 2005 when they did not total even one-tenth of adoptive placements. (See Table 6.1.)

Sending abroad those whose mental and physical ailments have rendered them "low quality" citizens in China has allowed government authorities to outsource intimacy to willing Westerners while seemingly keeping children's best interests in mind. Lu Ying, the director of the CCCWA, reasoned that the Waiting Child Program provides children with superior care and life

**Table 6.1.** Special needs adoptions from China, 2005–2009.

| World totals | 2005 | 2006 | 2007 | 2008 | 2009 |
|---|---|---|---|---|---|
| Total number of adoptions | 14,221 | 10,646 | 7,858 | 5,531 | 5,294 |
| Special needs adoptions | 1,285 | 2,131 | 2,365 | 2,604 | 2,583 |
| Total proportion special needs | 9% | 20% | 30% | 47% | 48.8% |

Data from Hague Conference on Private International Law Publication 33: Convention of 29 May 1993 on Protection of Children and Co-Operation in Respect of Intercountry Adoption. China (mainland) annual adoption statistics 2005–09. Available at www.hcch.net/index_en.php?act=publications.details&pid=5158&dtid=32.

opportunities they would not have access to in China. In light of the 2007 restrictions, he stated, "The new rules will help shorten waiting time for qualified foreigners and speed up the process for children, especially the disabled, so that they can go to their new families, where they can get better education and medical treatment, more quickly."[18] Although undeniably the case, this statement also glosses over Chinese state authorities' continued financial stake in providing children to Westerners. As Kristin Cheney argues, "States that allow adoption of poor children effectively privatize childcare by transferring a child internationally to a new home."[19] This rings even truer in situations where costly intensive or specialized medical care is needed. Moreover, Lu Ying's explanation ignores pervasive economic disparities and cultural stigmas against disability in China that contribute to the large-scale abandonment of special needs youth and deprive them of domestic opportunities for adoption. Rather than actively trying to match these children with families in the PRC, Chinese authorities have outsourced intimacy to Western NGOs that aim to prepare these children for foreign homes.

## Creating Adoptable Special Needs Youth in China

China-based Western humanitarian organizations provide abandoned youth with first-world care, knowledge, and resources that local state institutions typically cannot or will not perform. In the case of Tomorrow's Children, volunteers used first-world resources and practices that quietly assisted the Waiting Child Program by preparing kids for lives in Western families. In the special care units, this was performed through child-centeredness and the rigorous, highly individualized tracking of babies' physical health and development of their emotional well-being—practices that sought to develop children's intellectual, emotional, and physical potential. As I've detailed earlier, there was a fairly clear division of labor between Chinese caregivers and Western volunteers. *Ayis* performed reproductive tasks—including feeding and administering medication, bathing children, clothing them, changing diapers, and putting babies to sleep—whereas Western volunteers provided for the kids' medical and emotional needs. The application of intensive first-world, middle-class child-rearing methods heightened children's sociability, cognitive capacities, and ultimately their international adoptability.

The focus on enhancing children's global desirability was obvious in the daily English classes that all mentally capable toddlers began in the Beijing foster home when they turned two. Bearing an uncanny resemblance to a Western preschool classroom, the space was complete with tiny wooden tables and chairs, bilingual posters featuring animals and the English alphabet, and a soft tiled foam mat in the corner surrounded by shelves full of new toys. The classes were taught by a pleasant, bespectacled white British woman named Nicky who had moved to China with her husband a year earlier to serve as a full-time volunteer with Tomorrow's Children. The young Christian couple committed to stay for three years, though they eventually left after two. Nicky was not a trained teacher, nor did she speak much Mandarin, but she impressively managed to keep the group of six rambunctious two- to-four-year-olds organized and entertained for the full forty-five–minute class session.

In the classroom one morning, the little students greeted each other with a cheerful English "good morning." Three children quickly sat down at a table and began to form colorful shapes out of Play-Doh. The rest of the group sat at a different table, concentrating hard while composing pictures on red magnetic Etch A Sketch toys, which they shook fiercely every few minutes. Five adult women—the teacher, another British short-term volunteer, two Chinese *ayi*s, and myself—squeezed amusingly into tiny seats between the children. We observed some of the preschoolers display remarkable English skills. One three-year-old boy, who joined an American family several weeks later, was able to count to ten and could name all the parts of the face. Gazing at him fondly, the *ayi* who had cared for him since he was a baby commented on his intelligence, adding proudly that she had also taught him to count to fifty in Chinese.

The children engaged in highly supervised play for about half an hour. Afterward, they enjoyed a snack of cookies and juice and were asked to clean up after themselves. I overheard the adults discussing the disciplinary troubles caused by a three-year-old girl named Fang Fang, an otherwise healthy child living with a local foster family who came in daily for English classes. The girl often displayed oppositional behavior, at one point pushing one of her male classmates hard. As he broke down in tears, she whispered menacingly, "I'll kill you!" Though she didn't understand Mandarin, teacher Nicky spotted the commotion and pulled them apart. She instructed the students to sit down in a straight line on the foam mat and led them through several rounds of classic Western children's songs, including "Row, Row, Row Your Boat," "Head, Shoulders, Knees, and Toes," and "Twinkle, Twinkle Little Star." All of the children—even Fang Fang, whose aggression was now placated by the jaunty music—enthusiastically bobbed their heads and hummed along happily with the melodies.

While the preschoolers were occupied on the floor, I engaged in a short conversation with the two *ayis* at my table, Li Zhang and Yang Chen. Somewhat puzzled, Li Zhang asked me why foreigners liked to adopt Chinese children—a question that local people often asked me during my fieldwork. I provided my standard, if vastly oversimplified, response that foreign parents were sometimes unable to have their own offspring or that they wanted to give a needy child a home. The women glanced at one another, nonplussed. Fidgeting with an Etch A Sketch toy, Yang Chen stated, "Chinese people prefer to take care of their own [biological] children." Her friend nodded vigorously in agreement. I asked what they thought about the Western style of childrearing provided by the foster home. Clucking her tongue, Li Zhang criticized volunteers for always following the child's lead and for constantly trying to entertain them. As evidence, she pointed her chin in the direction of the preschoolers who were now rolling on the floor with laughter as Nicky exaggeratedly pretended to paddle a boat during the final round of songs.

## Financial Investment in Children

Providing for children's medical and daily life needs in a Western middle-class manner was not only labor intensive, it was also incredibly expensive. At the time, the organization was able to keep up with an estimated US$160,000 per month in operating costs through private donations from individuals, churches, schools, and even multinational corporations such as Shell, UPS, Virgin Atlantic, and General Electric. As a well-organized faith-based group with global reach, Tomorrow's Children was successful in raising funds from its constituents, including many Christian business leaders. Donating to the organization presented a "win-win" for multinational corporations able to benefit at-risk and needy children while participating in global corporate social responsibility in the PRC, the world's fastest-growing marketplace. In her study of Christian child-saving NGOs in Zimbabwe, Erica Bornstein contends that "ideas of helping and humanitarianism, although not capitalist per se, are correlative components of transnational accumulation. Transnational NGOs operate in the global economy, alongside multinational corporations."[20] Civil society–corporate partnerships in China like those held by Tomorrow's Children illustrate the neoliberal logic that can align such seemingly disparate sectors as global humanitarianism and private industry.

According to a financial report on its website, in 2012 alone, Tomorrow's Children received nearly US$3.6 million in contributions, of which it spent roughly US$500,000 on baby supplies for the 300 children in its care and US$2.15 million on payroll expenses for its 500 local employees.[21] Although hospitals and doctors working pro bono provided many surgeries and treatments, the organization spent large amounts of its own funds on major medical expenditures each year. For example, in 2011, Tomorrow's Children paid to treat forty-two heart issues, eighty cleft lips and palates, thirteen bowel defects, thirteen genital defects, and four liver transplants—altogether totaling more than half a million U.S. dollars. Legal scholar Anna Kloeden argues, "Surgical intervention provided by private orphanages often results in children becoming 'adoptable' who were previously destined to live out their childhoods in state facilities at state expense."[22]

Thus, the organization's investment in abandoned children involved a complex combination of care and commodified practices that required extensive financial resources, time, and professional expertise. Every time a child was sent out for international surgery—a process that could take months for preparation and recovery—*both* a Chinese caregiver and a Western volunteer accompanied the small patient. A Tomorrow's Children monthly newsletter recounted the story of a little boy named Brian who arrived at one of the units in 2008 at three months of age suffering from complex medical needs. Over a four-year period he was hospitalized ten separate times, both locally as well as in Hong Kong, to treat his multiple ailments. Just after his fourth birthday, Brian left China to "join his Forever Family." The newsletter emphasized his social, cultural, and emotional readiness to go abroad, noting that "his English is almost as good as his Chinese and he has an uncanny ability to grab onto your heart the moment you see him."[23] Costly outsourced intimacy remade Brian into a healthy, lovable Western family member.

### International Adoption as the End Goal

For myriad reasons, only a small percentage of the children cared for in the foster homes were ultimately sent abroad while others passed away or remained institutionalized. Nonetheless, the material and emotional investment involved in their care indicated that international adoption—rather than domestic—was the organization's ultimate objective. Founders Barbara and Peter Dunlop used a discourse of family and kinship, describing the medical units as "normal, home-like settings" where they treated each child like one of their own offspring. The organization promoted emotional bonds between *ayis* and children, noting on its website, "Nannies have the complete responsibility of feeding, bathing and playing with their babies . . . just like any mother."[24] Unsurprisingly, *ayi*s who cared for the same children around the clock for years at a time often became extremely attached. But in spite of these women's long-term involvement and deep emotional bonds, in reality they were treated as low-paid, temporary maternal substitutes until children could be retrieved by their foreign forever families.

Barbara Dunlop spoke candidly with me about her preference that children were sent abroad rather than placed locally. Revealing the assumption that Chinese people adopted out of self-interest whereas Western Christian families loved children unconditionally, she stated emphatically:

> Actually, I'm a bit fearful of domestic adoption. We have families willing to pay the fees for local people to adopt because they think it's a good idea, but sometimes I think Chinese people adopt for the wrong reasons. Like adopting a twelve-year-old to be a maid in your house, that kind of thing, and the fact that they might not treat these children the same as they would blood relatives. In China there's really no child protection laws; people don't know anything about this. Here we have Western Christian families who will love the child no matter what, and that is what I would prefer for these children.

Yet with many babies and caregivers spread across the five different special care units, some nannies did occasionally successfully adopt the children under their care. When local women expressed interest, however, Tomorrow's Children and orphanage officials were aligned in their disapproval of locals as prospective parents when compared to affluent foreign families. International adoption has thus infused market logic into Chinese authorities' considerations of children's best interests. Barbara described a situation in which an orphanage refused to allow one of her working-class *ayi*s to adopt a baby:

> The officials didn't see any reason to let her adopt a child when they could give it to a Western couple who would pay US$4,000 to the orphanage and be able to provide a good life and education for it. They didn't want to let a woman from the countryside adopt because they didn't think she could provide as good a life.

Tomorrow's Children placed a strong emphasis on providing unconditional love for special needs children regardless of the surrounding cultural context. In the process, the organization overlooked cultural stigmas against disability in China—stigmas that could have very real negative consequences for local adoptive families. Barbara described a recent situation in which one of her *ayi*s became interested in adopting a girl from the facility who was born with a bilateral clubfoot. However, the woman wanted to wait until the child started walking to make her final decision. Exasperated, Barbara explained:

> Basically, if the child had a limp, the *ayi* wouldn't want to adopt her. This made me really angry! *Because she wanted a perfect child instead of just loving her despite her problem.* I asked this woman why she wouldn't want to adopt a child with a limp, and she said it was because in the future her marriage and job prospects would be limited and she would be teased by her classmates at school. So here I'm thinking that you need to love the child no matter what, and she's just not willing to take the risk . . . So she didn't end up adopting her. You can't have a perfect child, I'm sorry!

Barbara used this and other stories to assert that, unlike local Chinese people, Westerners—and evangelical Christians in particular—love children despite their flaws, implying clear cultural superiority. Furthermore, due to assumptions about the "high quality" of first-world nations, local people— even those interested in adoption—often also shared the belief that children would be better off overseas. One afternoon at the Beijing foster home, I went for a walk with two *ayi*s and the children in their care. The nannies and I sat on a bench and chatted while the toddlers ran around a nearby playground. Wang Meili, a woman in her forties who already had a fifteen-year-old son, engaged me in a discussion about adoption. After asking the usual questions about why foreigners were so interested in obtaining Chinese children, she wondered aloud whether PRC citizens were also able to adopt. I explained that not only could local people adopt but also they could often choose the child themselves; as an additional benefit, there were international sponsors who were willing to pay the fee. Wang Meili's face lit up momentarily and then turned gloomy, as she quickly talked herself out of the possibility:

> I really like this little girl and would be interested in adopting her. I've been with her since she was little . . . but what kind of conditions (*tiaojian*) could I provide for her? What kind of life could she have here compared with being raised in a foreign country?

## The Christian Adoption Movement and the Rise of the "Global Orphan Crisis"

Tomorrow's Children's emphasis on preparing special needs youth for Western homes did not develop in a cultural vacuum but instead connects to larger trends in the American evangelical community. Although Chinese government incentives and shorter wait times are some of the reasons why American parents have chosen to adopt from the Waiting Child Program, many have also pursued this path in response to persuasive calls from prominent Christian leaders who, since the early 2000s, have made adoption a central focus of their ministries. This movement became prominent at a time of waning evangelical influence over traditional family life, as evidenced by increasing social acceptance of key issues such as gay marriage, abortion, and single motherhood. According to Kathryn Joyce, adoption provides a "perfect storm of a cause" that allows Christian conservatives to express a pro-life agenda under the guise of compassion and social justice.[25] Adoption serves as a doubly effective form of rescue, enabling evangelicals to save children twice: first by liberating them from desperate circumstances and second by redeeming their souls through religion. Adoption has consciously been used as a catalyst to "revitalize the faith of people in American churches."[26]

To convince followers of the magnitude of need, religious leaders continually refer to the "global orphan crisis," or "the idea that there are hundreds of millions of orphaned children across the world who are in need of American help and waiting to be adopted."[27] This so-called crisis is founded on official statistics released by UNICEF that estimated the number of orphans worldwide as 143 million in 2004 and 153 million in 2010.[28] Christian adoption advocates have used this figure as evidence of an urgent global catastrophe, despite the fact that official statistics define orphans far more broadly as children under the age of eighteen who have lost *one or both* parents. Therefore, the figure of 153 million includes primarily "single orphans," or children who have lost only one parent and most often still live with kin and receive other forms of community support. By contrast, the number of "double orphans"—girls and boys who have lost both parents—totaled only 17.8 million in 2010. This number, though tragically high, means that truly parentless children constitute less than 12 percent of the massive figure repeated in sermons, publications, and media campaigns to support the existence of a global catastrophe.

The call to adopt reaches its pinnacle every year during Orphan Sunday, a global event held in churches worldwide each November to spread awareness about the plight of orphans and to remind practitioners that they themselves were rescued and adopted by God. Founded by the Christian Alliance for Orphans, a coalition of more than 150 different prominent American ministries, Orphan Sunday frames adoption as a cause with immense potential to increase the strength and moral authority of the evangelical mission across the globe. Promotional materials explain:

As Christians see and respond to God's call to care for orphans, lives are transformed. Certainly, orphans and foster youth are changed forever. But it doesn't stop there. Individual Christians are drawn beyond a self-focused religion to vibrant, sacrificial discipleship. Their churches grow deeply, too, as the community catches the vision. Finally, a watching world is changed as it sees the Gospel story made visible in Christian adoption, foster care and global orphan care.[29]

Adoption advocates openly blame the reduction in available adoptable children on UNICEF and the Hague Convention, faulting them for emphasizing domestic placements and making the process more difficult for prospective parents. Harvard law professor Elizabeth Bartholet, one of the most vocal proponents of this perspective, has controversially claimed that increased regulations on adoption have robbed disadvantaged third-world kids of membership in nurturing Western families while depriving poor countries of much-needed income.[30] Adoption reformers such as legal scholar David Smolin have forcefully countered this viewpoint, arguing that the lack of legal regulation and accountability within the adoption industry and the huge potential for profit has encouraged systematic child trafficking—which he has termed "child laundering"—in many nations.[31]

Although the American adoption movement takes its primary inspiration from the biblical mandate to care for orphans and widows (originally considered one cohesive unit), in practice it has tended to focus more on saving individual children than on trying to keep poor families intact. In other words, the global adoption industry has incentivized the practice of taking children away from impoverished mothers rather than improving women's life conditions to support them to keep their offspring.[32] The evangelical mission to pluck non-Western kids out of difficult circumstances one by one and place them into Western families has been bolstered by neoliberal values that prioritize individual-level solutions over large-scale systemic change. As Cheney and Rotabi contend, although many charitable efforts and humanitarian responses are elicited "out of sympathy for parentless children, inflating orphan numbers to attract scarce resources ultimately does little to remedy the structural issues that lead to orphanhood in the first place."[33]

Influential megaministries such as Saddleback Church in Orange County, California, have taken the lead in advocating an individualized approach to social problems. Elizabeth Styffe, the Director of Orphan Care Initiatives at Saddleback, has appealed to members using the following logic:

If every church empowered their members to care for orphans in ways that helped and didn't hurt, the orphan crisis could be over . . . There are 163 million children at risk in the world today [note the inflated figure] but 2.4 billion people who claim the name of Jesus. This means the solution for every child is a church where all the members are caring about orphans.[34]

### The Adoption Movement as a Form of American Soft Power

Hotly contested ideological debates over children's best interests in an era of waning international adoptions have motivated a coalition of evangelical groups to promote federal legislation to make the global orphan crisis a central concern of American foreign policy. Combining efforts, faith-based groups such as Saddleback Church, the Christian Alliance for Orphans, and the Southern Baptist Convention created government legislation known as Children in Families First (CHIFF). The bill garnered strong bipartisan backing, introduced into the Senate in September 2013 by Mary Landrieu and Roy Blunt and into the House of Representatives by Kay Granger and Karen Bass the following month. Using language heavily inspired by the adoption movement, an official press release from Mary Landrieu's office in May 2014 described the need for the bill by linking the strength of American foreign policy with traditional Christian family values:

By some estimates, there are over 150 million orphans in the world. But the U.S. government, through our foreign policy and programming, isn't helping turn this around. Americans know that family is the bedrock of any society, and that children need the permanent love, care, and protection of a family to grow into healthy, productive adults. Although U.S. foreign policy in theory emphasizes preserving or creating safe, permanent families for children, through family preservation, reunification, and creation from domestic, kinship, or intercountry adoption, the structures and coordination aren't there to make it happen. We need change, and it will take legislation.[35]

The proposed measure, which ultimately did not pass, positioned the United States as the official guardian of the world's children. Theological scholars such as Sheryl Ryan have taken issue with this approach of the adoption movement for uncritically casting "Christian adoptive parents as messiah figures, and the United States church as analogous with heaven."[36] Furthermore, although the bill claimed to prioritize preserving or reunifying families, in effect it centered almost entirely on streamlining and

simplifying the process of foreign adoptions. The campaign urged supporters: "We need to retake control of U.S. foreign policy on this critical issue
and lead the way in shifting the world's focus on to the importance of family
for all children."[37]

If it had passed, CHIFF would have allocated roughly $60 million per year
to establish new offices in the State Department and the U.S. Agency for International Development (USAID).[38] Through international adoption, the bill
sought to extend America's moral influence by challenging globally agreed-
upon legal safeguards designed to prevent the unnecessary transfer of children between nations. Critics Cheney and Rotabi warn that "CHIFF implies
that the U.S. could link aid to developing countries to adoption policy—a
practice explicitly prohibited by the Hague Convention, to which the U.S. is a
signatory."[39] The substantial effort and financial resources that were expended
on this initiative are particularly problematic in light of America's own foster
care system in which over 100,000 children, primarily of color, are available
for adoption at any one time.[40] In a sad irony, while advocates fight to keep
the doors to international adoption open, the United States quietly adopts out
several hundred locally unwanted African American children in foster care to
Canadian and European families each year.[41]

Beyond governmental legislation, adoption advocates have found creative
ways to adjust their approach to the changing composition of available youth.
In recent years, they have directed attention toward older children—a group
that was generally overlooked when babies and toddlers were still readily accessible. Beginning in 2010, older orphan hosting programs began bringing
adolescents each summer and winter from orphanages in China, Ukraine,
and Latvia to do homestays with American families. Pioneered by the Christian nonprofit group Project 143, so-named for the "143 million orphans
worldwide," these four- to eight-week trips reportedly more than double an
older child's chances of adoption. Families that participate in this program
must be able to pay the required $2,750 fee to host a child for four weeks, not
including the cost of food or additional activities. The online FAQ page justi-
fies this price by comparing to traditional Christian missionary work, noting
that hosting fees "are similar to a mission trip overseas."[42]

Like CHIFF, Project 143 portrays membership in a standard middle-
class American family as the answer to children's lack of parental care in
their home countries. In the process it ignores larger structural dilemmas by

focusing only on individual orphans themselves, outside the context of their communities or other kin support. According to its website:

> Most orphans have never taken part in a vacation, shared in a game of catch with dad or gotten "made-up" with mom, much less experienced the life giving love of being connected to a family. What can 4 to 8 weeks spent in your family mean to these kids? HOPE. By simply opening your home this summer or winter and sharing some love and encouragement to a child who needs it more than you will ever be able to imagine, you will simply be amazed at the miracles that happen. We hope that you will join us and help to combat the global orphan crisis—ONE child at a time.[43]

Because of the age of older youths, many advocates, agencies, and prospective parents believe that this group poses little risk of involvement in fraudulent adoption. Yet in an overarching system of child circulation fueled by market logic, the possibility of corruption remains. The motivations of the evangelical adoption movement are clearly well intentioned. Nonetheless, as Kathryn Joyce contends, because systemic global inequalities have gone unacknowledged, hundreds of millions of dollars have inadvertently been directed "into a system that already responds acutely to Western demand—demand that can't be filled, at least not ethically or under current law."[44]

In the case of China, state-run orphanages in Luoyang, Beijing, and Guangzhou were found to have illegally sent older adolescents abroad. Many of these youths were over the age of fourteen—the official cutoff age for adoption in the country—and some had birth parents who did not agree to these custody transfers. Brian Stuy found that government officials in certain areas with long-standing international adoption programs offered poor Chinese families a chance to educate their offspring in local orphanages. Unbeknownst to these parents, soon after arrival their daughters and sons were made available for international adoption. After a foreign match was located, birth parents were allegedly told that their child had received the opportunity to study abroad and were pressured to sign relinquishment papers. In at least one case, the birth family was not even notified that their daughter had left the country, believing instead that she had simply disappeared. Thus, even though the composition of adoptable children has changed, Stuy argues that the considerable potential financial gain from adoption fees and postadoption donations creates "strong incentives for orphanages to internationally adopt as many children as possible, even if those children enter the orphanage through extra-legal channels."[45]

### The "Rehoming Controversy" and the Invisible Aftermath of Failed Adoptions

Although the push to increase international adoptions has incentivized un-ethical behavior in many sending countries, a disturbing absence of regula-tion in the United States leaves many newly arrived adoptees without ade-quate protection should their family placement go awry. In September 2013, Reuters news agency published a lurid exposé of an underground practice known as "private rehoming"—a term borrowed from the language of ani-mal adoptions—in which parents transfer custody of adopted children they no longer want to strangers encountered on Internet forums.[46]

The investigation's cover story highlighted the transfer of a sixteen-year-old Liberian girl from parents unable and/or unwilling to deal with her se-vere behavioral problems to a couple accused of child sexual abuse. At the time, these custody transfers required only a notarized power of attorney, bypassing the child welfare system altogether. This was a bafflingly simple legal scenario given the lengthy and costly process of formal adoption, which involves home inspections, interviews, background checks, and training. Prior to the exposé, there were no state or federal laws prohibiting rehoming, although a number of states quickly moved to increase restrictions following the investigation.[47]

Over the course of an eighteen-month-long investigation, Reuters jour-nalists identified eight different American web forums established specifically for these purposes. They analyzed requests to rehome 261 children that were posted onto a Yahoo group called Adopting-From-Disruption, which has since been shut down. Roughly 70 percent of the children had been adopted internationally, and most were between the ages of six and thirteen. The mes-sages conveyed clearly how overwhelmed some adoptive parents were by the reality of their child's emotional and medical needs. Many posts mentioned children's diagnoses of reactive attachment disorder—an often lifelong condi-tion in which, due to early traumatic experiences or lack of care, individuals are unable to form sincere emotional attachments to others. Parents described lacking adequate time and financial resources to care intensively for the child, as there were often other biological and adopted children in the home.[48]

A number of the online postings referred to Chinese adoptees who had ar-rived through the Waiting Child Program. The two different messages below (reproduced verbatim) provide representative examples of the advertisements found on the Yahoo forum:[49]

*We adopted an 8-year old girl from China on 9/4 and felt from the beginning that her needs were going to be more than we could manage, but we just couldn't send her back to the orphanage. We believed that with structure, family and education she could come around. Unfortunately, We are now struggling having been home for 5 days with also adopting a 13 year old who needs our attention along with our 5 other children . . . [W]ith both of us working full time and the number of other children in our home—we do not believe we can provide the full attention that she needs and deserves. Please share with anyone you think may be interested. (Posted 9/26/11)*

*Hello, We are a family in Michigan who is looking to re-home our almost 3 yr. old son. We brought him home from China this past July and since then we have had many, many issues. First off we had many problems with bonding and attachment, both on his part and ours but mainly with me. I have yet, as his mother, been able to form a bond or any attachment to him whatsoever . . . we knew he had special needs (premature birth, developmental delays) but there have been sensory issues, eating issues, defiance, stubborn attitude, and he is severely speech delayed. Even as a special ed. teacher, I have been unable to deal with all these issues. After dealing with students with cognitive delays at work all day, coming home to a child with these same delays has been more than I can bear. (Posted 1/31/10)*

The adoption movement has influenced many well-intentioned people to rescue and redeem special needs and older youth from other countries. Unfortunately, the ideal of saving a needy girl or boy through adoption is often incompatible with the reality of parenting a disabled and/or emotionally traumatized child. Because the United States lacks adequate postadoption services for parents and legal protection for adoptees once they arrive in their new country, this disjuncture has sometimes led children to be abandoned by families for a second time.

## Conclusion

International adoption cannot be considered solely a practice that matches unwanted babies with willing families. Instead, this legal market in children involves a constellation of constantly shifting local and global social, political, and economic factors. Though the trend has been waning in recent years, international adoption has created a financial incentive for the PRC to maintain a consistent population of accessible youth. By outsourcing the care of abandoned youth to foreign humanitarian organizations, Chinese state authorities have effectively relieved themselves of responsibility for these children's welfare while reaping financial and other benefits when babies are rehabilitated and sent overseas.

The physical process of migration from poor to rich nations is often assumed to be the catalyst that transforms children from neglected social outcasts into first-world subjects deserving of rights, privileges, and social recognition. For the tens of thousands of healthy Chinese girls adopted by foreign families, this may indeed be the case. However, the global appeal of sick and disabled children is the result of much behind-the-scenes effort performed on both sides of the Pacific. Groups such as Tomorrow's Children ensure the attractiveness of special needs youth through intensive material expenditure and emotional care that transforms them into "priceless" daughters and sons who can be readily incorporated into white Western families.[50] Though state authorities and Western child savers may disagree on the personal potential of disabled individuals, their goals align in placing children in foreign families. There is no doubt that foreign adoption benefits many children who may have little chance of finding permanent families in their birth countries. Nonetheless, inspired by the American adoption movement, many parents' desire to take a disabled or ill child into their homes extends from a larger first-world commitment to help the less fortunate that focuses on individual solutions rather than resolving structural inequalities. Like much of global humanitarianism, this undertaking allows those from more developed regions to perform moral superiority and altruism through their care of marginalized Others.[51]

Shifts in the PRC's adoption industry are deeply symbolic of the nation's rapid global rise. Placing children in loving families has helped China create a lasting bridge to the global north in general and the United States in particular.[52] It is highly significant that, as the country's global economic position has improved, the number of children it sends abroad has declined dramatically. It thus remains to be seen whether international adoption from China will continue and what form it might take. Perhaps one day we will look back on this trend as a remarkable, but short-lived, phase in the nation's path to modernization.

# 7 Conclusion

*Retying the Red Thread*

INTERNATIONAL ADOPTION IS AN INFLUENTIAL POLITICAL and economic institution that has mirrored China's own rise to prominence. Although countries that allow their vulnerable children to be cared for by outsiders are typically considered less powerful, the PRC has instead demonstrated its rising global influence through outsourcing the care of its orphans to Western families and organizations. Operating as part of a transnational circuit that began with the exportation of mostly healthy girls out of the country via adoption, outsourced intimacy has paved a route for the importation of first-world actors, resources, and practices into orphanages. But what are the implications of outsourced intimacy in a global age?

Western humanitarian organizations now care for many of China's primarily special needs population of abandoned children. Despite their lack of visibility, these transnational partnerships place institutionalized youth squarely at the intersection of public and private spheres, state and civil society, and local and global agendas. The Chinese state authorities and Western volunteers I worked with entered these partnerships with very different—and often conflicting—objectives. My observations of the NGOs Tomorrow's Children and Helping Hands suggest that, due to their divergent logics of care, China's outsourced intimacy to humanitarian organizations intent on "saving" local children was not always straightforward. Using their own funds, volunteers attempted to impose a normative Western middle-class view of appropriate childhood and childcare onto local people. Yet, in practice, state authorities and *ayi*s often pushed back or even rejected these standards.

The evangelical group Tomorrow's Children was motivated by an intensive logic of care grounded in ideologies of individualism, child-centeredness, and concerted cultivation of children's potential. The group's religious orientation inspired a larger set of objectives that included caring for sick and dying babies and using their work to transform Chinese cultural values from the ground up. This vision, however, was disrupted by poor and working-class local *ayi*s who subscribed to a pragmatic logic of care. Influenced by China's increasingly competitive economy in which disabled people lack guaranteed rights or a viable future, many questioned the purpose of investing such large amounts of money, time, and energy into these unwanted youth. Though this perspective did not negate their emotional attachments to the children, it incited them to focus on short-term physical health and well-being. Meanwhile, volunteers treated children as they would in their own countries. With activities such as art and English lessons, these Westerners sought to cultivate free thinking, creative, and expressive individuals who could be easily absorbed into first-world societies—even though few would ever be sent abroad.

Since I first began fieldwork, Tomorrow's Children has expanded at lightning speed. In late 2007, it opened a third medical unit in Henan with room for eighteen sick and dying babies. Less than two years later, with the financial backing of a Western evangelical organization affiliated closely with the American adoption movement, the group opened a massive six-story hospital for ill and disabled youth that replaced the Haifeng special care unit where I spent most of my time. Opening to great fanfare and local publicity, this hospital could house 140 to 150 children organized into three separate groups: those needing palliative care, those needing long-term chronic care, and babies with operable conditions.

In the midst of these changes, I kept in touch with nurse Cathy Marks and her husband Brian—the couple who ran the Henan special care units when I was there. Anxious and overworked, they were engaged in battles with the NGO's founders in Beijing over the organization's rapid expansion. Brian's usually jovial demeanor was overtaken by worry as he explained:

The founders of Tomorrow's Children rush into new projects and get them started without having a long-term plan. This puts people like us in the position of having to clean up messes when they occur. If they just took a bit more time, then they could figure out how to prevent these problems in the first place.

Due to ongoing conflicts with the founders, Cathy and Brian made the difficult decision to leave the organization and opened their own infant palliative care unit in a different province in 2010. Because my main connection to the NGO was through this couple, I also lost touch with Tomorrow's Children. But, according to its website, the group opened yet another palliative care unit with forty-five beds in one of Henan's largest child welfare institutes in 2010. Impressively, over the course of only fifteen years, this nonprofit organization built and opened five different facilities that cared for roughly 350 children at a time and employed over 500 local people.

As a prime example of outsourced intimacy, Tomorrow's Children alleviated a tremendous financial burden from Chinese welfare institutes and contributed to economic development by turning the care of unwanted kids into a small local industry. Yet, even with China's low labor costs, providing intensive Western-style care to hundreds of sick and disabled babies is incredibly expensive. The couple who founded Tomorrow's Children passed the financial responsibility for its four Henan-based units to the other, much larger Christian organization, but they have still struggled to keep up with operating costs for their original facility near Beijing. In March of 2015, I received an urgent email update from the organization asking supporters to help keep this facility open. A recent drop in donations had forced them to let go of thirty-four Chinese caregivers and relocate twenty-two babies to other units. The message laid out the dire situation in plain terms, asking for US$350,000 to pay outstanding bills and staff salaries and to build up three months of operating costs. By May the organization had received enough donations to keep its doors open for another few months, but its reliance on large gifts from private foreign donors raises questions about its long-term feasibility.

By contrast, the expatriate wives who comprised the majority of Helping Hands volunteers subscribed to an emotional logic of care that was grounded in the desire to provide maternal nurturance to the children of Yongping Orphanage. However, their engagement in charity work was largely self-serving, intended to create a sense of purpose while they supported their husbands' careers in China. Their unpredictable schedules also resulted in a lower level of commitment to their volunteer work. Like the booming volunteer tourism industry, which has been critiqued for reinforcing material inequalities between aid givers and receivers, it was not always clear whom this type of temporary altruism was actually assisting.

Helping Hands' efforts were also impeded by the socialist institutional structure, which prioritized a custodial logic of care that treated children as objects to be maintained only minimally. This lack of investment reflected the broader Chinese societal context in which abandoned special needs youth have been categorized as "low quality" citizens undeserving of extensive governmental resources. Compounding these issues, the orphanage director regarded the Westerners with deep suspicion, producing a chilling effect that permeated down through the hierarchy of the institution. The resulting sense of ambivalence forced the collaboration into a stalemate despite the abundant resources the Western group offered.

Helping Hands' collaboration with the Yongping Orphanage went through a series of stops and starts after the 2008 Beijing Summer Olympics. The volunteers were allowed to visit intermittently until 2011, when foreign volunteers were permanently barred from the facility—a decision that reflected the government's provision of more funds to welfare institutes around Beijing. Helping Hands continued to perform charity work, refocusing its attention on a local school and privately run orphan care centers.

In the summer of 2014, I was able to visit the children and caregivers at Yongping one last time. Having returned to Beijing for a short period, I coincidentally arrived only a few days before Helping Hands founder Marjorie Lee was scheduled to permanently retire to the United States. I accompanied her as a special guest on her own final visit to the orphanage.

At Yongping, little had changed in terms of physical appearance, but there were now several key improvements in care that related to the hiring of a new orphanage director. The first person we ran into was Big Mother *Ayi*, one of the first caregivers I had met there. With her long hair pulled up into its characteristic bun, the middle-aged woman was surprised and delighted to see us. She was watching over a large group of toddlers, several of whom stared at us calmly from their perches in new baby walkers. Instinctively, I knelt down and held out my arms to a little girl who had recently undergone eye surgery. As I moved toward her, the startled child began to cry, clearly unaccustomed to strangers. Glancing at Big Mother *Ayi* she called out in alarm, "Mama, Mama!" In any other environment, her reaction may have been upsetting. Here, however, I was immensely gratified to see the children differentiating between strangers and trusted adults. It also struck me that this was the very first time I had heard anyone use a familial term at Yongping, suggesting that the institution had shifted away from its earlier custodial approach to care.

Our group headed down the hallway toward the older kids' playroom, passing two Chinese physical therapists working intently with several children who had cerebral palsy. As we entered the playroom, another long-term *ayi* greeted us with warm hugs—a pleasant surprise after the many years of tension between the caregivers and volunteers. Scanning the room, I recognized roughly three-quarters of the kids. There were still more boys than girls. We passed out boxes of Cracker Jack to the children, who crunched with glee as they worked on an activity. Out of the corner of my eye I spotted Dang Yan, the wheelchair-bound girl with spina bifida who had been barred from attending school due to her disability, *walk into the room* with the help of arm braces. No longer needing full-time care, the girl was now permitted to attend the local school with some of the older youths. Clad in a green and white school uniform, Dang Yan beamed at us proudly as she slowly made her way across to a table in the corner to do homework.

With the other kids happily situated, I went over to greet three older boys with cerebral palsy who had grown up at Yongping. Seated uncomfortably in aging wheelchairs, their bodies were bent and contorted. Usually left alone in the back corner of the playroom for hours on end, the adolescents were starved for interaction. Noticing their long, sharp fingernails, I quickly located a nail clipper and set to work trimming them. Overjoyed with the attention, the boys smiled and laughed as I provided them with this most basic form of care. My thoughts drifted back to the Helping Hands volunteers, who cut children's nails, spread lotion on their chapped cheeks, and held babies on short two-hour stints. Their efforts felt superficial to me back then. But with the passage of time, I could appreciate that the women performed a fundamentally important service for kids with few other sources of love and affection in their lives. Although their collaboration ultimately did not last, it's possible that the volunteers planted seeds for longer-term investments in these children that were beginning to take root.

## Addressing Underlying Causes, Not Just Symptoms

Aiding in the physical and/or spiritual "rescue" of marginalized orphans is the central mission of many foreign aid organizations. Indeed, "international responses to child suffering, and orphans in particular, can easily become a barometer for global humanitarianism."[1] Some of the volunteers I met, such as Marjorie Lee and Cathy and Brian Marks, approached their work as a vocation, making enormous personal and financial sacrifices to pursue their cause. As an observer and participant, my purpose was not to measure the "success" of these transnational partnerships but rather to examine the forces that shape points of conflict and cooperation as well as to track their longer-term outcomes.

Foreign NGOs in China negotiate uneven political terrain, forging ahead with seemingly unchecked momentum and accomplishing incredible feats only to run up against unforeseen difficulties that can cause them to collapse altogether. Moreover, the local response to Western involvement is highly unpredictable. For example, state authorities treated Tomorrow's Children as a symbol of modernity while viewing Helping Hands as a threat. How can one objectively assess success or failure in such a contingent environment?

There is no doubt that Western involvement in China's state orphanages has improved and even saved the lives of many children. Nonetheless, the unstable and unsustainable nature of the NGOs I worked with meant that they were sometimes counterproductive for those they sought to help. As I watched these collaborations unfold over time, I thought often about Henry, the teenager with cerebral palsy at the Haifeng special care unit who appeared at the beginning of this book. First-world resources and practices nursed this intelligent adolescent back to excellent physical health, yet he remained severely disabled and would always require costly intensive care (most recently, I was told that he was being moved to the new hospital built by Tomorrow's Children and would remain under full-time supervision). Henry's rehabilitation allowed him to flourish into a healthy, happy person with a vastly improved quality of life. But what does his future have in store if the organization caring for him ever completely runs out of funding or leaves the country? What will happen after he turns eighteen and ages out of the child welfare system? There are many thousands of other children like Henry who face a host of challenges that have yet to be resolved.

The Chinese government's improvisational approach toward economic development has created a dynamic environment for humanitarian organizations. Facing relatively few major bureaucratic hurdles, Western volunteers can accomplish personal and professional objectives abroad that would be impossible (perhaps even illegal) in their home countries. Reflecting back on my time in the field, it seems unfathomable to me now that I—as someone with absolutely no medical training—was given the responsibility of escorting dying babies to the hospital, giving them shots of morphine when their pain levels became unbearable, and changing their dressings after surgery.

This raises larger questions about the possibilities and limits of global humanitarianism within non-Western, and especially authoritarian, contexts. Collaborations between state-run welfare institutes and international NGOs give the impression that the Chinese government is more open to outside influences, even as these partnerships actually facilitate state efforts to modernize the local population. Put another way, as Western child-savers devote personal resources to caring for and rehabilitating the PRC's unwanted kids, they also bolster Chinese state authority through their willing participation in outsourced intimacy.

Because global humanitarians exist in a legal gray zone, they have only been able to tackle the symptoms of larger social problems that have led certain families to give up their offspring rather than address root causes. From my perspective, this means organizations like Tomorrow's Children and Helping Hands are unlikely to represent much more than a stopgap solution. Ultimately, the power to change the fate of marginalized youth lies with the Chinese government. Rather than building new orphanages and physical infrastructure, state authorities should focus instead on developing a coherent, organized system to protect the rights of vulnerable children—especially those with special needs. Even now, all major decisions regarding treatment are left solely to parents, some of whom decide that it would be better to allow their child to perish rather than continue life with a disability. Until the government creates a comprehensive protection system, babies with cognitive and/or physical impairments run the risk of abandonment by family members who see it as the best—or only—alternative for them to receive care.

The Chinese government must also offer financial assistance and other social services to families throughout the child's lifetime. Ideally, the money that currently flows into the country through adoptions, which realistically has an impact on only a small fraction of vulnerable youths, could be used to support and keep intact a much larger number of affected families. As social welfare scholars Karen Fisher and Xiaoyuan Shang warn, "Unless Chinese parents are convinced that their children's needs will be addressed through social support, reduced discrimination, and shared financial costs, they may continue to rationalize that life [itself] is not in their children's best interests."[2]

In addition to increased government support and policy changes for children and their families, active challenges to the broader social stigmatization of disability in China are necessary. This will be an uphill battle, as state authorities themselves continue to perpetuate the notion that sick and disabled babies represent a major societal burden. Nevertheless, this should not prevent us from envisioning new ways of retying the red thread into a social safety net capable of protecting all vulnerable children.

## Outsourced Intimacy Comes Full Circle: Adoptees Return to China

With the vast declines in foreign adoption from the PRC, the large cohorts of healthy female adoptees who arrived in the United States during the 1990s and early 2000s symbolize a particular historical moment of Chinese development. These mostly young girls and women represent the global face of the now discontinued one-child policy; as such, their international image is linked to broader perceptions about the PRC. Because they occupy a unique space between cultures and identities, they are well positioned to serve as bridges between Western societies and their country of birth should they so choose.

Thousands of adoptees who had no input into the decision to leave China as babies are making the conscious choice to return as adolescents and adults. One such journey was captured in the documentary "Somewhere Between" (2011), which follows four adoptees as they come of age in the United States. In this film we meet fourteen-year-old Haley Butler, a pretty beauty pageant contestant who speaks in a soft Southern lilt. Adopted from Anhui Province at six months of age and raised in a white Christian family in Nashville, Tennessee, she states earnestly, "I would like to be the first Chinese person to play on the Grand Ole Opry. That's like my life goal." Similar to many other Asian Americans—adopted or not—Haley describes herself as a "banana," or someone who is "yellow on the outside and white on the inside."

Despite her assimilation into white mainstream American culture, the girl began asking questions about her birth parents at a young age. "I just told her there was no way that we would ever know anything," her blond adoptive mother recalls. "And that may be how it turns out; we may never know anything," the woman's words foreshadowing a trip that the Butler family was going to make to Haley's Chinese hometown. They planned to search for the girl's birth parents by putting up a poster with her pictures and story of relinquishment at her official "finding spot"—the place where official records state she was abandoned.

The cameras follow Haley as she strides down a dusty side street past a row of shops and parked mopeds. They are in her hometown of Ma'anshan, a "small" industrial city in Anhui Province of roughly two million inhabitants. As the girl tapes her poster to the side of a building, curious locals gather around. Almost immediately, a middle-aged woman begins speaking animatedly in sharply accented Mandarin. Amidst the commotion, the translator conveys that the woman thinks that Haley "looks like the daughters of her cousin." Motioning with her arms as if dumping a pail of water on the ground, the translator speculates that "maybe she was thrown away" by the woman's relatives. Within hours, Haley learns that a man has stepped forward claiming to be her birth father. He and one of his other daughters are heading over to their hotel right away to meet them.

In the hotel lobby, Haley holds a small hand-held video camera and records the reunion. She is seated next to a thin Chinese man whose weathered face has the deep baked-in tan of an outdoor laborer. Their physical resemblance is uncanny. "So this is the guy that I think is my dad," Haley narrates, her voice wavering uncertainly. Silently, the man pulls her close and presses their heads together, his red-rimmed eyes filled with tears. The camera pans the other way, centering on a solemn-looking young woman in a white t-shirt and ponytail who is standing uncomfortably to one side. "And that's my sister, I think, over there, maybe. Who knows?" Haley's combination of emotion and bewilderment is palpable. DNA testing later confirms what they already felt was true: They were indeed related by blood.

Haley Butler's reconnection with her birth parents shows how outsourced intimacy is beginning to come full circle. Media coverage typically highlights only the most positive aspects of adoptee–birth parent reunions, representing the initial meeting as the joyful end of a long, emotional journey for both sides. Yet the political sensitivity of China's international adoption program and its intertwined relationship with controversial issues such as fertility regulations, child abandonment, and baby trafficking can raise many more difficult and ethically fraught questions for adoptees who seek to know more about their early lives. Reunions mark the beginning—rather than the end— of an emotionally and logistically complex process in which adopted individuals must navigate geographic, cultural, language, and social class divides to establish bonds with biological kin.[3]

Although these types of reunions are exceedingly rare due to the lack of reliable knowledge surrounding children's origins, Haley's story has nonetheless instilled hope in other adoptees that they, too, might someday follow suit. Moreover, it appears that many birth parents are themselves eager to be found. Jenna Cook, another girl featured in "Somewhere Between," returned to China to conduct her own search when she was a sophomore at Yale University. The young woman garnered intense local interest by documenting her journey on Weibo, China's popular microblogging site. In response, no less than forty-four sets of parents who relinquished their baby girls came forward publicly in the hopes of reconnecting with their long-lost daughter. Even though none was a match, Jenna stated that she continues to look for them because "they gave life to me. I feel very grateful, and I love them and miss them very much."[4] Now that the nation has switched to an official two-child policy, it is likely that many more birth parents and adopted children will seek ways of finding one another.

Adoptees who may not want to pursue a birth parent search are also returning to China in increasing numbers, both with their adoptive families and on their own, to travel, volunteer, and study abroad.[5] In 2015, my research team conducted a large-scale survey of adolescent and young adult adoptees (ages thirteen through twenty-one) that demonstrates this group's keen interest in reconnecting with their Chinese origins. Of the 211 primarily female respondents, nearly 70 percent had returned to the PRC at least once since being adopted, and roughly half had visited their orphanages and abandonment locations. Significantly, 45 percent stated that they would like to find their birth parents, pointing to the wave of travel to the PRC that is yet to come.[6] Although this trend is an unintended outcome of adoption, it will nonetheless help to reinforce China's soft power in Western countries. Furthermore, these new forms of return migration highlight the ways in which adoption is an ongoing, transnational cycle rather than a process that ends when a child joins her or his "forever family."

I've argued that foreign adoption has allowed China to extend its state-driven project of creating high quality citizens across national borders. Nevertheless, the country has yet to follow the example of South Korea, which began welcoming back its foreign adoptees in the late 1990s by granting them special citizenship privileges—rights that were granted, at least in part, due to the activism of adult Korean adoptees. Eleana Kim has shown that perceptions of transnational adoption in Korea have changed alongside economic development. Once considered a shameful failure, adoption has since been positively reframed as a clever investment in the nation's human capital, and adoptees are now seen as valuable assets to their birth country. An official press release for the Overseas Korean Act, which extended special citizenship rights to foreign adoptees, notes that while adoptees may be "Korean in a biological sense, their American culture and lifestyles serve as a precious resource for the international development of Korea."[7]

Granted, adoptions from Korea began much earlier in the twentieth century, and the percentage of the population in the sending country affected by the practice has been far higher. The PRC also does not recognize dual citizenship. Nonetheless, like their Korean counterparts, most Chinese adoptees are native English speakers and experts in Western cultural norms—skills that are highly valued in the globalizing world economy. Due to primordial understandings of race and ethnicity that cause adoptees to be considered Chinese regardless of nationality, as these individuals become working professionals Chinese state authorities may proactively encourage them to contribute their talents and abilities to their country of birth.

## Retying the Red Thread

The red thread myth has come to symbolize the relationship between foreign adoptive parents and their children. In the absence of details about children's early lives, it has reinforced the sense that adoption was somehow inevitable or simply "meant to be." Often paired with a generalized explanation of the one-child policy, this origin story has come to stand in for the many personal and structural reasons why some Chinese parents make the difficult decision to relinquish their babies. In doing so, it elides the inequalities of gender, class, and ability that have rendered certain offspring more socially valuable than others in the PRC.

Untying this myth requires understanding why daughters and sons who were devalued in China have been constructed as deserving of love and care on a global scale. Yet it has not been my aim to critique adoption or adoptive parents. Indeed, since beginning this research in the late 1990s, I looked forward to eventually adopting a daughter of my own from China—a dream that has since been dashed by the ever-increasing restrictions on foreign parents and the changing demographics of available babies. I have sought, however, to question this feel-good narrative of predestination because it focuses only on what children have gained and closes off their ability to openly grieve what they have lost through abandonment and international migration. We are, however, finally beginning to hear more of adoptees' own voices and perspectives. On her anonymous blog, one young woman poignantly dissects the red thread myth:

The problem with saying that children are connected to the people "destined" to become their adoptive parents is that it is also saying birthmothers are equally destined to be in situations in which they have to relinquish their children and that these children are destined to lose their first families, countries, cultures, and everything they know.[8]

I'll end this book with a recent conversation I had with Zoe, a twenty-five-year-old adoptee raised by white Christian parents in California who returned to China after college to work with abandoned children. She reached out to me by email after having read some of my previous research. By sheer coincidence, Zoe had volunteered in Tomorrow's Children's hospital in Henan Province for several months. There, she "really wrestled with the concept and purpose of these medical facilities that seemed to groom children specifically for international adoption." The young woman then found work with a Western NGO in Beijing that places abandoned children in local long-term foster care. "Although I am the product of international adoption," Zoe explained, "my own insecurities and struggles in identity have compelled me to seek out other options for children other than staying in an orphanage or being adopted overseas."

Growing up in the United States, adoptees are repeatedly told how "lucky" they are to have been raised in American families. Ironically, Zoe hears similar comments from Chinese people in Beijing who envy her Western education and English language fluency, advantages that they desire for their own children. The young woman noted that, although immensely grateful for her life opportunities, she still feels as if something is missing. It is this yearning (one that nonadopted people find difficult to understand, she notes) that sparked her desire to return to China. Rather than conducting a birth parent search, which she has little interest in doing at this point, Zoe instead returned to prove herself worthy of her adoption. "Part of my desire to come back to China was almost like an 'Aha, I made it' kind of declaration, that even though I wasn't seen to have value and was rejected as a child, I was able to do something with my life."

After leaving in 1992, when the PRC was just beginning to modernize, Zoe has returned to a country whose surging economy is soon expected to surpass that of the United States. Experiencing contemporary Chinese society on her own terms as an adult has dissipated any naïve childhood fantasies she once held of a long-lost homeland, which have been replaced instead by the actual lived experience of the country. Even though Zoe feels more like a "white American" than a Chinese American, she is enthusiastically taking part in Beijing's dynamic atmosphere. Having grown up feeling rejected by the PRC, the young woman marvels at how influential the nation has become. Thoughtfully, she reflects that this new reality "makes me proud to be Chinese." With hope, adoptees like Zoe will one day be able to derive even more pride from seeing China take on a role as a moral leader, and not just an economic powerhouse, that gives its most vulnerable children a bright future within their own country of birth.

# Notes

## Chapter 1

1. Notes on terminology: In China, the official designation for a state-run facility that cares for parentless children is "Children's Welfare Institute" (facilities that care only for children) or "Social Welfare Institute" (facilities that usually house the elderly, the disabled, and children in separate buildings). The Chinese Ministry of Civil Affairs manages all of these institutions. Although some scholars object to the negative connotations associated with the Western term *orphanage*, I use it interchangeably with the other two terms in this book.

2. To protect the identities of individuals and organizations, all proper names have been given pseudonyms unless otherwise specified.

3. Anthony J. Spires, "Contingent Symbiosis and Civil Society in an Authoritarian State: Understanding the Survival of China's Grassroots NGOs." *American Journal of Sociology* 117, 1 (2011): 1–45.

4. Peter Selman, "The Global Decline of Intercountry Adoption: What Lies Ahead?" *Social Policy and Society* 11 (2012), 381–397.

5. "China Overview," The World Bank. Retrieved on May 13, 2015, from www .worldbank.org/en/country/china/overview.

6. Michael Elliott, "China Takes on the World," *Time Magazine*, January 11, 2007. Available at www.time.com/time/magazine/article/0,9171,1576831,00.html.

7. On October 29, 2015, the Chinese Communist Party officially announced that it will allow all families to have two children, thus ending the one-child policy after thirty-five years. It should be noted, however, that the effects of decades of stringent fertility regulations, including labor shortages, a rapidly aging population, and skewed sex ratios, might not be resolved with the dissolution of this policy. Martin

King Whyte, Wang Feng, and Yong Cai, "Challenging Myths about China's One-Child Policy," *The China Journal* 74 (2015), 144–159.

8. Kenji Minemura, "China's One-Child Policy Creates Wimpy Military Recruits, Deserters." *Asahi Shimbun*, February 26, 2013. Available at http://ajw.asahi.com/article/asia/china/AJ201302060009?_ga=1.155980667.173550494.1404841202.

9. Vanessa Fong, *Only Hope: Coming of Age under China's One-Child policy*. Stanford, CA: Stanford University Press, 2000, 30.

10. Ann Anagnost, "The Corporeal Politics of Quality (Suzhi)." *Public Culture* 16, 2 (2004): 189–208, 194.

11. Barbara Demick, "China Blames Pollution for Surge in Birth Defects," *Los Angeles Times*, February 2, 2009. Available at http://articles.latimes.com/2009/feb/02/world/fg-china-birth-defects2.

12. "Baby with Defects Born Every 30 Seconds in China," *People's Daily Online*, September 13, 2010. Available at http://en.people.cn/90001/90782/7138970.html.

13. Terry Ellen Woronov, "Transforming the Future: 'Quality' Children and the Chinese Nation." ProQuest. Chicago: UMI Dissertations Publishing, 2003, 16.

14. "Would You Choose to Have a Second Child?" (*Ni Hui Xuanze Sheng Er Hai Ma?*). Retrieved on November 9, 2015, from http://survey.news.sina.com.cn/result/111331.html.

15. "Orphans." UNICEF Press Centre. Retrieved on June 10, 2015, from www.unicef.org/media/media_45279.html.

16. Liu Meng and Zhu Kai. "Orphan Care in China." *Social Work & Society* 7, 1 (2009): 43–57. Rather than taking into account all at-risk or parentless youth in China, I focus on a much smaller subset of children, those who reside in urban welfare institutes that received aid from foreign NGOs. Although a variety of organizations are devoted to caring for street children, HIV/AIDS orphans, and youths with incarcerated parents and deserve detailed investigation, they are not included in this analysis.

17. Xiaoyuan Shang and Jianpeng Cheng, "Analysis of the Situation of China's Orphans" ("*Zhongguo gu'er zhuangkuang fenxi*"). *Youth Studies* 10 (2006): 8–12.

18. *Child Welfare in China—Stocktaking Report 2011* (中国儿童福利政策 告2011). Beijing: UNICEF China. Available at www.unicefchina.org/cn /uploadfile/2012/0207/20120207020819518.pdf.

19. Catherine Keyser, "The Role of the State and NGOs in Caring for At-Risk Children: The Case of Orphan Care." Pages 45–65 in *State and Society Responses to Social Welfare Needs in China: Serving the People*, edited by Jonathan Schwartz and Shawn Hsieh. New York: Routledge, 2009.

20. Keyser, "The Role of the State and NGOs in Caring for At-Risk Children," 2009.

21. Nathan Vanderklippe, "The Tragic Tale of China's Orphanages: 98% of Abandoned Children Have Disabilities," *The Globe and Mail*, March 21, 2014. Available

at www.theglobeandmail.com/news/world/the-tragic-tale-of-chinas-orphanages-98-of-abandoned-children-have-disabilities/article17625887/.

22. Shang and Fisher, *Caring for Orphaned Children in China*, 2014.

23. Matthew Crenson, *Building the Invisible Orphanage: A Prehistory of the American Welfare System*. Cambridge, MA: Harvard University Press, 2009.

24. Norman D. Apter, "All in the Family: New Approaches to Child Relief in Post-Mao China." *Modern China* 40, 1 (2014): 3–39.

25. "The Dying Rooms and Return to the Dying Rooms," True Vision Films. Retrieved on May 14, 2015, from www.truevisiontv.com/films/details/57/the-dying-rooms-return-to-the-dying-rooms.

26. Robin Munro, Jeff Rigsby, and Human Rights Watch Asia, *Death by Default: A Policy of Fatal Neglect in China's State Orphanages*. New York: Human Rights Watch, 1996, 3.

27. People's Daily, "The Description and Accusations about China's Children's Welfare Institutions by Britain's Channel Four and the Human Rights Watch/Asia Do Not Hold Water." Retrieved on February 29, 2016, from http://english.peopledaily.com.cn/whitepaper/13appendix.html.

28. Human Rights Watch/Asia. "Chinese Orphanages: A Follow Up." Retrieved on May 14, 2015, from www.hrw.org/sites/default/files/reports/china96.pdf.

29. Sharon Stephens, *Children and the Politics of Culture*. Princeton, NJ: Princeton University Press, 1995, 4.

30. Anne Thurston, "In a Chinese Orphanage." *The Atlantic Monthly*, April 1996. Available at www.theatlantic.com/magazine/archive/1996/04/in-a-chinese-orphanage/376563/.

31. Keyser, "The Role of the State and NGOs in Caring for At-Risk Children," 2009.

32. Grace Lin, *The Red Thread: An Adoption Fairy Tale*. Morton Grove, IL: Albert Whitman and Company, 2007.

33. Lin, *The Red Thread*, 2007.

34. Gonzalez and Wesseling, "The Stories We Adopt By," 261.

35. Joseph S. Nye, "Soft Power." *Foreign Policy*, 80 (1990): 153–171.

36. For a more detailed explanation of why Chinese orphanages received a large number of children in the 1980s and early 1990s, see Kay Ann Johnson, *Wanting a Daughter, Needing a Son: Abandonment, Adoption, and Orphanage Care in China*. St. Paul, MN: Yeong & Yeong, 2004.

37. Peter Selman, *International Adoptions from the People's Republic of China, 1992–2012*. Working paper, 2014. Newcastle University, UK.

38. Shang and Fisher, *Caring for Orphaned Children in China*, 2014.

39. David L. Eng, "Transnational Adoption and Queer Diasporas." *Social Text* 21, 3 (2003): 1–37.

40. Brian H. Stuy, "Open Secret: Cash and Coercion in China's International Adoption Program." *Cumberland Law Review* 44 (2013): 355.

41. Sara K. Dorow, *Transnational Adoption: A Cultural Economy of Race, Gender, and Kinship*. Nation of Newcomers. New York: New York University Press, 2006, 25.

42. Michelle King, *Between Birth and Death: Female Infanticide in Nineteenth-Century China*. Stanford, CA: Stanford University Press, 2014.

43. Norman Apter, "From Charity to Welfare: Restructuring Child Relief in the Early People's Republic of China." Paper prepared for Association for Asian Studies Annual Meeting, Chicago, IL, 2009, 6–7.

44. Catherine Keyser, "The Role of the State and NGOs in Caring for At-Risk Children: The Case of Orphan Care." Pages 45–65 in *State and Society Responses to Social Welfare Needs in China: Serving the People*, edited by Jonathan Schwartz and Shawn Hsieh. New York: Routledge, 2009.

45. Carolyn Hsu, "Chinese NGOs in Child Welfare: State Pawns or Savvy Partners?" Paper prepared for Association for Asian Studies Annual Meeting, Chicago, 2009, 3.

46. The *wu bao* protection system provides food, fuel, clothes, and health care to orphaned children, older residents, or disabled people incapable of supporting themselves. Xiaoyuan Shang, Morris Saldov, and Karen R. Fisher, "Informal Kinship Care of Orphans in Rural China." *Social Policy and Society* 10, 1 (2011): 103–116.

47. Linda Wong, *Marginalization and Social Welfare in China*. London: Routledge, 1998.

48. Keyser, "The Role of the State and NGOs in Caring for At-Risk Children," 2009, 50.

49. Nathalie Rothschild, , "China Doesn't Need the West in Loco Parentis." *Spiked Online*, October 9, 2007. Available at www.spiked-online.com/newsite/article/3946#.VJHRd4ffIVU.

50. China Scherz, *Having People, Having Heart: Charity, Sustainable Development, and Problems of Dependence in Central Uganda*. Chicago: University of Chicago Press, 2014.

51. Frayda Cohen, "Tracing the Red Thread: An Ethnography of Chinese–United States Transnational Adoption." ProQuest. Pittsburgh, PA: UMI Dissertations Publishing, 2007.

52. The tenuous nature of NGOs in China has led many of these groups to register as businesses in other countries such as Hong Kong, making it difficult to locate accurate statistics on international orphan relief organizations.

53. The Half the Sky Foundation focuses specifically on aiding institutionalized children in China and should not to be confused with the Half the Sky Movement started by journalist Nicholas Kristof.

54. Although there may be other Western faith-based orphan aid organizations in China that are not Christian, I did not encounter any during my fieldwork.

55. Miwa Hirono, *Civilizing Missions: International Religious Agencies in China.* New York: Palgrave Macmillan, 2008.

56. "Foreign NGOs Doing Good." *Economist Magazine*, June 19, 2014. Available at www.economist.com/news/china/21604609-foreign-charity-shows-how-thrive-china-doing-good.

57. Anna Jane High, "China's Orphan Welfare System: Laws, Policies and Filled Gaps." *East Asia Law Review* 8 (2013): 127–176, 173.

58. Spires, "Contingent Symbiosis and Civil Society in an Authoritarian State," 2011.

59. I was not able to formally interview any Chinese caregivers or spend time with them outside of the institution. Yongping's proximity to the central government in Beijing created a highly politicized climate that made it difficult to ask questions without possibly jeopardizing the group's tenuous relationship with the orphanage.

## Chapter 2

1. Frank Dikötter, *Imperfect Conceptions: Medical Knowledge, Birth Defects and Eugenics in China.* New York: Columbia University Press, 1998.

2. Viviana Zelizer, *Pricing the Priceless Child: The Changing Social Value of Children.* Princeton, NJ: Princeton University Press, 1985.

3. Viviana A. Zelizer, "The Price and Value of Children: The Case of Children's Insurance." *American Journal of Sociology* 86, 5 (1981): 1036–1056, 1037.

4. Charlotte Ikels, *Filial Piety: Practice and Discourse in Contemporary East Asia.* Stanford, CA: Stanford University Press, 2004.

5. Susan Greenhalgh, "Planned Births, Unplanned Persons: 'Population' in the Making of Chinese Modernity." *American Ethnologist* 30, 2 (2003): 196–215, 196.

6. Lisa Rofel, *Other Modernities: Gendered Yearnings in China after Socialism.* Berkeley: University of California Press, 1999, 10.

7. Quoted in Ellen R. Judd, *The Chinese Women's Movement between State and Market.* Stanford, CA: Stanford University Press, 2002, 20.

8. King, *Between Birth and Death*, 2014.

9. Gary Sigley, "*Suzhi*, the Body, and the Fortunes of Technoscientific Reasoning in Contemporary China." *positions: east asia cultures critique* 17, 3 (2009): 537–566.

10. Jim Yardley, "No Spitting on the Road to Olympic Glory," *New York Times*, April 17, 2007. Retrieved on December 30, 2014, from www.nytimes.com/2007/04/17/world/asia/17manners.html?_r=2&oref=slogin&.

11. Ann Anagnost, "A Surfeit of Bodies: Population and the Rationality of the State in Post-Mao China." Pages 22–41 in *Conceiving the New World Order: The*

*Global Politics of Reproduction*, edited by Faye Ginsburg and Rayna Rapp. Berkeley: University of California Press, 1995, 24.

12. Vanessa L. Fong, *Only Hope: Coming of Age under China's One-Child Policy*. Stanford, CA: Stanford University Press, 2004, 3.

13. Lisa Handwerker, "The Hen That Can't Lay an Egg (*Bu Xia Dan De Mu Ji*): The Stigmatization of Female Infertility in Late Twentieth Century China." ProQuest. Berkeley, CA: UMI Dissertations Publishing, 1993, 55.

14. Christopher Smith, *China in the Post-Utopian Age*. Boulder, CO: Westview Press, 2000, 70.

15. "400 Million Births Prevented by One-Child Policy." *People's Daily Online*. October 28, 2011. Available at http://en.people.cn/90882/7629166.html.

16. "Fertility Rate, Total (Births Per Woman)," The World Bank. Retrieved April 25, 2015, from http://data.worldbank.org/indicator/SP.DYN.TFRT.IN.

17. "China Past Due: One Child Policy," narrated by Marco Werman, PRI, NPR, April 15, 2013. Available at www.theworld.org/2013/04/china-past-due-one-child/.

18. Borge Bakken, *The Exemplary Society: Human Improvement, Social Control, and the Dangers of Modernity in China*. London: Oxford University Press, 2000.

19. Terry Ellen Woronov, "Transforming the Future: 'Quality' Children and the Chinese Nation." ProQuest. Chicago: UMI Dissertations Publishing, 2003, 18.

20. Jun Jing, *Feeding China's Little Emperors: Food, Children, and Social Change*. Stanford, CA: Stanford University Press, 2000, 4.

21. "Marriage Law of the People's Republic of China." Consulate General of the People's Republic of China in New York. Retrieved April 29, 2015, from http://newyork.china-consulate.org/eng/lsqz/laws/t42222.htm.

22. Ann Anagnost, *National Past-Times: Narrative, Representation, and Power in Modern China*. Durham, NC: Duke University Press, 1997, 197.

23. Sigley, "Suzhi, the Body, and the Fortunes of Technoscientific Reasoning in Contemporary China," 2009, 538–539.

24. Xiaoyuan Shang, Xiaoming Wu, and Haiyan Li. "Social Policy, Social Gender and the Problem of Infant Abandonment in China" ("*Shehui zhengce, shehui xingbie yu zhongguo de ertong yiqi wenti.*") *Youth Studies* 4 (2005): 32–35, 35.

25. Judith Banister, "Shortage of Girls in China Today." *Journal of Population Research* 21, 1 (2004): 19–45.

26. Rachel Murphy, "Fertility and Distorted Sex Ratios in a Rural Chinese County: Culture, State, and Policy." *Population and Development Review* 29, 4 (2003): 595–626.

27. Wei Xing Zhu, Li Lu, and Therese Hesketh. "China's Excess Males, Sex Selective Abortion, and One Child Policy: Analysis of Data from 2005 National Intercensus Survey," *British Medical Journal* (2009), 338.

28. Banister, "Shortage of Girls in China Today," 2004.

29. "China's Mainland Population Grows to 1.3397 Billion in 2010: Census Data." *Xinhua News*, April 28, 2011. Available at http://news.xinhuanet.com/english2010/china/2011-04/28/c_13849795.htm.

30. Wei Xing Zhu, Li Lu, and Therese Hesketh, "China's Excess Males," 2009.

31. Zhang Kun and Zhang Songlin, "Estimates of Sex-Selective Abortion of Female Fetuses in China" (*"Wo guo xuanze xing rengong yinchan zaocheng de yinchan nuying shu guji"*). *Statistical Research* 11 (2006): 48–51.

32. Amartya Sen. "Missing Women." *British Medical Journal* 304, 6827 (1992): 587–588.

33. Zhang Kun and Zhang Songlin. *"Wo guo xuanze xing rengong yinchan zaocheng de yinchan nuying shu guji"* ("Estimates of Sex-Selective Abortion of Female Fetuses in China"). *Statistical Research* 11 (2005): 48–51.

34. Chu Junhong. "Prenatal Sex Determination and Sex-Selective Abortion in Rural Central China." *Population and Development Review* 27, 2 (2001): 259–281.

35. Kay Ann Johnson, *Wanting a Daughter, Needing a Son: Abandonment, Adoption, and Orphanage Care in China*. St. Paul, MN: Yeong and Yeong Company, 2004.

36. Sulamith Potter and Jack Potter. *China's Peasants: The Anthropology of a Revolution*. Cambridge, UK: Cambridge University Press, 1990.

37. Elizabeth Croll, *Endangered Daughters: Discrimination and Development in Asia*. Hoboken, NJ: Routledge, 2002, 112.

38. Croll, *Endangered Daughters*, 2002.

39. Pang Lihua et al. "Working until You Drop: The Elderly of Rural China." *The China Journal* 52 (2004): 73–94.

40. Zhang Erli,*"Cong 'wupu' dishi shuju kan shengyu zhengce dui chusheng xingbie bi he ying you'er siwang lu xingbie bie de yingxiang"* ("Using the 5th Census to Analyze the Influence of Birth Control Policies on the Sex Ratio at Birth and Infant Mortality Rate"). *Population Research* 29 (2005): 11–18.

41. Tyrene White, "Domination, Resistance and Accommodation in China's One-Child Campaign." *Chinese Society: Change, Conflict and Resistance* (2000): 102–119. New York: Routledge.

42. Kay Johnson, Huang Banghan, and Wang Liyao, "Infant Abandonment and Adoption in China." *Population and Development Review* (1998): 469–510.

43. Susan Greenhalgh, "Controlling Births and Bodies in Village China." *American Ethnologist* 21, 1 (1994): 3–30.

44. Johnson, *Wanting a Daughter, Needing a Son*, 2004.

45. Johnson et al., "Infant Abandonment and Adoption in China," 1998.

46. Ann Anagnost, "Imagining Global Futures in China: The Child as a Sign of Value." *Figuring the Future: Globalization and the Temporalities of Children and Youth* (2008): 49–72, 57.

47. Vanessa L. Fong, "China's One-Child Policy and the Empowerment of Urban Daughters." *American Anthropologist* 104, 4 (2002): 1098–1109.

48. Hong Zhang, "China's New Rural Daughters Coming of Age: Downsizing the Family and Firing Up Cash_Earning Power in the New Economy." *Signs* 32, 3 (2007): 671–698.

49. "Desperate Parents Now Overwhelming China's 'Baby Hatches.'" YouTube video, 3:04, posted by ITV News, June 11, 2014. Available at www.youtube.com/watch?v=bKRAIXSiFrY.

50. "Suspension of Baby Hatch Highlights Abandoned Infants Dilemma." March 17, 2014. Retrieved December 27, 2014, from http://news.xinhuanet.com/english/indepth/2014-03/17/c_133193247.htm.

51. Frank Dikötter, *Imperfect Conceptions: Medical Knowledge, Birth Defects, and Eugenics in China.* New York: Columbia University Press, 1998.

52. Zhou Xun, "The Discourse of Disability in Modern China," *Patterns of Prejudice* 36, 1 (2002): 104–112.

53. Yinan Hu, "Baby Born with Birth Defects Every 30 Seconds," *China Daily,* October 30, 2007. Available at www.chinadaily.com.cn/cndy/2007-10/30/content_6214736.htm.

54. Barbara Demick, "China Blames Pollution for Surge in Birth Defects," *Los Angeles Times,* February 2, 2009. Available at http://articles.latimes.com/2009/feb/02/world/fg-china-birth-defects2.

55. Yinan Hu, "Baby Born with Birth Defects Every 30 Seconds."

56. David Blumenthal and William Hsiao, "Privatization and Its Discontents—The Evolving Chinese Health Care System." *New England Journal of Medicine* 353, 11 (2005): 1165–1170.

57. Ibid.

58. Winnie Yip and William C. Hsiao. "The Chinese Health System at a Crossroads." *Health Affairs* 27, 2 (2008): 460–468.

59. Wong, *Marginalization and Social Welfare in China,* 2005.

60. Yip and Hsiao, "The Chinese Health System at a Crossroads," 2008, 460–461.

61. Shanlian Hu, Shenglan Tang, Yuanli Liu, Yuxin Zhao, Maria-Luisa Escobar, and David de Ferranti. "Reform of How Health Care Is Paid for in China: Challenges and Opportunities." *The Lancet* 372, 9652 (2008): 1846–1853.

62. Wang Jing. "China's 'Baby Hatch' Project Swamped by Abandoned Children," *WorldCrunch,* December 19, 2014. Available at www.worldcrunch.com/china-2.0/china-039-s-039-baby-hatch-039-project-swamped-by-abandoned-children/babies-family-birth-orphans-health-policy/c9s17651/#.VJ781EBYB3A.

63. Eleanor E. Holroyd, "Chinese Cultural Influences on Parental Caregiving Obligations toward Children with Disabilities." *Qualitative Health Research* 13, 1 (2003): 4–19, 10.

64. Ibid., 18.

65. "Rising Birth Defects," *China Daily*, September 15, 2009, Available at www .chinadaily.com.cn/opinion/2009-09/15/content_8691526.htm.

66. Yinan Hu, "Baby Born with Birth Defects Every 30 Seconds," 2007,

67. Gail Kligman, *The Politics of Duplicity: Controlling Reproduction in Ceausescu's Romania*. Berkeley: University of California Press, 1998, 25.

68. Linliang Qian, "Consuming 'the Unfortunate': The Violence of Philanthropy in a Contemporary Chinese State-Run Orphanage." *Dialectical Anthropology* 38, 3 (2014): 247–279, 263.

69. Qiu Renzong and Frank Dikötter, "Is China's Law Eugenic?" *Unesco Courier* 52 (1999): 9.

70. "Chinese Sterilizing Retarded Who Marry," *Chicago Tribune*, August 15, 1991. Available at http://articles.chicagotribune.com/1991-08-15/news/9103280857_1_ eugenics-retarded-sterilization.

71. Alice Yan, "End to Checkups Fuels Fears of More Disabled Babies," *South China Morning Post*, May 5, 2004. Available at www.scmp.com/article/454526/end-checkups-fuels-fears-more-disabled-babies.

72. Dikötter, *Imperfect Conceptions*, 1998.

73. Ibid., 69.

74. "Rising Birth Defects," *China Daily*, September 15, 2009. Available at www .chinadaily.com.cn/opinion/2009-09/15/content_8691526.htm.

75. Susan Greenhalgh, *Cultivating Global Citizens: Population in the Rise of China*. Cambridge, MA: Harvard University Press, 2010, 49.

76. Sara L. Friedman, "Embodying Civility: Civilizing Processes and Symbolic Citizenship in Southeastern China." *The Journal of Asian Studies* 63, 3 (2004): 687–718, 688.

77. Tamara Jacka, "Approaches to Women and Development in Rural China." *Journal of Contemporary China* 15, 49 (2006): 585–602.

## Chapter 3

1. In 2006 the China Center for Adoption Affairs reported having adoption ties with sixteen countries: the United States, Spain, Canada, the Netherlands, Sweden, Norway, France, Australia, Belgium, Denmark, Finland, Iceland, Ireland, New Zealand, the United Kingdom, and Singapore. In 2008 an adoption agreement was made with Italy.

2. Peter Goodman, "Stealing Babies for Adoption," *Washington Post*, March 12, 2006. Available at www.washingtonpost.com/wp-dyn/content/article/2006/03/11/ AR2006031100942.html.

3. Scott Tong, "The Dark Side of Chinese Adoptions." *Marketplace*, National Public Radio, May 5, 2010. Available at www.marketplace.org/topics/life/dark-side-chinese-adoptions.

4. Patricia J. Meier and Xiaole Zhang, "Sold into Adoption: The Hunan Baby Trafficking Scandal Exposes Vulnerabilities in Chinese Adoptions to the United States. (Symposium: The Baby Market)." *Cumberland Law Review* 39, 1 (2008): 87.

5. Goodman, "Stealing Babies for Adoption," 2006.

6. Barbara Demick, "A Family in China Made Babies Their Business," January 4, 2010. Retrieved on June 14, 2014, from http://articles.latimes.com/2010/jan/24/world/la-fg-china-adopt24-2010jan24/2.

7. Michele Goodwin, ed., *Baby Markets: Money and the New Politics of Creating Families.* Cambridge, UK: Cambridge University Press, 2010.

8. Goodman, "Stealing Babies for Adoption," 2006.

9. Joseph S. Nye, "Soft Power." *Foreign Policy*, 80 (1990): 153–171.

10. Lynn Pan, *Sons of the Yellow Emperor: A History of the Chinese Diaspora.* New York: Kodansha International, 1994, 267.

11. Meier and Zhang, "Sold into Adoption," 2008, 87.

12. David L. Eng, "Transnational Adoption and Queer Diasporas." *Social Text* 21, 3 (2003): 1–37, 6.

13. Eleana Kim, *Adopted Territory: Transnational Korean Adoptees and the Politics of Belonging.* Durham, NC: Duke University Press, 2010.

14. The 2010 U.S. census found that there were more than two *million* adopted youth under age eighteen. In total, only about 13 percent were adopted internationally. See Rose M. Kreider and Daphne A. Lofquist, "Adopted Children and Stepchildren: 2010." *Adoption Quarterly* 13 (2010): 268–291.

15. Elizabeth Croll, *Endangered Daughters: Discrimination and Development in Asia.* Hoboken, NJ: Routledge, 2002.

16. U.S. Department of State, "International Adoption Statistics." Retrieved on May 3, 2015, from http://travel.state.gov/content/adoptionsabroad/en/about-us/statistics.html.

17. These provinces also bear some of the most abnormal sex ratios at birth in the nation, which correlates to the higher number of abandoned girls in these areas. However, why son preference appears to be stronger in southern China than in other regions has not yet been systematically investigated.

18. Nili Luo and David M. Smolin, "Intercountry Adoption and China: Emerging Questions and Developing Chinese Perspectives." *Cumberland Law Review* 35, 3 (2005): 598.

19. Viviana Zelizer, *Pricing the Priceless Child: The Changing Social Value of Children.* Princeton, NJ: Princeton University Press, 1985, 193.

20. Mariagiovanna Baccara et al. *Child-Adoption Matching: Preferences for Gender and Race.* No. w16444. Cambridge, MA: National Bureau of Economic Research, 2010, 3.

21. Abbie E. Goldberg, "Heterosexual, Lesbian, and Gay Preadoptive Parents' Preferences about Child Gender." *Sex Roles* 61, 1–2 (2009): 55–71.

22. John Gravois, "Bringing Up Babes: Why Do Adoptive Parents Prefer Girls?" *Slate.com*, January 1, 2004. Available at http://www.slate.com/articles/news_and_politics/hey_wait_a_minute/2004/01/bringing_up_babes.html.

23. Gordon Dahl and Enrico Moretti, "The Demand for Sons." *Review of Economic Studies* 75 (2008): 1085–1120.

24. Love Without Boundaries, "Adopt Special Needs." Retrieved on April 25, 2015, from www.adoptspecialneeds.org/special-needs/.

25. LWB Videos, "Adopting a Boy," YouTube video, 4:40, April 25, 2011. Available at www.youtube.com/watch?v=5ijggNs2Ask.

26. Baccara et al., "Child-Adoption Matching," 2010, 3.

27. Ana Teresa Ortiz and Laura Briggs, "The Culture of Poverty, Crack Babies, and Welfare Cheats: The Making of the 'Healthy White Baby Crisis.'" *Social Text* 21, 3 (2003): 39–57.

28. Sara Dorow, "Racialized Choices: Chinese Adoption and the 'White Noise' of Blackness." *Critical Sociology* 32, 2–3 (2006): 357–379.

29. Toby Alice Volkman, "Embodying Chinese Culture: Transnational Adoption in North America." *Social Text* 21, 1 (2003): 29–55.

30. Ortiz and Briggs, "The Culture of Poverty," 41–42.

31. Dorow, "Racialized Choices," 2006.

32. Mia Tuan, *Forever Foreigners or Honorary Whites? The Asian Ethnic Experience Today.* New Brunswick, NJ: Rutgers University Press, 1998.

33. Kazuyo Kubo, "Desirable Difference: The Shadow of Racial Stereotypes in Creating Transracial Families through Transnational Adoption." *Sociology Compass* 4, 4 (2010): 263–282.

34. Aki Uchida, "The Orientalization of Asian Women in America." *Women's Studies International Forum* 21, 2 (1998): 161–174, 162.

35. Andrea Louie, "'Pandas, Lions, and Dragons, Oh My!': How White Adoptive Parents Construct Chineseness." *Journal of Asian American Studies* 12, 3 (2009): 285–320.

36. Dorow, "Racialized Choices," 2006, 364.

37. Arthur P. Wolf and Jieshan Huang, *Marriage and Adoption in China, 1845–1945.* Stanford, CA: Stanford University Press, 1980.

38. Sten Johansson and Ola Nygren, "The Missing Girls of China: A New Demographic Account." *Population and Development Review* 17, 1 (1991): 35–51.

39. Weiguo Zhang, "Child Adoption in Contemporary Rural China." *Journal of Family Issues* 27, 3 (2006): 301–340.

40. Jihong Liu, Ulla Larsen, and Grace Wyshak, "Factors Affecting Adoption in China, 1950–87." *Population Studies* 58, 1 (2004): 21–36.

41. Kay Ann Johnson, *Wanting a Daughter, Needing a Son: Abandonment, Adoption, and Orphanage Care in China.* St. Paul, MN: Yeong & Yeong Book Company, 2004.

42. Kay Ann Johnson, "Politics of International and Domestic Adoption in China." *Law & Society Review* 36, 2 (2002): 379–396, 386.

43. Weiguo Zhang, "Child Adoption in Contemporary Rural China," 2006.

44. Agence France-Presse in Beijing, "China Promises Rights to Citizens Born in Violation of One-Child Policy." *The Guardian*, December 10, 2015. Available at www .theguardian.com/world/2015/dec/10/china-promises-rights-citizens-born-violation-one-child-policy.

45. Susan Greenhalgh and Jiali Li, "Engendering Reproductive Policy and Practice in Peasant China: For a Feminist Demography of Reproduction." *Signs* 20, 3 (1995): 601–641.

46. Dandan Ni, "Chinese Parents Compete with Foreign Applicants to Adopt Healthy Babies," *Global Times*, April 2, 2014. Available at www.globaltimes.cn/content/852341.shtml.

47. Zhang, Weiguo. "Who Adopts Girls and Why? Domestic Adoption of Female Children in Contemporary Rural China." *The China Journal*, 56 (2006): 63–82.

48. Johnson, "Politics of International and Domestic Adoption in China," 384.

49. Zhang, "Who Adopts Girls and Why?" 78.

50. Meier and Zhang, "Sold into Adoption," 2008, 99.

51. Frayda Cohen, *Tracing the Red Thread: An Ethnography of China–U.S. Transnational Adoption.* PhD dissertation, University of Pittsburgh, 2007.

52. Meier and Zhang, "Sold into Adoption," 2008.

53. Although preference was granted to childless individuals, foreigners who already had their own birth children were allowed to adopt children who were older or had some form of special need.

54. Johnson, "Politics of International and Domestic Adoption in China," 389.

55. Nili Luo and Kathleen Ja Bergquist, "Born in China: Birth Country Perspectives on International Adoption." *Adoption Quarterly* 8, (2005): 21–39.

56. Li Xiaohua, "200,000 Children Need More Support." *China.org.cn*, October 24, 2005. Available at www.china.org.cn/english/2005/Oct/146340.htm.

57. Personal communication with Brian Stuy, June 14, 2010. His estimate is based on the locations of children's "finding ads" that are placed in local Chinese newspapers, which is a key step in allowing a child to become eligible for international adoption.

58. Meier and Zhang, "Sold into Adoption," 2008, 106.

59. Ibid.

60. David Smolin, "Child Laundering: How the Intercountry Adoption System Legitimizes and Incentivizes the Practices of Buying, Trafficking, Kidnaping, and Stealing Children." *Wayne Law Review* 52 (2006): 113–200, 115.

61. Brian Stuy, "Domestic Adoption in China's Orphanages." January 19, 2006. Available at http://research-china.blogspot.com/2006/01/domestic-adoption-in-chinas-orphanages.html.

62. Ni, "Chinese Parents Compete with Foreign Applicants to Adopt Healthy Babies," 2014.

63. Sara Dorow, *Transnational Adoption: A Cultural Economy of Race, Gender and Kinship.* New York: NYU Press, 2006, 98.

64. Anqi Shen, Georgios A. Antonopoulos, and Georgios Papanicolaou, "China's Stolen Children: Internal Child Trafficking in the People's Republic of China." *Trends in Organized Crime* 16, 1 (2013): 31–48, 32.

65. Beth Lloyd, "China's Lost Children," *ABC News*, May 12, 2008. Available at http://abcnews.go.com/International/story?id=4774224&page=1&singlePage=true.

66. Sophie Brown and CY Xu, "Chinese Police Save Hundreds of Babies from Online Trading Racket," *CNN.com*, February 28, 2014. Available at www.cnn.com/2014/02/28/world/asia/china-online-baby-trafficking-crackdown/.

67. Shen et al., "China's Stolen Children," 2013, 45.

68. Weiguo Zhang, "Child Adoption in Contemporary Rural China."

69. Sara Dorow, *Transnational Adoption*, 82.

70. Peter Selman, "The Rise and Fall of Intercountry Adoption in the 21st Century." *International Social Work* 52, 5 (2009): 575–594.

71. "Can Homosexual Adopt Children in China?" ChinaDaily.com, May 30, 2006. Available at www.chinadaily.com.cn/china/2006-05/30/content_604309.htm.

72. Nili Luo and David M. Smolin. "Intercountry Adoption and China: Emerging Questions and Developing Chinese Perspectives." *Cumberland Law Review* 35, 3 (2005): 598–618, 608.

73. FCC New York, "Letter to Chinese Government," April 15, 2008. Available at www.fccny.org/HelpPopUp.asp?202.

74. Beth Nonte Russell, "The Mystery of China's Baby Shortage," *New York Times*, January 23, 2007. Available at www.nytimes.com/2007/01/23/opinion/23russell.html?pagewanted=all.

75. Eleana Kim, "Wedding Citizenship and Culture: Korean Adoptees and the Global Family of Korea." *Social Text* 21, 1 (2003): 57–81, 63.

76. Nancy E. Riley, "American Adoptions of Chinese Girls: The Socio-Political Matrices of Individual Decisions." *Women's Studies International Forum* 20, 1 (1997): 87–102.

77. Tony Tan and Xiaohui Fan, "Chinese Views on International Adoption." Pages 327–337 in *From Home to Homeland: What Adoptive Families Need to Know before Making a Return Trip to China*, edited by Debra Jacobs, Iris Ponte, and Leslie Wang. St. Paul, MN: Yeong and Yeong, 2010, 331.

78. Meier and Zhang, "Sold into Adoption," 2008.

79. Luo and Smolin, "Intercountry Adoption and China," 2005.

80. Legacy Journey, "CCCWA Summer Tour 2016." Retrieved on May 3, 2015, from www.legacyjourney.org/package/cccwa-summer-tour/.

81. Eleana Kim, "Wedding Citizenship and Culture: Korean Adoptees and the Global Family of Korea." *Social Text* 21, 1 (2003): 57–81, 58.

82. Great Wall China Adoption Travel Agency agreement. Retrieved on May 3, 2015, from www.gwca.org/GWCAguide/CCCWATravelAgreement.pdf.

## Chapter 4

1. Tomorrow's Children Foundation website.

2. Erica Bornstein, "Developing Faith: Theologies of Economic Development in Zimbabwe." *Journal of Religion in Africa* 32, 1 (2002): 4–31.

3. Sara K. Dorow, *Transnational Adoption: A Cultural Economy of Race, Gender, and Kinship*. New York: New York University Press, 2006, 100.

4. Stated in a publication of the Haifeng CWI.

5. Olga Nieuwenhuys, "Growing up between Places of Work and Non-Places of Childhood." *Children's Places: Cross-Cultural Perspectives* (2003): 99–118, 100.

6. Sharon Hays, *The Cultural Contradictions of Motherhood*. New Haven, CT: Yale University Press, 1996.

7. Annette Lareau, *Unequal Childhoods: Class, Race, and Family Life*. Berkeley: University of California Press, 2011.

8. Dorow, *Transnational Adoption*, 2007, 103.

9. Ibid.

10. Martin Woodhead, "Psychology and the Cultural Construction of Children's Needs." Pages 63–84 in *Constructing and Reconstructing Childhood*, edited by Allison James and Alan Prout. London: Falmer, 1997, 63.

11. David Wu, "Chinese Childhood Socialization." Pages 143–154 in *The Handbook of Chinese Psychology*, edited by Michael Harris Bond. New York: Oxford University Press, 1996.

12. Ruth K. Chao, "Beyond Parental Control and Authoritarian Parenting Style: Understanding Chinese Parenting through the Cultural Notion of Training." *Child development* 65, 4 (1994): 1111–1119.

13. Hays, *The Cultural Contradictions of Motherhood*, 1996, 94.

## Chapter 5

1. See Chapter 3 for the gender composition of Yongping's inhabitants.

2. Erving Goffman, *Asylums: Essays on the Social Situation of Mental Patients and Other Inmates.* London: Penguin, 1961.

3. Christina J. Groark, Rifkat J. Muhamedrahimov, Oleg I. Palmov, Natalia V. Nikiforova, and Robert B. McCall, "Improvements in Early Care in Russian Orphanages and Their Relationship to Observed Behaviors." *Infant Mental Health Journal* 26, 2 (2005): 96–109.

4. Samantha L. Wilson, "Post-Institutionalization: The Effects of Early Deprivation on Development of Romanian Adoptees." *Child and Adolescent Social Work Journal* 20, 6 (2003): 473–483, 474.

5. Linda G. Tirella, W. Chan, S. A. Cermak, A. Litvinova, K. C. Salas, and L. C. Miller, "Time Use in Russian Baby Homes." *Child: Care, Health and Development* 34, 1 (2008): 77–86.

6. Linda M. Richter and Amy Norman, "AIDS Orphan Tourism: A Threat to Young Children in Residential Care." *Vulnerable Children and Youth Studies* 5, 3 (2010): 217–229.

7. Rosie Read, "Labour and Love: Competing Constructions of 'Care' in a Czech Nursing Home." *Critique of Anthropology* 27, 2 (2007): 203–222.

8. Ibid., 209.

9. Ibid., 209–210.

10. Anthony J. Spires, "Contingent Symbiosis and Civil Society in an Authoritarian State: Understanding the Survival of China's Grassroots NGOs." *American Journal of Sociology* 117, 1 (2011): 1–45, 20.

11. Roderick L. Stirrat and Heiko Henkel. "The Development Gift: The Problem of Reciprocity in the NGO World." *Annals of the American Academy of Political and Social Science* 554, 1 (1997): 66–80, 72.

12. Carrie Kahn, "As 'Voluntourism' Explodes In Popularity, Who's It Helping Most?" *National Public Radio,* July 31, 2014. Available at www.npr.org/blogs/goatsandsoda/2014/07/31/336600290/as-volunteerism-explodes-in-popularity-whos-it-helping-most.

13. Mary Conran, "They Really Love Me! Intimacy in Volunteer Tourism." *Annals of Tourism Research* 38, 4 (2011): 1454–1473; Mary Mostafanezhad, "The Geography of Compassion in Volunteer Tourism." *Tourism Geographies* 15, 2 (2013): 318–337; Richter and Norman, "AIDS Orphan Tourism," (2010): 217–229.

14. Julie Clothier, "Voluntourism: The Benefits and Pitfalls You Need to Know," CNN.com, June 18, 2010. Available at www.cnn.com/2010/TRAVEL/06/18/voluntourism.pros.and.cons/.

15. Anne-Meike Fechter, *Transnational Lives: Expatriates in Indonesia.* Hampshire, UK: Ashgate Publishing Limited, 2007, 33.

16. Hilary Callan and Shirley Ardener, eds., *The Incorporated Wife*. London: Croom Helm, 1984.

17. Kathleen D. McCarthy, ed., *Lady Bountiful Revisited: Women, Philanthropy, and Power*. New Brunswick, NJ: Rutgers University Press, 1990, xi.

18. Katie Walsh, "Travelling Together? Work, Intimacy and Home amongst British Expatriate Couples in Dubai." *Gender and Family among Transnational Professionals* (2008): 63–89.

19. Brenda S. A. Yeoh and Louisa-May Khoo, "Home, Work and Community: Skilled International Migration and Expatriate Women in Singapore." *International Migration* 36, 2 (1998): 159–186.

20. Daniella Arieli, "The Task of Being Content: Expatriate Wives in Beijing, Emotional Work and Patriarchal Bargain." *Journal of International Women's Studies* 8, 4 (2013): 18–31.

21. Arieli, "The Task of Being Content," 2007, 20.

22. Fechter, *Transnational Lives*, 2007, 5.

23. Judith Van de Bovenkamp. "Getting Happiness from a Smile." *China Now (China Nu)*, Summer, 2009.

24. Fechter, *Transnational Lives*, 2007, 51.

25. Kay Bratt, *Silent Tears: A Journey of Hope in a Chinese Orphanage*. Las Vegas, NV: AmazonEncore, 2007, 41.

26. Ibid., 271.

27. Conran, "They Really Love Me," 2011, 1454.

28. Richter and Norman, "AIDS Orphan Tourism," 2010.

29. Kristen Cheney and Karen S. Rotabi, 2015. "'Addicted to Orphans': How the Global Orphan Industrial Complex Jeopardizes Local Child Protection Systems." In *Conflict, Violence and Peace, Volume 11: Geographies of Children and Young People*, edited by C. Harker, K. Horschelmann, and T. Skelton. Singapore: Springer.

## Chapter 6

1. Eleana Kim, *Adopted Territory: Transnational Korean Adoptees and the Politics of Belonging*. Durham, NC: Duke University Press Books, 2010.

2. Michele Goodwin, "Baby Markets." In *Baby Markets: Money and the New Politics of Creating Families*, edited by Michele Goodwin. Cambridge, UK: Cambridge University Press, 2010.

3. David Eng, "Political Economics of Passion: Transnational Adoption and Global Woman: Roundtable on Global Woman." *Studies in Gender and Sexuality* 7, 1 (2006), 49–59.

4. Karen Rotabi, "Fraud in Intercountry Adoption: Child Sales and Abduction in Vietnam, Cambodia, and Guatemala." *Intercountry Adoption: Policies, Practices and Outcomes* (2012): 67–76.

5. Lynette Clemetsen, "Adoptions from Guatemala Face an Uncertain Future." *New York Times*, May 16, 2007. Available at www.nytimes.com/2007/05/16/us/16adopt.html?_r=0.

6. "Adoption Illegalities in Guatemala: What the U.S. Government Knew—and What Was Said and Done." The Schuster Institute for Investigative Journalism. Retrieved on May 7, 2015, from www.brandeis.edu/investigate/adoption/US-embassy-cables-reveal-adoption-fraud-in-Guatemala.html.

7. "Outline: Hague Intercountry Adoption Convention." Hague Conference on Private International Law. Retrieved on May 7, 2015, from www.hcch.net/upload/outline33e.pdf.

8. Intercountry Adoption Statistics. U.S. Department of State Bureau of Consular Affairs. Retrieved on May 8, 2015, from http://travel.state.gov/content/adoptions abroad/en/about-us/statistics.html.

9. Peter Baker and Ellen Barry, "US Penalizes Russians for Human Rights Violations." *New York Times*, April 12, 2013. Available at www.nytimes.com/2013/04/13/world/europe/us-issues-penalties-against-russians-for-rights-violations.html?pagewanted=all&_r=0.

10. Ultimately, Hansen was sued by her own adoption agency. In 2012 she was ordered to pay child support for the boy—now living in a group home for children in Moscow—because he is still legally her son as well as an American citizen.

11. Holly Yan and Susannah Palk, "Russia Slams Texas Prosecutors for Not Charging Parents of Dead Adopted Boy." CNN.com, March 19, 2013. Available at http://edition.cnn.com/2013/03/19/us/texas-russian-adoption-death/index.html.

12. Tony Xing Tan, Kofi Marfo, and Robert F. Dedrick, "Special Needs Adoption from China: Exploring Child-Level Indicators, Adoptive Family Characteristics, and Correlates of Behavioral Adjustment." *Children and Youth Services Review* 29, 10 (2007): 1269–1285.

13. European Adoption Consultants website. Retrieved on May 10, 2015, from www.eaci.com/site/informationCenter/PreadoptiveParents/Programs/China.

14. "China's New Adoption Rules to Protect Children, not Deter Foreign Adopters." People.com.cn, January 4, 2007. Available at http://en.people.cn/200701/04/eng20070104_337980.html.

15. "Special Focus Program (Adopting Two Children)." CCAI Adoption Services. Retrieved on November 15, 2015, from www.ccaifamily.org/WaitingChild/Special Focus.aspx.

16. "Qualifications to Adopt from China." CCAI Adoption Services. Retrieved on May 10, 2015, from www.ccaifamily.org/WaitingChild/WCP-Qualification.aspx.

17. "China Requirements." America World Adoption Services. Retrieved on November 15, 2015, from www.awaa.org/programs/china/requirements.aspx.

18. "New Adoption Rules Not to Deter Foreign Adopters." *Xinhua News*, January 3, 2007. Available at http://news.xinhuanet.com/english/2007-01/03/content_5562016.htm.

19. Kristen Cheney, "'Giving Children a Better Life?': Reconsidering Social Reproduction, Humanitarianism and Development in Intercountry Adoption." *European Journal of Development Research* 26, 2 (2014): 247–263, 255.

20. Erica Bornstein, *The Spirit of Development: Protestant NGOs, Morality, and Economics in Zimbabwe*. Stanford, CA: Stanford University Press, 2003, 69.

21. Tomorrow's Children Foundation website.

22. Anna Jane Kloeden, "Government Beyond Law: Exploring Charity Regulation and Spaces of Order in China." PhD dissertation, Oxford University, 2012, 240.

23. Tomorrow's Children Foundation newsletter, January 2013.

24. Tomorrow's Children Foundation website.

25. Kathryn Joyce, *The Child Catchers: Rescue, Trafficking, and the New Gospel of Adoption*. New York: PublicAffairs, 2013, xii.

26. Sheryl J. Ryan, "A Wolf in Sheep's Clothing? A Missiological Examination of the United States Evangelical Adoption and Orphan Care Movement." *Missiology: An International Review* 42, 4 (2014): 412–424, 413.

27. Joyce, *The Child Catchers*, 2013, xiii.

28. UNICEF, UNAIDS, and World Health Organization. "Children and AIDS: Fifth Stocktaking Report." 2010. Available at www.unicef.org/aids/files/ChildrenAnd AIDS_Fifth_Stocktaking_Report_2010_EN.pdf.

29. Christian Alliance for Orphans, "What Is Orphan Sunday?" Retrieved on May 10, 2015, from http://orphansunday.org/wp-content/uploads/What-is-Orphan-Sunday.pdf.

30. Elizabeth Bartholet, "International Adoption: The Human Rights Issues." In *Baby Markets: Money and the New Politics of Creating Families*, edited by Michele Bratcher Goodwin. (2010): 94–117.

31. David M. Smolin, "Child Laundering: How the Intercountry Adoption System Legitimizes and Incentivizes the Practices of Buying, Trafficking, Kidnapping, and Stealing Children." *Wayne Law Review* 52, 1 (2006): 113.

32. David M. Smolin, "Orphan Rescue or Child Trafficking?" Paper presented at the Herbert and Elinor Nootbaar Institute on Law, Religion and Ethics Conference on Intercountry Adoption: Orphan Rescue or Child Trafficking? Malibu, California, February 8–9, 2013.

33. Kristen Cheney and Karen S. Rotabi. 2016. "'Addicted to Orphans': How the Global Orphan Industrial Complex Jeopardizes Local Child Protection Systems." In *Conflict, Violence and Peace, Volume 11: Geographies of Children and Young People*, edited by C. Harker, K. Horschelmann, and T. Skelton. Singapore: Springer, 4.

34. "Orphan Care." Saddle Back Church. Retrieved on May 10, 2015, from http://orphancareinitiative.com/getinformed/.

35. "Children in Families First—CHIFF." Retrieved on March 7, 2016, from http://childrendeservefamilies.com/wp-content/uploads/2014/02/CHIFF-Summary.pdf.

36. Ryan, "A Wolf in Sheep's Clothing?" 416–417.

37. "Chiff Legislation Gaining Momentum." American World Adoption. January 15, 2014. Available at http://adoptedbydesign.typepad.com/blog/2014/01/chiff-legislation-gaining-momentum.html.

38. Nila Bala. "The Children in Families First Act: Overlooking International Law and the Best Interests of the Child." Stanford Law Review Online, April 18, 2014. Available at www.stanfordlawreview.org/online/children-families-first-act-overlooking-international-law-and-best-interests-child.

39. Cheney and Rotabi, "Addicted to Orphans," 2016, 6.

40. Congressional Coalition on Adoption Institute Statistics. Retrieved on May 10, 2015, from www.ccainstitute.org/index.php?option=com_content&view=category&layout=blog&id=25&Itemid=43.

41. Rebecca Buckwalter-Poza, "America's Unseen Export: Children, Most of Them Black." *Pacific Standard Magazine.* June 24, 2014. Available at www.psmag.com/navigation/politics-and-law/outgoing-adoption-americas-unseen-export-children-black-84084.

42. "Hope Program Frequently Asked Questions." Project 143. Retrieved on May 10, 2015, from http://www.projectonefortythree.org/about/faq/.

43. "Who We Are." Project 143, Retrieved on May 10, 2015, from www.projectonefortythree.org/about/who-we-are/.

44. Kathryn Joyce, "Christian Adoption Crusade Ignores Dark Side." Women's E-News, May 26, 2013. Available at http://womensenews.org/story/books/130522/christian-adoption-crusade-ignores-dark-side#.VF-56effIVU.

45. Brian H. Stuy, "Open Secret: Cash and Coercion in China's International Adoption Program." *Cumberland Law Review* 44, 3 (2014): 355–422.

46. "The Child Exchange: Inside America's Underground Market for Adopted Children." Reuters News Agency, September 9, 2013. Available at www.reuters.com/investigates/adoption/#article/part1.

47. Alicia Bayer, "States Moving to Ban Private Re-homing of Adopted Children," Examiner.com, April 18, 2014, Available at www.examiner.com/article/states-moving-to-ban-private-re-homing-of-adopted-children.

48. Even though rates of reactive attachment disorder (RAD) are high among internationally adopted children, most adoptive parents would never consider this route. Instead, some have turned to a controversial technique known as attachment therapy that aims to emotionally rehabilitate adopted children with RAD. See Rachael

Stryker, *The Road to Evergreen: Adoption, Attachment Therapy, and the Promise of Family*. Ithaca, NY: Cornell University Press, 2010.

49. All of these messages are available on the Reuters website: www.reuters.com/ investigates/adoption/#article/part1/sidebar/emails/email/75.

50. Viviana A. Rotman Zelizer, *Pricing the Priceless Child: The Changing Social Value of Children*. New York: Basic Books, 1985.

51. Joyce, *The Child Catchers*, 2013.

52. Nili Luo and David Smolin, "Intercountry Adoption and China: Emerging Questions and Developing Chinese Perspectives." *Cumberland Law Review*, 35, 3 (2005): 597–618.

## Chapter 7

1. Kristen Cheney and Karen S. Rotabi, 2016. "'Addicted to Orphans': How the Global Orphan Industrial Complex Jeopardizes Local Child Protection Systems." Page 2 in *Conflict, Violence and Peace, Volume 11: Geographies of Children and Young People*, edited by C. Harker, K. Horschelmann, and T. Skelton. Singapore: Springer.

2. Karen R. Fisher and Xiaoyuan Shang, "Protecting the Right to Life of Children with Disabilities in China." *Journal of Social Service Research* 40, no. 4 (2014): 560–572, 562.

3. Leslie Wang, Iris Chin Ponte, and Elizabeth Weber Ollen, "Letting Her Go: Western Adoptive Families' Search and Reunion with Chinese Birth Parents." *Adoption Quarterly* 18, 1 (2015): 45–66.

4. Feng Shu, "On the Trail of Your Parents," *Global Times*, July 15, 2012. Retrieved on April 11, 2015, from www.globaltimes.cn/content/721142.shtml.

5. Iris Ponte, Leslie Wang, and Serena Fan, "Returning to China: The Experience of Adopted Chinese Children and Their Parents." *Adoption Quarterly* 13, 2 (2010): 100–124.

6. Leslie Wang and Iris Chin Ponte, "Adolescent Birth Parent Search." Web survey, University of Massachusetts Boston, 2015. Available at http://surveymonkey.com.

7. Eleana Kim, "Our Adoptee, Our Alien: Transnational Adoptees as Specters of Foreignness and Family in South Korea." *Anthropological Quarterly* 80, 2 (2007): 497–531, 507.

8. "Red Thread Broken." Online blog. Retrieved on April 11, 2015, from https:// redthreadbroken.wordpress.com/about/this-site/.

# Index

abandonment, 13, 28, 35, 64–65, 84, 85, 89, 104, 113, 157, 159; in baby hatches (*ying'er anquandao*), 39–40, 42; healthy boys, 62–63; healthy girls, 6, 23, 30, 37, 38–39, 48–49, 51, 62–63, 71, 172n17; special needs children, 1–3, 6–7, 8, 23, 39–46, 41, 61, 76–81, 95–98, 99, 135, 149, 155; and state modernization goals, 15, 23, 30

abortion: as coerced, 31; as sex-selective, 6, 36–37, 38, 39, 46, 71. *See also* sterilizations

Addis Ababa, Ethiopia: foreign NGOs in, 88

Adopting-From-Disruption (Yahoo group), 146–47

adoption, domestic, 58–63; cost of, 59, 65–66; of girls vs. boys, 8, 59, 62–63, 72; as informal, 37, 58–60; kidnapping for, 67; number in PRC, 58, 68; PRC policies regarding, 50, 59, 63, 64, 67–68, 139; urban vs. rural areas, 58–59, 60. *See also* adoptive parents; birth parents; orphanages

adoption, international, 1, 3, 16, 79, 99; adoption fees, 14, 49, 65–66, 145–46; attitudes of Chinese people toward, 71, 129, 137, 160; and Chinese identity, 50; of girls, 4, 8–9, 14–15, 23–24, 48–49, 50, 51–63, 66, 71–72, 75, 132, 134, 148, 149, 156; and HCIA, 131; kidnapping for, 131; number of Chinese state orphanages sending children abroad, 64–65, 174n57; of older adolescents, 144–45; as

outsourced intimacy, 14, 47, 49–50, 134, 135; PRC policies regarding, 14, 23–24, 49, 50, 51, 60, 63–64, 67, 68–69, 71–72, 74–75, 131, 132–35, 139, 140–41, 147, 149; and racial relations in U.S., 55–56; reactive attachment disorder (RAD) in, 146, 181n48; as redemption, 2, 20–21, 51, 56, 57, 141, 147; and red thread myth, 13–14, 130, 159–61; in relation to child trafficking, 14, 48–49, 53, 64, 66–67, 75, 142, 157; as soft power for PRC, 14, 23–24, 69, 72, 74, 130; as soft power for U.S., 130, 143–45; of special needs children, 24, 49, 72, 76, 99, 128–30, 132–35, 138, 139–40, 141, 146–47, 174n53; statistics on, 14, 48, 49, 51, 68, 73, 134, 156; visits to PRC by adoptees, 24, 156–58, 159, 160–61; wait time, 72; in Western media, 2, 14, 51; and Western NGOs, 4, 18–19, 21, 103–4, 115, 138. *See also* adoptive parents; birth parents; orphanages

adoption movement, 24, 130, 132, 140–45, 147, 148, 150

adoptive parents: daughter preference among, 51, 53–54, 60, 72; desires of, 8, 23, 51, 53–54, 55, 60, 62–63, 72, 132, 135–36, 148; PRC policies regarding, 63–64, 69–70, 74–75, 132, 134, 159, 174n53; single women as, 55, 56–57, 63–64, 68, 70, 134

Anhui Province, 51, 156–57, 172n17

Apter, Norman, 15

183